WHAT USERS SAY ABOUT
THE INTERACTION METHOD

"Getting people to speak up and participate was like pulling teeth. About five weeks after introducing the Interaction Method, I started to notice changes. People began speaking up more. Now, four months later, it's like a new organization. It's not just the meetings; the whole department is getting more done."

—Insurance company vice-president

"More people started showing up because they felt the union leadership was listening more and talking less. With these techniques we developed a high degree of consensus on many issues that previously split us down the middle."

—Representative of a civil service union

"It takes a lot to keep everyone right on the main point. Using the Interaction Method, I succeeded in doing this, and many good ideas were brought out."

—President of a church choir

"Better meetings have definitely created a good feeling of teamwork, and we now have relatively few and minor problems. A lot of group rivalries have ceased. People are taking care of things by themselves. I don't have to get involved in all the details. Before, people were constantly referring everything to me."

—Manager of a federal agency

THE NEW
INTERACTION
METHOD

HOW TO MAKE MEETINGS WORK

MICHAEL DOYLE
DAVID STRAUS

A JOVE BOOK

This Jove book contains the complete text
of the original hardcover edition.

HOW TO MAKE MEETINGS WORK

A Jove Book / published by arrangement with
the authors

PRINTING HISTORY
Playboy Press edition published 1976
Five previous paperback printings
Jove edition / September 1982
Second printing / June 1983

ISBN: 0-515-07539-6

Jove books are published by The Berkley Publishing Group,
200 Madison Avenue, New York, N.Y. 10016.
The words "A JOVE BOOK" and the "J" with sunburst
are trademarks belonging to Jove Publications, Inc.

PRINTED IN THE UNITED STATES OF AMERICA

To Patricia and Alice

Contents

Acknowledgments

Several institutions have supported and encouraged us over the last seven years. Specifically, we would like to thank the Carnegie Corporation of New York for supporting us during our first three years of research and The Rockefeller Foundation for funding our work with the Citizens Master Plan Committee of the Oakland Public Schools. We are also grateful to the Western Program Service Center of the Social Security Administration for its support in developing and refining the Interaction Method.

It would be impossible to list all the individuals who have contributed to the development of our ideas. We would like to acknowledge and thank Geoff Ball, who did some of the earliest work with group graphics and coined the phrase "group memory." We are indebted to Sally Keen, who helped us adapt the Interaction Method to the realities of a large organization, along with Bert Baylin, Jane Presley, and Walter Baum of Social Security.

We would like to express our appreciation for the contributions of all who assisted in the development and testing of these ideas while working at Interaction Associates: Jerold C. Kindred, Rudie Tretten, Julie Jansen, Catherine McEver, Ted Mitchell, Suzanne Wexler, Ethan Gluck, Chris Thorsen, Ruth Thorsen, and Georgine Kifer. In particular, we want to acknowledge the writing contributions of Penelope Wong who worked on earlier versions of this book.

Few authors have received more attention and assistance from their editor. Peter Wyden has patiently worked with us through several drafts of this book and has vastly improved its quality.

To Mary Beth Crenna, who has supported us in countless ways, we offer our warmest thanks and appreciation. Finally, this book might never have made it to print without two very special people who facilitated the facilitators: Patricia Straus and Justine Fixel.

HOW TO MAKE
MEETINGS WORK

CHAPTER 1

Why Meetings Are Important

We are a meeting society—a world made up of small groups that come together to share information, plan, solve problems, criticize or praise, make new decisions or find out what went wrong with old ones. Governments, businesses, schools, clubs, families—all are built up from *groups* of men, women and children. Regardless of their values or goals, individual members of these groups must get together in order to function. When three or more people work together face to face we call this a "meeting."

Look around you—every person alive belongs to any number of different groups. You may be the manager of a division in your organization, a member of your local PTA or labor union or grocery cooperative, the committee chairperson of a club, a member of a civic task force or local church council, or the head of your household. Each of these groups meets—perhaps once a month or so, perhaps a few times a week, perhaps several times daily. When you add up how much time you actually spend in meetings, you may surprise yourself. Taking a conservative estimate of four hours of meetings a week, you will sit through more than 9,000 hours of meetings in your lifetime— that's over 365 days!

Do you have any idea of how many meetings are held every day in the United States alone? More than 11 million! Just taking that staggering figure by itself, you can see there is a good chance your life is going to be full of meetings.

As you know, the more successful you become in your organization, the more time you spend in meetings. So if you are in middle management, you probably spend about 35 percent of your working week in meetings; if you are in top management, that figure may grow to more than 50 percent of your work week. That means you may spend over half of the rest of your organizational life attending or conducting meetings.

MEETINGS ARE EXPENSIVE

If you like to think in dollars and cents, you can compute how much money your organization spends on meetings. While the figures vary from one kind of organization to another, most organizations spend between 7 percent and 15 percent of their personnel budgets directly on meetings. So if your organization has a personnel budget of $100,000, approximately $7,000 to $15,000 of it is spent on people sitting in meetings. This does not include time spent preparing for meetings or attending training programs and conferences. A major California corporation with a $350 million personnel budget estimates it spends $30 million a year on meetings alone.

If you are involved with organizations in your community, you know that a major portion of your time is spent in meetings. Community organizations are literally run by meetings. While most of this time is volunteered and doesn't cost these organizations much money, your time is valuable to *you*. Time spent attending a meeting is time taken away from all the other things you might like to be doing. Your time is one of your most valuable resources, and naturally you want to spend it wisely.

WHY HAVE MEETINGS AT ALL?

A lot of of people groan, inwardly or out loud, at the mere thought of another meeting. So why have meetings? Couldn't we do without them? Of course, many meetings held every day are unnecessary. Either they are poorly prepared for, or the wrong people are there, or there is no reason to meet, or things could be accomplished just as well by other means. On the other hand, many meetings that should be held aren't.

Since people must communicate in groups to get many things done, it's a fact that the vast majority of groups and organizations couldn't function without meetings. They'd wither away and die without getting together, which is why many groups are required by law to meet, perhaps once a month or once a year: boards of directors, school boards, boards of supervisors, legislative bodies, stockholders, appointed committees. Like it or not, sitting down face to face with members of your group really is the most effective way to accomplish many tasks.

A meeting is often the best way to communicate information to others in a group when face-to-face interaction is necessary —when what you say depends on what another person says. It is almost always much harder and more time-consuming to convince someone of something by letter than it is to convince him face to face, when you can react immediately to objections and omit arguments that are clearly unnecessary. In groups, creative dynamics—new alternatives and solutions—emerge that don't occur to you when you sit by yourself at your desk, and so a group becomes more than the sum of its parts. A group can develop solutions collectively that the members could not have come up with individually, and for good reason. A problem that requires the knowledge and experience of several people often can be solved best by bringing them all together in a meeting.

HOW MEETINGS AFFECT YOUR LIFE

Just think of all the decisions made by small groups of men and women that directly affect your life. Issues are being discussed and decisions made at this moment which will have a tremendous impact on the future of all of us. A Congressional committee may be considering whether to increase your taxes, or a school board may be deciding if there should be cutbacks in the number of teachers in your school, or a regional planning committee may be setting guidelines for the growth of your community. Like it or not, most important decisions made in the United States every day are made in meetings of small groups.

There are also psychological reasons for meeting: a need to feel part of a group or a member of a team; a need for a sense of togetherness, trust, and belonging; a need to ease the loneliness and burden of responsibility and to develop a sense of commitment—and even sometimes a need to pass the buck.

Meetings are an intensive way of involving others in solving problems and making decisions. Involving someone in the process of solving a problem is the most effective way to ensure that he or she will accept and support a solution.

WE'RE ALL IN THIS TOGETHER

Families, organizations, our cities are all becoming more interdependent, interconnected, and complex. A change in one part affects all other parts. If a government lowers taxes, it may decrease unemployment but increase inflation. If an industrial-products division builds a new plant, the consumer-products division may have to cut back on its research and development. If a city builds a convention center downtown, revenues and taxes and tourism may increase, but so may traffic and parking problems, and what happens to the citizens who have to be displaced from the building site? Because of this complexity we are losing our power to act independently and unilaterally. In many parts of our society people are forced to work together to find common solutions, and working together always involves meeting together.

Everybody knows that men and women of all ages are demanding more say in decisions that affect their lives. Wives and children are no longer willing to have the man in the house make all decisions. Students aren't willing to accept decisions handed down by faculty and administration. Employees are demanding involvement in decisions made by management. Citizens are demanding involvement in decisions at all levels of government. As society becomes more complex and interdependent, the number of meetings you attend may even increase. That is why it is increasingly important to make the most of them.

WHEN DOES A MEETING WORK?

How do you know if a meeting works? What is an effective meeting, anyway?

There are two ways of judging the success of a meeting.

First, what happened? Did you get the results you wanted? What did you get done, what problems did you solve, what decisions did the group make? Were the solutions or decisions innovative? Obviously, you must judge the real importance of your meetings by the results you get from them. The results directly affect the functioning of your organization or group and its ability to achieve its objectives, whether the objectives are profits, delivery of services, survival, or member satisfaction.

Second, you will find it worthwhile to look at how the meeting went—the process of the meeting. How did problems get solved? How did decisions get made? How well did the group work together? How did people feel about the meeting? Did everyone get a chance to participate, or did one person dominate the meeting? Was the meeting a pleasure to attend? Did you have fun? Were you stimulated or challenged? Did people draw and build on each other's ideas, or was the meeting a battle of egos?

WATCH OUT FOR THE RIPPLE EFFECT

If your meetings are more than window dressing or hot air, they are critical to the health of your group or organization. This is the only time that members of a group actually see themselves as a group—when everyone is sitting in the same room working together. These group experiences directly affect how individuals feel about their group, how committed they are to decisions, and how well they work as a team and individually. And many meetings generate a ripple effect. A meeting of fifteen people can affect how 300 people work—or don't work—for the rest of the day or week or even permanently.

Obviously, this effect can be positive or negative on an organization. When a meeting blows up, when nothing gets accomplished or people become frustrated and angry, the participants take the frustration back with them to their jobs or homes. Not only do the participants of the meeting waste time cooling off, but they waste other people's time griping about what happened.

These are some of the hidden costs of unsuccessful meetings. Harold Reimer, a researcher in this field, estimates that the cost of time lost *after* ineffective meetings amounts to $800,000 per year for every 1,000 employees. We call this the "meeting recovery syndrome."

On the positive side, meetings can have a tremendous beneficial effect on how well an organization functions. If you can improve the meetings in your organization you will improve teamwork, communications, morale, and productivity as well.

SO WHAT'S THE TROUBLE WITH MEETINGS?

Many people live with meetings as a necessary evil. You've heard them say, "Oh no. Not another meeting! Meetings are a waste of time."

Why do meetings have such a terrible reputation? What *is* the trouble with meetings?

Just think for a moment of all the technological advances of the last twenty years. Color television, commercial jet planes, pocket calculators. Think of all the social changes. Civil rights, women's liberation, the emergence of the Third World. In almost every field remarkable advances have come in the last decade, but there has been no major improvement in the way meetings have been run in the last twenty years—in fact, not even in the last century.

Most meetings have their roots in some version of parliamentary procedure. The manager or chairperson sits at the head of the conference table, controlling the discussion, while a secretary takes minutes (or each person takes his or her own notes). Some formal meetings, particularly in government, are run according to Robert's Rules of Order: chairpersons, points of order, old business, new business, minutes, motions, ayes, nays. All these terms date back to the British Parliament of the nineteenth century.

Parliamentary procedure is fine for formal debate; the televised debate of the impeachment of President Nixon by the House judiciary committee was a good example. But parliamentary procedure is not at all suited to solving problems more or less informally, collaborating, working together to reach agreement, and coping with complex, interdependent issues. If you recall, new resolutions and compromises during the Watergate hearings were worked out in small private caucuses between the formal, televised meetings and then debated in the official sessions. You can be sure there were no stuffy rules of order to get things moving (or even twist an arm or two) in these unofficial sessions.

So it's no wonder meetings generally don't work very well. Our environment has grown vastly more complex in the last half-century, so it's time to update how we deal with it when we get together in meetings.

NOW: THE INTERACTION METHOD

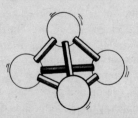

There is a better way. We have designed a new method to run meetings. It *works.* We call it the Interaction Method, and it has worked for thousands of people in all kinds of meetings and all kinds of organizations. At the time of this writing, we have trained over 10,000 people in the Interaction Method in businesses like I.B.M., Xerox, and the Bank of America; in government agencies like the Department of Health, Education and Welfare, Social Security Administration, and the National Institute of Drug Abuse; in community organizations like the Urban League and the Spanish Speaking Unity Council; and in religious organizations like the Archdiocese of Los Angeles and the Unitarian Church.

Its tools and techniques have helped these people to become more effective leaders and participants in the meetings they attend. They get more done in less time, and their meetings are more enjoyable. The Interaction Method can work for you, too.

This book will give you practical tools and techniques that will improve the quality of your meetings and make you more effective, whether you are a leader of a group or a participant. Regardless of the objectives of your meeting, the number of people involved, or the kind of organization in which you work, our system can be adapted to meet your needs. It has worked for directors of government agencies, business executives, civic leaders, managers, union leaders, supervisors, rank and file workers, educators, students, community organizers, parents, and senior citizens; for people of all ages, all educational levels, and all ethnic backgrounds.

WHO SAYS IT WORKS?

Here are some comments that people have made to us after trying the Interaction Method.

"Getting people to speak up and participate was like pulling teeth. Most of my people sat there like bumps on a log waiting to be told what to do," complained a vice-president of a Southern insurance company. "About five weeks after introducing the Interaction Method, I started to notice changes. People began speaking up more. Fred volunteered an idea for the first time in years, and Dorothy actually cracked a joke about the filing system she hates so much. Now, four months later, it's like a new organization. It's not just the meetings; the whole department is getting more done. We've reduced our backlog of cases to be processed. It's hard to believe it's the same old department."

"We've used the Interaction Method to run our school district meetings and have greatly increased staff participation," reported the superintendent of a Santa Cruz County school district in California. In the words of one principal, "I like it. I can sit back and hear more. In meetings last fall the bilingual-bicultural parent committee developed their own priorities for learning, which were so coherent they were written into the district's Title I proposal almost intact."

"The union meetings were not very effective. They were disorganized and rowdy. Often people claimed they were being manipulated and that the union wasn't serving their best interest," said a representative of the civil service union who had seen the Interaction Method used by management in the government agency where he worked and was impressed. "I decided to introduce the Interaction Method into the union meetings—not all at once, but gradually. It took several months, and some people complained about changing the ground rules. I think they had more to gain by keeping the meetings chaotic. Well, anyway, things got better. More people started showing up because they felt the union leadership was listening more and talking less. With these techniques we developed a high degree of consensus on many of the issues that previously split us down the middle."

"I learned to appreciate people in meetings," said the head of a Baptist choir in New Orleans. "As president of the choir I found that in meetings people get off the main subject very easily, and it takes a lot to keep everyone right on the main point. Using the Interaction Method I succeeded in doing this, and many good ideas were brought out."

A director of a large civic organization in Minneapolis used to spend 40 percent of her time with meetings. "I always felt it was my responsibility to set up a meeting, to get whatever it was out in the open to talk about, and to follow through and make sure it was done. Now I don't have to do all that work because the Interaction Method has specific roles and responsibilities for taking care of it. It relieves my time considerably —my whole time in running the agency, not just the meetings."

"I have become closer to my supervisors and it has strengthened line supervision. Better meetings have definitely created a good feeling about teamwork, and we now have relatively few and minor problems," reported a manager of a federal agency after it had introduced the Interaction Method into its operations department. "A lot of group rivalries have ceased and the technical and clerical groups have blended together. There is a very good sense of togetherness in the meetings which has spread to the whole department. People are taking care of things by themselves. Things are running smoothly. I don't have to get involved in all the details. Before people were constantly referring everything to me."

PRODUCTIVITY GOES UP

By using the Interaction Method, the divisions of some organizations have been able to increase their overall productivity by 15 percent. Groups have also been able to confront and resolve problems more creatively. By increasing participation and teamwork they have increased commitment to organization-wide decisions and consequently decreased the length of time required to get action on the decisions.

We know you may be skeptical at this point. No, our approach is *not* a new kind of encounter or sensitivity game, and it's *not* a panacea for all the problems of your group or organization. It is a set of tools and techniques that will help you plan and conduct more effective meetings.

What we have done is really simple. After attending and analyzing hundreds of meetings, we began to see that certain forces are common to all groups. A board of directors, a governmental task force, a student council, a citizens' committee, an administrative staff, a radical political group may have different values and objectives, but they all face similar problems when they hold a meeting. After studying the behavior of successful leaders and participants in meetings and assembling ideas from such new fields as cognitive psychology, group dynamics, organizational development, information processing, communications, and design methodology, we designed a simple system that will work immediately to increase the effectiveness of meetings.

We got rid of most of the jargon and translated the new behavioral ideas into language that everybody can understand. Then we tested and refined the Interaction Method while conducting thousands of successful meetings and analyzing the responses of people we have trained who have run more thousands of meetings in all kinds of organizations. The roles, behaviors, and techniques of our method have proved effective. It's as simple as that.

While this book focuses on running task-oriented gatherings of three to thirty people—the kind you attend day in and day out—most of the principles and techniques can be adapted to other kinds of meetings (sales meetings, training programs, public hearings, and rap groups) as well as meetings of more than thirty people. By "task-oriented" we mean meetings in which people come together to accomplish a goal—to do work. Task-oriented meetings include a range of work sessions from information sharing and problem-solving to planning, evaluation, and decision-making. Over 10.5 million of the 11 million meetings held every day in the United States fall into this category.

Moreover, we believe that some of our ideas about problem

solving, participation, leadership, and decision-making are useful above and beyond meetings. They apply to the way we behave as individuals, families, organizations, and as a society.

WHICH TYPE OF ORGANIZATION IS YOURS?

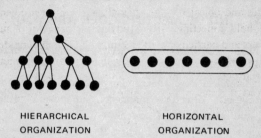

HIERARCHICAL
ORGANIZATION

HORIZONTAL
ORGANIZATION

All groups and organizations (and their meetings) are hierarchical or horizontal. At each level of a hierarchical organization the authority and responsibility for making decisions rests in one individual. Most large organizations are hierarchies: corporations, government agencies, educational institutions, hospitals, etc. In a hierarchical meeting, only one person has the final say. When the President of the United States meets with his advisers, he must be the one to decide. The same is true of a manager and staff, principal and administrators, chief executive officer and vice-presidents.

In horizontal groups and organizations, the authority and responsibility for making decisions rests with a specific *group* of people; final decisions can only be made by a vote of a quorum. Horizontal organizations include boards of directors, boards of supervisors, legislatures, chambers of commerce, student councils, membership organizations like PTA's, Junior Leagues, and Lions Clubs, and many task forces and committees.

We would like to be able to address this book to you personally and focus on your own needs the way we do in our workshops, but we know that "you," the reader, is not one you, but many, with different needs, concerns, and expectations of meetings. Since the printed page cannot address each of you personally, we will attempt to address four categories. You will be able to identify with one or more of these.

WHAT KIND OF MEETING-GOER ARE YOU?

1. Those of you who *conduct* meetings in *hierarchical* organizations. In most meetings you attend you are responsible for making final decisions. This category includes those of you who are presidents, directors, managers, supervisors, principals, deans, and other types of leaders.

2. Those of you who are generally *participants* in meetings in *hierarchical* organizations. This category includes all of you who see yourselves primarily as staff or employees. In meetings you may be able to suggest courses of action but don't have the power to make final decisions.

3. Those of you who *conduct* meetings in *horizontal* organizations: chairpersons. You are official members of your group but are also responsible for running meetings.

4. Finally, those of you who are *members* of *horizontal* groups or organizations, responsible for participating in decision-making but not for running meetings.

You may find yourself belonging to more than one of our categories. You might be a manager in a hierarchical organization, conducting meetings with your staff but participating in meetings with the senior managers to whom you report. After work, you may attend meetings as a member of the board of directors of a grocery cooperative while being chairperson of a school advisory committee, another horizontal group.

WHAT YOU WILL GET FROM THIS BOOK

No matter whether you run meetings or are a participant, whether you are in a hierarchical or horizontal organization, the tools and techniques in this book will make you more effective in groups.

If you are a meeting leader, you will learn how to get meetings to start and end on time, how to design a practical agenda, how to keep the meeting on track, how to deal with people who talk too much or criticize too much, how to increase group participation, how to generate more creative solutions, how to nail down accountability, and how to develop consensus.

If you are a meeting participant, you will learn how to restore a common focus to a meeting, how to create a positive atmosphere, how to suggest appropriate problem-solving techniques, how to guard against manipulation, how to give effective presentations, and generally how to be more effective yourself.

SOME WORDS OF CAUTION

At this point we must introduce some words of caution. First of all, things are not going to change suddenly. Making meetings work requires some doing. There is a big difference between understanding how to make meetings work and actually making them work better. You too are going to have to do some changing, and changing behavior is rarely easy. Things may seem strange and uncomfortable at first, just like a new suit of clothes. It will take time, patience, and a willingness to take some risks. While it will take commitment on your part, the rewards will come soon and will continue to grow.

Secondly, we are counting on you to use your own good judgment. Once you understand our concepts you must adapt the techniques to your own personality and needs. Our method is flexible and pragmatic. You can use the whole system or begin by trying parts of it. The tools and techniques will work by themselves. We're not purists. We have seen our techniques adapted and applied successfully in many different combinations in a wide variety of situations. We believe that if a tool works for you, fine; if it doesn't, adapt it, modify it, or try a new one.

HOW TO USE THIS BOOK

This book itself is a tool. Take it to your meetings. Feel free to underline important parts, to put tabs on various sections for easy reference. Read it through once and then begin to start applying the techniques. After some practical experience, we suggest that you review the entire book again, and you will find new meaning and relevance.

CHAPTER 2

What Goes Wrong at Meetings

Productivity, creativity, efficiency, participation, and commitment are results. If you want these results from your meetings, you have to understand the process that produces them. You don't get better at doing something unless you stop to think about what you've been doing—to analyze your process.

Take the example of athletes. Joe Namath and Billie Jean King don't go out every day and play for real. Even the best performers spend most of their time practicing. A football team may practice forty hours for every one that counts. After every game the players analyze the films to figure out what worked and what didn't. That's how they develop teamwork. They break down the complex activity of football into fundamentals and plays, practice them, and then put them all together in a game.

Meetings are one of the most complex activities you "do." The success or failure of a meeting has a significant impact on you and your group. When things go wrong in a meeting, does your group stop and analyze what worked and what didn't? Do you know and practice the "fundamentals" of meetings? Probably not. Even though you may attend many meetings every week, if you are like most people, you have never had any formal training in how to conduct (or participate in) meetings. When you first began attending meetings, you probably picked up skills by osmosis, by modeling your behavior on the behavior of other meeting participants, who, in turn, may have learned the same way. One generation has taught the next without questioning what it learned from the generation that came before; it's the blind leading the blind.

That's why we will look at some of the most common things that go wrong with meetings. We are going to stop and analyze why, and what the consequences are. We are going to illustrate some basic meeting problems, but our discussion will not be exhaustive. After our analysis, we will introduce those parts of the Interaction Method that are designed to cope with these problems, show you how they work, and discuss some of the benefits.

THE MULTI-HEADED ANIMAL SYNDROME

THE MULTI-HEADED ANIMAL

THE TENDENCY TO GO OFF IN ALL DIRECTIONS SIMULTANEOUSLY

You've heard it and we've heard it—"You can't do anything in a meeting. Everyone wants to do it his own way." Or: "The more people, the more impossible it becomes." Or: "A committee is a collection of the unfit chosen from the unwilling by the incompetent to do the unnecessary."

Why are all that many people all that down on meetings? Why do things seem to get more complicated with each additional person at a meeting? Let's listen in on a couple of fairly typical meetings.

Mr. Roberts, the chairperson of a fund-raising committee for a nonprofit organization, has called a meeting.

Mr. Roberts, insistently: It's clear to me our problem is that we need to raise membership dues by $5 a year.

Mr. Peters, aggressively: Our membership would drop if we did that. What we need to do is change our name to something that's more appropriate to our real function.

Mr. Roberts, less insistently: What would happen if we raised our membership dues by only $1 a year in all categories?

Ms. Orlando, hopefully: I know the name of a good fund-raiser we could hire.

Mr. Peters, returning to his agenda: What about changing "association" to "committee." That sounds more contemporary.

Ms. King, jumping in for the first time: Couldn't we cut our budget for this year? What is it, anyway?

What was going wrong here? Everyone was trying to be helpful, but each person saw the fund-raising problem differently and had a preconceived solution to his or her version of the problem. Mr. Roberts saw the problem as "how to raise more money" and had the solution "raise membership dues." Mr. Peters saw the problem as "a poor name for the organization" and offered some ideas about how the name could be changed.

And Ms. Orlando and Ms. King had other solutions. Each of these perceived problems may have been valid, but the meeting won't go anywhere until they decide to focus on one problem for a period of time and put all their creative energies into investigating it.

ONE ITEM AT A TIME

We've just illustrated one reason why individuals in a group can have more difficulty solving a problem than they would experience by themselves. One of the useful features of your mind is that it allows for just one point of attention. You can think about only one thing at any instant in time. Try listening to two conversations at once. You will find yourself jumping back and forth between the two. You can't listen to two people at the same time. Now, try mentally to feel your left ear and your right big toe at the same time. Can you catch yourself vibrating between the two? What this means is that all the stimuli from your environment and from your subconscious must line up and file by your attention in single, discrete chunks. This is useful because it keeps you from getting overloaded and scattered. True, when you get harried, you can feel like a chicken with its head cut off, running frantically around and not getting anywhere; still, it could be much worse if you were mentally to become twenty chickens running around. Your single point of attention is a built-in safety device.

A group has no such single focus. In fact, there are as many foci as there are individuals in the group. Each person can be focusing on a different problem at a given time. If everyone mentally heads off in different directions, the result can be confusion, tension, and lack of productivity—the multi-headed animal syndrome. To work effectively, a group needs a single focus.

Let's look at another example.

This is a PTA committee meeting of fifteen people in Oakland, California.

President of the PTA, opening the meeting: Good evening. Our principal called me today to say that he had an unavoidable conflict and wouldn't be able to attend this meeting. But he did request that we put together a list of school problems as we see them. So, who wants to begin?

Ms. Brown, trying to get the ball rolling: Violence in the corridors.

Ms. Elliott, reacting: I think the solution to that problem is more monitors.

Mr. Jones, sarcastically: They tried that last year and it didn't work.

Ms. Elliott, indignantly: I think it would have. They didn't try it for long enough.

Ms. Brown, still trying to keep the ball rolling: The use of drugs in the school.

Ms. Frank, out of the blue: My Johnny came home with a bloody nose just last week.

The meeting isn't working. They aren't getting anywhere. We can discover one of the reasons for this lack of progress if we analyze this segment of the PTA meeting step by step.

SEPARATING THE "WHAT" FROM THE "HOW"

The example begins with the president suggesting a problem for the group to work on, but she has fallen into one of the most common traps of meetings. She has posed a problem, but she is in difficulty. The group has not agreed to work on it. More important, she has not gotten agreement on how to approach the problem. To achieve a common focus the group must agree on what they are going to discuss for the next period of time as well as how they are going to discuss it.

This distinction between the content (the *what:* problem, topic, or agenda) and the process (the *how:* approach, method or procedure) is a difficult but vitally important concept to grasp if you are going to understand why meetings don't work well.

The PTA president had suggested a content focus for the meeting, but not a process focus (a way for the group to work on the problem.) Let's look at what happened.

Ms. Brown immediately agreed to the content focus—a list of issues for the principal—and implicitly decided that the best process was to toss out suggested issues. So she volunteered an item for the list. It all might have worked out all right, but Ms. Elliott, rather than following Ms. Brown's lead and suggesting a further item, decided to offer a solution to Ms. Brown's problem of violence in the corridors. Ms. Elliott thus changed her content focus from a list of problems to the specific problem of violence in the corridors.

Then, to make things worse, Mr. Jones came along and evaluated Ms. Elliott's solution, and everything began to fall apart. The multi-headed animal began to bite itself. Naturally, Ms. Elliott came back to defend her solution, and before Mr. Jones could counter, Ms. Brown valiantly plugged on with her listing process and offered another item: drugs in the schools. At the end of this portion of the PTA meeting Ms. Frank tosses in an example in support of something. It's not clear what. Perhaps she is only lamenting that violence is still a problem.

"PROCESS" IS LIKE CHEWING GUM

It's worthwhile to discuss this process/content distinction in more depth. The process of melting is not the state of ice nor the state of water; it's what happens in between. In problem-solving, the *process* is how an individual or group solves the problem. The problem and solution is whatever is acted on; it is the *content*. If you want an easy way to remember it, suppose you are chewing gum: chewing is the process, gum is the content.

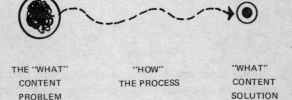

THE "WHAT"	"HOW"	"WHAT"
CONTENT	THE PROCESS	CONTENT
PROBLEM		SOLUTION

In our sample PTA meeting, making a list is the process. The list itself is the content or object. Another way of putting it would be: listing, evaluating, and solving are processes; what is listed, evaluated, or solved is content.

The important thing to keep in mind for now is: in meetings, a group must agree on a common problem and a common process or it will fall prey to the multi-headed animal syndrome.

Let's look at another common problem.

The setting is a high school faculty meeting in the Midwest. The topic of discussion is the recent buildup of racial tensions in the school.

Dick (a black-studies teacher), angrily: Man, I've said this over and over, until this faculty begins to reflect the student population, until more black men and women are hired, there's going to be nothing but trouble around here.

Bob (a black athletic coach), chiming in: Last year there wasn't one black hired.

Peter (a math teacher): Hey, we've heard this before. You know that there wasn't a qualified black for—

Dick, interrupting: Says who?

Mary (an English teacher): But how is this going to help our racial problems now?

Peter, turning toward Dick: According to our committee on hiring—

Mary, still trying to be constructive: I think that we should set aside a day for student/faculty dialogue.

Dick: What a dumb idea! More of your touchy-feely stuff. We want action. *(Turning to Peter)* How many blacks were on that hiring committee? Huh?

Peter: Don't run that number on me again.

Mary gives up and pulls out some student papers and begins to correct them. Dick and Bob continue to fight it out with Peter.

This exchange illustrates a problem common to many meetings, particularly those without a chairperson or discussion leader. The floor is grabbed by whoever can talk loudest and fastest. People who are basically not outspoken (like Mary) have a hard time being heard. Yet it's often these individuals who put a lot of thought into what they say and whose contributions would be valuable if they could just get a fair hearing. Moreover, when a quiet participant of a meeting finally gets the floor and then is jumped upon, he or she may give up and pull out of the meeting altogether, as did Mary.

"GROUP RAPE" CAN GET YOU

Think how many times you have been in a meeting and have had to devote energy merely to pick a good time to jump into the conversation so you'd be heard. When you finally did manage to get the attention of the group, it was either too late to make your point or you had forgotten what you were going to say in the first place.

And haven't you ever been in a meeting and volunteered a suggestion, only to be attacked so hard that you wished you could crawl into the woodwork? The response to your suggestion didn't exactly encourage your participation, did it? In situations like that, other members become guarded, too, because they know they could be attacked next. They are afraid of what we call the "group rape syndrome."

So, two things seem clear. You won't participate in a meeting if you feel you are not going to receive protection from attack or don't feel confident that you can protect yourself. Second, in a meeting of more than four to five people without some kind of guidance, a good deal of your energy is wasted trying to time your jump into the conversational flow.

To maneuver your way out of this trap, think of vehicular traffic. When there is light traffic at an intersection, stop signs are adequate; when traffic is heavy in all directions, a great deal of skill is required to time your entry into (or across) the traffic flow, and accidents are more likely to happen. Some kind of signaling system, traffic lights or a policeman, ensures safety and also increases the rate of flow through the intersection. You heave a sigh when you discover a policeman at a busy intersection and don't have to poke the front part of your car into cross traffic and pray that the other cars will stop.

The same is true of a meeting. If you know someone is concerned with seeing that everyone is heard, that no one is attacked, that individuals can signal for entry into the conversational flow, you are relieved of a great deal of unneccessary tension. You can devote more of your energy to listening to others and thinking about what you want to contribute.

EVERY MEETING NEEDS A TRAFFIC COP

A human system of regulating flow is almost always more responsive than a mechanical one. Have you ever had to sit at a red light when there was a lot of traffic on your street and none on the cross street? A policeman would immediately see the situation and adjust the directional flow to meet the momentary need. The same applies to rigid rules in a meeting, like speaking in a fixed order. It is hard to get a constructive dialogue going. A human system—a sensitive moderator—could adjust to the moment-by-moment needs of the individuals in the group without letting anyone dominate the meeting for long.

Clearly, every meeting of more than four or five people needs a leader who will keep an open and balanced conversational flow and protect individuals and their ideas from personal attack.

WHO DOES WHAT

One of the biggest barriers to effective meetings is the lack of clarity about roles and responsibilities. You've probably been in a meeting and heard some of the following complaints: "Who is he and what is he doing here?" "Are you making the decision or are we going to vote?" "I thought you were just going to be an observer." "I don't want any so-called expert in here telling us what to do." "I thought the discussion leader was supposed to limit discussion to this one subject." "I thought we were going to have the final say."

For specific periods in a meeting you can accept almost any role for yourself or someone else, as long as it is clear in advance who is playing what role; you can agree to remain silent or participate fully or to speak only when called on by the group. But if you enter a meeting with one understanding only to discover that everybody else is playing by different rules, then naturally you are going to feel confused and perhaps deliberately deceived.

While it's hard to generalize, it tends to be true that the more you change your role, the more you are going to inhibit the effective functioning of a group. If a meeting begins with the understanding that you are to be a silent observer but you get so excited that you can't help making your own contributions, sooner or later members of the group are likely to get irritated. At that point, you should either see if the group will agree to let you change your role from silent observer to active participant or you should leave the room. This problem of multiple roles is particularly true for managers in meetings, as we'll see in the next case history.

HOW POWER IS MISUSED IN MEETINGS

A meeting of a division manager of the Acme Widget Co. and his supervisors.

Joe, division manager: I have been directed by the president to cut our production costs by 15 percent within the next three months. It's going to be tough, but we are going to do it. Here's what I think we should do: Ask all employees to pitch in, direct all employees to keep coffee breaks to fifteen minutes, cut out free coffee and doughnuts for supervisors in the morning, place a hiring freeze on temporary employees, and stop Sunday overtime. Well, that's it. What do you think, Bill?

Bill, nodding his head mechanically: Oh, certainly, Joe. Sounds fine. Those changes should do it.

Joe: How about you, Juan?

Juan, cautiously: I'm not sure about the idea of stopping coffee and doughnuts. It won't save us much, and coffee and doughnuts are good for morale.

Joe, abruptly: Yes, I know it's only a token gesture, but we've got to set an example. How about you, Rico? What do you think?

Rico: I don't think the crews are going to like not being able to work Sunday overtime. Besides, I don't see how we can keep up our monthly output that way.

Joe, defensively: Dammit. I have looked at all the alternatives and that's the only one that will make a major dent in lowering our costs. I know it's going to be unpopular, but it's the way it has to be. You got any ideas, Marta?

Marta: Well, as you were suggesting when we talked the other day, we could reduce inspections from every third item to every fifth.

Rico, jumping in: If we do that, our quality control will be shot to hell. And you damned well know how those consumer groups have been getting on our backs lately.

Juan: Yeah, I agree. I don't think—

Joe, breaking in: I think you are absolutely right, Marta. Let's make inspections on every fifth item. Well, that's about it.

I'll prepare the paperwork and you can tell your people what we've decided. Meeting adjourned.

Exchanges like this are common in meetings, particularly in hierarchical organizations. This one illustrates several major problems. Joe, the manager, probably went back to work feeling that it was a good meeting. It was short, quick, and to the point. He might have thought to himself, "I gave them my ideas, got their reactions, and made my decisions." He did give them his ideas and made some decisions, but did he get meaningful reactions?

TELLING THE BOSS WHAT HE WANTS TO HEAR

When Joe said, "Here's what I think we should do. What do you think, Bill?" he placed his subordinate in a classic double bind. Bill thought to himself, "Do I tell him what I think, or do I tell him what he wants to hear?" He decided, as many subordinates do, on the latter and safer course: reinforce the boss's ideas, don't stick out your neck.

THE MANAGER PLAYS

A DUAL ROLE

A POWER ROLE
AND
A PROCESS ROLE

Did Joe really want an honest answer? Was he willing to be told that his ideas might not work? The way he abruptly and defensively dealt with the objections of Rico and Jaun indicated that, in fact, he was convinced his ideas were good and only wanted them rubber-stamped and supported.

In fairness to Joe and the thousands of managers like him who are under constant pressure to perform, he probably did want to know if there were any real dangers in implementing his ideas or if there were even better solutions to the problem. Didn't he ask every member of the group for his opinion? Yes, but he didn't give them the chance to develop their own ideas. As a result of his heavy-handedness, Joe cut himself off from the accurate information he needed to make his decisions. He wasted his time and the time of his staff by having a meeting and not tapping their creative potential. He wasn't making the most of the meeting and the talents of the people in it. It would be like going to an orgy and staying with your date.

FIVE INGREDIENTS OF AN EFFECTIVE MEETING

So far in this chapter we have established five basic criteria for a good meeting:

1. There must be a common focus on content.
2. There must be a common focus on process.
3. Someone must be responsible for maintaining an open and balanced conversational flow.
4. Someone must be responsible for protecting individuals from personal attack.
5. And, in general, for the duration of the meeting everyone's role and responsibility must be clearly defined and agreed upon.

Clearly, a good meeting needs structure and leadership. But what kind of leadership?

The position of leading a group, determining who speaks and how the meeting is to proceed, is obviously very powerful.

Process control can result in content control; by controlling the process of a meeting, you can determine to a large extent what is going to happen.

To return to the traffic analogy: If a cop is stationed at a point where many lanes converge on an approach to a bridge and allows certain lanes to go ahead and deliberately ignores other lanes, he not only will impede the overall flow of traffic, but also is likely to encounter some damned angry motorists. If a meeting's chairperson selectively permits certain people to talk and ignores others, he or she can manipulate a group in a preferred direction. That is just what happened when Joe asked Marta for her thoughts, discovered that Marta's idea was the one that he had suggested himself, and then quickly cut off any objections to the idea.

WHY BOSSES SHOULDN'T RUN THEIR OWN MEETINGS

Some bosses may find this difficult to live with at first, but it is almost impossible to run a fair, nonmanipulative meeting when you have a personal investment in the subject matter. There is no way you can objectively lead a group that is considering whether or not to discontinue a project of your own. Even if you try not to influence the group, you will find that your body language reinforces those who want to keep your project going. Your eyes will light up when someone says something reinforcing. You will shrug or frown when you disagree—or more likely, openly object. It is only human. You should be in the group fighting for your ideas, not trying to lead the group toward a rational decision.

It is also easy to use the leadership role as a way of "keeping the floor" and doing all the talking—which can result in a rubber-stamp meeting. Managers who run their own meetings tend to be the most active participants by far; we find that they talk on the average more than 60 percent of the meeting time. That doesn't leave much opportunity for others to contribute, and it's one more reason why participation in meetings is low.

To summarize, then, in most meetings of hierarchical organizations run by conventional methods, the manager with the most authority and decision-making power is generally the chairperson. As such, this manager controls how the meeting proceeds, deals with conflict between participants/subordinates, talks more than anyone else, and is responsible for making all final decisions. The result is often low participation and morale, poor data, and a waste of the manager's and group's valuable time.

Aside from all these handicaps, the big trouble is that the manager attempts to play too many roles at one time. It is like trying to be referee and scorekeeper as well as captain of the team. No matter how experienced, efficient, and smart he is, a manager can't do a good job of filling all these important and conflicting positions at once. As we have seen, it is almost impossible to be heavily invested in the subject of a meeting and run the meeting without bias. As a manager, since you are responsible for all decisions made by your staff, you must participate in a meeting and must continue to be captain of your team, but you cannot at the same time function as a competent referee and scorekeeper.

Picture yourself, for a moment, as President of the United States on the way to the airport in your limousine with your top advisers, having a last-minute meeting with them. You wouldn't want to be driving the limousine at the same time, would you? Having to deal with traffic would be a distraction, a waste of your time. In a similiar way, you are too important to your group or organization to run your own meetings. Steering a meeting, like steering a car, demands total concentration. We therefore strongly recommend that managers and chairpersons not run their own meetings.

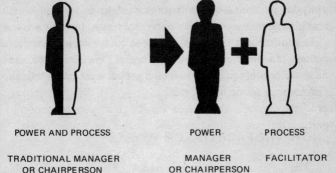

POWER AND PROCESS

TRADITIONAL MANAGER
OR CHAIRPERSON

POWER

MANAGER
OR CHAIRPERSON

PROCESS

FACILITATOR

ENTER THE FACILITATOR

The key to solving the problems of authority, participant contribution, and managerial overload is to separate the process role (often played by the manager as chairperson) from the power or decision-making role. The manager maintains his or her involvement in issues and responsibility for making decisions and delegates all the procedural functions to another person—the facilitator.

The facilitator is a meeting chauffeur, a servant of the group. Neutral and nonevaluating, the facilitator is responsible for making sure the participants are using the most effective methods for accomplishing their task in the shortest time. The manager, as decision maker, participates fully in the meeting, fights for his or her ideas, sets constraints, and does not give up any power and responsibility.

In the Interaction Method the role of facilitator in both hierarchical and horizontal organizations is to deal with the common problems we have discussed so far. For instance, to avoid the multi-headed animal syndrome—the tendency of group members to go off in different directions—the facilitator gets the group to stick to a common subject and a common process at all times. The facilitator might say, "Hey, wait a minute. You've agreed to work on problem A, but how are you going to tackle it? Are you going to try to define it in more detail? If so, how are you going to begin? Do you want to make a list of possible causes? Does each person want to describe the problem in his or her terms?"

HOW THE FACILITATOR WORKS

The facilitator holds the group back, offers a menu of possible ways of attacking the problem, and waits until there is agreement on one particular process. Then the facilitator helps keep the group on track until it has accomplished what it set out to do or wants to change direction. By getting all the group members to use the same tool at the same time on the same problem, the facilitator can transform a group from a multi-headed animal to a creative, coordinated organism.

To make sure that all participants have an opportunity to participate, that everyone will be protected from personal attack, and that no one is allowed to dominate the meeting, the facilitator is empowered to act as a cop. When the group is working well together, the facilitator may not need to do much and lets group members speak spontaneously. When things become heated or bogged down, the facilitator steps in and becomes more forceful in his or her use of power to direct the meeting process, signaling who should speak next, cutting off aggressive behavior, and keeping the group to its agreed-upon task.

Don't confuse our definition of a facilitator with others you may have heard. The Interaction Method is designed to accomplish tasks. It is not, as we have said, encounter or sensitivity training. The facilitator oils the tracks for groups to work effectively in meetings—to accomplish something. When a group is able to concentrate its creative energy, to work hard, and to accomplish a task in a positive and constructive fashion, group members feel better about themselves and each other.

The facilitator agrees to remain neutral, not to contribute his or her own ideas, and not to evaluate the ideas of others. At times it can be very hard not to get involved in the content of a meeting, so if you are a facilitator, do ask your group to let you know if you are favoring a point of view, criticizing an idea, not letting certain people speak or cutting them off too soon, or in any other way manipulating the meeting. It is obvious that nobody can be totally neutral; you are going to have feelings and opinions about what is being said in the meeting.

It is the responsibility of group members to make sure that your thoughts and feelings are not allowed to influence the meeting; ultimately, they have the right to remove you from the role of facilitator.

This nonmanipulation pact between the facilitator and the rest of the group is one of a set of social contracts that is distinctive about the Interaction Method. It creates a self-correcting system.

Three of the four key roles have now been introduced: the facilitator, the group member, and the manager/chairperson. It is the responsibility of the facilitator to make sure that group members work together and to protect them and the manager/chairperson from personal attack. It is the responsibility of the group members and the manager/chairperson to keep the facilitator from manipulating the group in any way. And it is the role of the manager/chairperson to keep the group focused on the agenda, to set realistic time limits and to be clear about organizational constraints.

CHAPTER 3

The Case for a Group Memory

Which of the following situations sounds familiar to you?

1. One person keeps reminding the meeting over and over about a pet peeve.

2. The group spins its wheels, covering the same old territory over and over again.

3. So much information is being discussed that you are overwhelmed, confused, and ask (or feel like asking), "What are we talking about now? Where are we?"

4. Somebody comes in late and you have to start dealing with the topic all over again.

5. You flash on an idea, but forget it by the time you have a chance to speak.

There is a connection between all these common situations —an underlying deficiency that keeps many meetings from working effectively. It has to do with a lack of memory.

Before we demonstrate why a group needs a memory, let's

look at why you as an individual need a memory. Suppose you couldn't remember anything that happened longer than one minute ago. And suppose you have mislaid a piece of clothing someplace in your home and start to look for it. You begin in the bedroom, and don't find it, so you look in the bathroom, and then go on to the living room. But by the time you are in the living room, you can't remember whether you looked in the bedroom, so back you go. At this rate, it could take a long time to find your lost possession. Or suppose you can't remember anything longer than a second ago; you would not be able to finish even a single sentence! This kind of memory—remembering what happened a short while ago—is called by psychologists "short-term memory," and is essential for any kind of communication or purposeful effort.

SHORT-TERM VS. LONG-TERM MEMORY

Short-term memory is different from long-term memory, the recall of important events or information that you learned or memorized some time ago: your name, language, life history, telephone number, basic mathematics, etc. Short-term memory has several interesting features. It really is short because it automatically erases itself.

For example, when you read this sentence, you will remember the phrase "for example" until you finish this sentence. And maybe even into the next sentence. But by the time you read *this sentence* you probably remember the phrase "by the time" but have forgotten "for example"—unless you try to remember it. You might do this by repeating it over and over to yourself, and thereby refreshing your short-term memory. Or by now, we hope, we have made such a fuss over the phrase "for example" that you have moved this event into your long-term memory, and will be able to remember what short-term memory is for a long time.

Short-term memory can be refreshed by repeating a piece of information, say, from the time you close the telephone book to the time you dial the number. But as you know, this can take a lot of mental energy, and you don't like to be interrupted by a question until you have finally dialed the number. That is why when someone else is talking to you, and you get a great idea, you can become preoccupied and stop listening to what the other person is saying until you have a chance to get out your thoughts.

Short-term memory has a very limited capacity. Try remembering the following random list of numbers: 7, 5, 8, 2, 3, 8, 9, 3, 1, 6. How far did you get? It turns out that most people can remember only about seven pieces or "bits" of information at one time. There are ways of combining pieces of information into larger chunks—such as the telephone number 5318937 into (531)–(8937)—and other memory tricks, but basically you are stuck with severe limits to your short-term memory. No matter how hard you try, it will always be difficult to divide 352 into 82,596 in your head. There are too many steps and temporary pieces of information to juggle and remember.

GROUPS NEED SHORT-TERM MEMORIES, TOO

The point is that groups also need short-term as well as long-term memories. Traditionally, in formal meetings, the long-term memory function is served by the minutes as recorded by the secretary. But the minutes represent the memory of one individual who remembers what he or she thinks was important. The record is not available to the group until the next meeting. More frequently, individuals take notes for themselves. So after a meeting, there is no accepted memory or record of what happened and what was decided. This leads to the common problem of people who come to the next meeting and argue about who was supposed to do what: "I thought it was decided that you were going to do that." "No, I thought it was supposed to be you." And many good ideas get lost because no one remembers or writes them down.

The short-term memory problem in meetings can be even more frustrating and disabling. Most groups don't have a collective short-term memory. You remember what you think is important, usually your own ideas and supporting facts. Just the process of refreshing your short-term memory to retain approximately seven pieces of information involves mental energy, as we have seen. When you are concentrating on holding on to your own ideas, it is hard to be open to new ideas. And so people are off in different directions and the multi-headed animal syndrome emerges again.

Most organizational meetings are very rich in information. In the first ten minutes, hundred of facts and figures may be brought up. Without some kind of collective memory, it is very easy to come down with a case of data overload—to be overwhelmed by the amount of information and terribly confused.

In our research we investigated a wide range of the most advanced space-age technologies. We looked at overhead projectors, computer and video systems, and all kinds of displays. But in the end, we discovered that the most powerful tool for assisting meetings was the combination of large sheets of blank paper and magic markers. You can display more information on a large sheet of paper than on any TV screen yet developed, and it is inexpensive enough to be available to any group.

ENTER THE RECORDER

So the fourth essential role in the Interaction Method is the role of recorder. Like the facilitator, the recorder is a neutral, nonevaluative servant of the group. The role of the recorder is to create a combined short-term and long-term memory by writing down in full view of the group the main points of what

is said, using the words of the group members. A good recorder
in no way inhibits or slows down the flow of the meeting.

A skillful recorder will produce a clearly legible record capturing the key ideas of the meeting on large sheets of paper
taped or pinned to the walls of the meeting room. We call this
record the "group memory." The group is seated in a semicircle
facing the group memory. However, most of the time members
of the group are not preoccupied by the process of recording.
A record of the meeting just appears in the background. By
referring to it, you can check or recall what just happened or
what happened back at the beginning of the meeting.

It is the responsibility of each group member and the mana-
ger/chairperson to see that ideas are recorded accurately. This
is the final social contract that completes the self-correcting
mechanism built into the Interaction Method. The recorder

agrees to try to capture the main ideas of the participants in the group memory and not to paraphrase or use this central position to editorialize or to contribute personal ideas. It is up to the others to make sure the recorder is fair and accurate.

The supporting relationships between the four key roles (facilitator, recorder, group member, and manager/chairperson) allow a novice group to try the Interaction Method and to learn and correct itself as it goes along. It is like the automatic pilot on an airplane. When the plane gets blown off course, the automatic pilot makes the necessary adjustments to get the plane back on course. So, too, if the facilitator steps out of his or her role and begins to evaluate ideas, the group members will gently push the facilitator back into position and the meeting will proceed on course.

WHY THE GROUP MEMORY IS POWERFUL

The very presence of the group memory has many beneficial effects. It provides a physical focus for the group. Rather than sitting in a closed circle around a conference table, channeling their energies toward each other, the members sit in a semicircle and automatically focus their energies on the problem as represented by the group memory. This simple change can make a tremendous difference.

The group memory can also be a great benefit to you personally. You no longer have to hold on to an idea in your short-term memory. Once you have had a chance to express it to the group and have seen it recorded in the group memory, you know that your idea is captured and "remembered." You will feel a great psychic release—you can let go because you know that the group has heard you and that you can recall your ideas simply by looking up at the record in front of you. There they are up on the wall in full view of everyone—they won't be forgotten.

For the facilitator, the group memory is a great asset, because it is a record of the process as well as of the content of the meeting. If the group has agreed to cover three agenda items and all material on the walls only deals with the first item, the facilitator can demonstrate that fact graphically by pointing to the group memory.

For the manager/chairperson the group memory is ideal because it takes care of many of the sticky problems of accountability. When a decision has been reached, it can be circled and starred, and if there is a task to be done, the name of the person who is responsible for taking care of this task (and the date by which it is to be accomplished) can be written next to the item. At the next meeting, when action items are reviewed by consulting the group memory of this meeting, it is very clear who is supposed to have done what.

Now let's begin to get a sense of how the Interaction Method works in practice. We will go into this in much more depth later in this book. Let's return to the same PTA meeting we observed in Chapter 2. But this time let's assume that the PTA president has read about the Interaction Method and that she and Ms. Chin and Mr. Rosenthal had tried it a few times previously in other settings. Let's see how the meeting might have gone.

PTA President, opening the meeting: Good evening. As we agreed in our last meeting, we are going to try running this meeting by the Interaction Method. Ms. Chin has volunteered to be the facilitator and Mr. Rosenthal has kindly agreed to be our recorder. I am going to participate as a member of the group. If there aren't any questions, we can begin immediately. . . . It's all yours, Ms. Chin.

Ms. Chin, walking to the head of the room: Good evening. I am going to be your facilitator tonight. It's a difficult job, and I'm just learning, so please help me. My role is to stay neutral and to help you focus your energy on your task. I promise to try not to evaluate your ideas or toss in my own.

I'll suggest some ways of tackling the problem, but it is your meeting and I'm here to help you. If you catch me stepping out of my role, please let me know. Mr. Rosenthal, will you please introduce yourself and explain your role.

Mr. Rosenthal: I'm still learning, too, so please help me out. I'm going to be your recorder. I will try to write down your ideas in your own words on these large sheets of newsprint you see taped to the walls. Please let me know if I haven't heard you correctly or if I didn't capture your idea. I may lag behind the conversation, but don't worry about waiting for me. If I get too far behind, I may ask you to stop for a moment until I catch up. If you can't read my writing, let me know.

Facilitator: Does anyone have any questions about how the meeting is going to be run? . . . Okay, let's begin. *(She turns to the president of the PTA.)* Judith, just so that we're all clear about what we're supposed to be doing, please state our topic for discussion this evening and the reasons for dealing with this subject.

President: The principal called me today to say that he had an unavoidable conflict and would be unable to attend this meeting. But he requested that we put together a list of school problems as we see them. It is my understanding he and the staff will use our list in developing school priorities for the coming year.

Facilitator: Thank you, Judith. Okay, the recorder has written down our problem on page two of the group memory: a list of school problems. Do we all agree to work on this problem this evening? *(Heads nod.)* Now, let's see if we can agree on how to go about making this list. Any suggestions?

Ms. Brown: We could discuss what's happening in the school and see if we can agree on some problems.

Mr. Jones: Why don't we just toss out whatever's been bugging us?

Ms. Elliott: We could try brainstorming like they do in my husband's advertising agency.

Ms. Frank (still obsessed by what has happened to her son): My Johnny came home with a bloody nose last week.

Facilitator: Okay, Rosaline. The recorder got that down on the group memory. I'm sure we will have lots to say, but let's wait until we can agree on a way of going about making this list. What do you think about trying brainstorming? Any objections? *(All nod their heads.)* Okay, let's brainstorm a list of problems that we think exist in the school today. In brainstorming you toss things out and you don't evaluate each other's ideas. The recorder will write them down and later we will come back and review them, discuss them, and try to give them priorities. Let's see if we can get a list of twenty problems up on the wall in the next five minutes. Any questions? . . . All right, let's begin.

Ms. Brown: Violence in the corridors.

Mr. Jones: Overcrowded classrooms.

Ms. Elliott: Thirty to a classroom is normal—

Facilitator, jumping in: Hold it, Louise. We agreed we weren't going to criticize each other's ideas. Do you have a problem you would like to add to the list?

Ms. Elliott: Yes. Not enough locker space.

Facilitator: Thank you. Okay, you're next, Mary Lou.

Ms. Brown: The use of drugs in the school.

Facilitator: Good, keep the suggestions coming.

Mr. Jones: Teacher apathy.

Ms. Frank: There's broken glass all over the playground.

Mr. Jones: Improve the level of basic skills.

Ms. Elliott: Not enough supplies.

Ms. Frank: The school is dirty.

Ms. Brown: Not enough parent contact with our principal and teachers.

Facilitator: Fine, that's ten problems. We're halfway there. I'm sure you can think of ten more.

WATCH THE MEETING IN SLOW MOTION

Let's leave the meeting now and discuss what has been going on. Notice how the facilitator and recorder admitted that they were still learning and asked for help. Before beginning the meeting, they explained their roles and checked to make sure everyone understood. If you are the facilitator and make the social contract between you and your group clear from the start, many of the natural fears of a new process and of potential manipulation are put to rest. Members who don't trust this process at first will lie in wait to catch you evaluating or pushing too hard and will call you on it. They will watch for your reaction. If you are not defensive, thank them for their help, and correct whatever was bothering them, the doubters will relax and get more involved in the process. (That's what happened later in the meeting when Ms. Elliott caught the recorder editorializing and not using her own words. The recorder thanked Ms. Elliott for her help and corrected what he had written in the group memory.)

Next, notice how the facilitator got the group to focus and agree on the procedure by which they were going to generate a list of problems, rather than letting them rush off in all directions as in the earlier meeting without facilitation. She made sure the group wanted to go with the process of brainstorming before they got into content, i.e. school problems. She also made sure that everyone understood the ground rules of brainstorming before getting started. When Ms. Frank interrupted the meeting with a comment about Johnny's bloody nose, the facilitator didn't put her down but made sure the comment was recorded and then refocused the discussion.

HOW ANONYMITY HELPS

Since ideas are written down *without the name of the author,* an individual's ideas become the group's ideas. After a while, group members will tend to forget who originally made a particular suggestion. This depersonalization makes it much easier for the group to adopt a particular solution.

You might ask what happens if the facilitator or recorder flashes on a brilliant idea. What can they do about it?

We have found that group members become very possessive about their role and resent too many intrusions by the facilitator or recorder into a meeting's substantive content. One technique we have found works well when you are the facilitator and can't hold on to an idea any longer: just ask the group's permission to step out of your role ("Is it all right if I take off my facilitator hat for a moment?"). You then offer your idea and immediately step back into your role.

Often you will find that your ideas fall on deaf ears. We remember a session in which one of us, as facilitator, offered what he thought was a perfect solution to the problem. The suggestion was dropped like a hot potato, but fifteen minutes later a group member came up with a similar idea, worded slightly differently, that the group accepted.

Returning to our discussion of the PTA meeting, notice that when Ms. Elliott criticized Mr. Jones' idea, the facilitator leapt to Mr. Jones defense and reminded Ms. Elliott that the group had agreed to brainstorm and that during brainstorming all evaluation is deferred until everyone's ideas have been on the record. This intervention reassured Mr. Jones that the facilitator was there to guard against personal attacks, keep the group focused, and keep the momentum of the brainstorming going without the meeting degenerating into an argument over whether thirty was too large a size for a class.

WHEN MANAGERS DON'T RUN THEIR MEETINGS

Now let's return to the Acme Widget Company and see how division manager Joe's meeting might have gone using the Interaction Method. You may remember that he was meeting with his supervisors to talk about ways to reduce production costs. Let's assume that Joe has since had some positive experience using the Interaction Method; that he recognizes the value of having somebody run his meetings who has no personal investment in the outcome; that the Acme Widget Company has trained a pool of managers in the Interaction Method; and that these managers are free to act as facilitators for meetings in other departments during a few hours each month.

Since Joe realized that this might be an important and emotionally charged meeting, he requested an outside facilitator. So Tom from the Accounting Department was released to facilitate the meeting. Mary, a department secretary, had received some training as a recorder and was called in to assist at the meeting. (The conditions we are assuming here are now becoming commonplace in a growing number of private and public organizations with which we have worked.)

Sometimes the facilitator can provide pre-meeting assistance to the manager or chairperson. In this case, a few days before the meeting, Tom, the facilitator, met with Joe, the manager, to help him develop a clear agenda. Next, the most effective way to deal with each agenda item was considered, and they developed a content agenda (*what* they were going to talk about) as well as a suggested process agenda (*how* they were going to approach the subject). It was decided that the problem that the president of the Acme Widget Company had given Joe would be faced in a collaborative problem-solving session and that the meeting might begin with brainstorming alternative solutions. Also, some background information (as well as a report on the previous month's production levels) were to be written up and handed out before the meeting to avoid wasting valuable meeting time with an oral report by Joe.

The meeting begins. Tom, the facilitator, introduces himself.

Facilitator: Good morning. I'm Tom Layton from accounting. I've been asked to act as facilitator. I know your department uses the Interaction Method regularly, but just to be on the safe side I want to be sure you understand that I'm only here to help you do what you want to do. I'm your meeting chauffeur today. I'll try to remain neutral and not offer any of my own ideas or evaluate yours. But please help me—call me if you catch me taking sides and cutting you off. Mary is going to be the recorder. Make sure she gets down on the group memory what you actually say— not what she thinks you said.

As you can see on your agenda, the meeting will last an hour. It's going to be a problem-solving session. We're not going to try to make any decisions today—just come up with as many solutions as we can. Next Monday I understand Joe has agreed to another meeting to see if you can reach some consensus on what should be done. Is everything clear? Okay, Joe, can you begin by briefly reviewing the problems we are going to tackle today.

Joe, the manager: Acme is experiencing serious financial difficulties. Our materials and labor costs have skyrocketed—

Rico, interrupting: But not as much as the cost of living index—

Facilitator: Wait a minute, Rico. Will you let Joe finish, please?

Joe, regaining composure: As I was saying, material and labor costs have gone way up. We are in the red for the first time in years. We are in a very competitive market, and unless we can produce less expensively, we are going to be forced to discontinue the product line. The president has asked our division to cut costs by 15 percent while maintaining current production levels, and I feel personally obligated to develop a plan of action by next Monday afternoon. It's going to be very difficult to do this, but I want to involve all of you as much as possible. If we can't come up with something we all like by next Monday, I'm going to have to go ahead and make some decisions on my own. Do you understand me?

Juan: It's really that bad, huh?

Joe: Yup.

Facilitator: Joe, let's get the problem stated on the group memory. Could you state it concisely as a question?

Joe: All right: "How to cut costs by 15 percent." No, I said 15 percent, recorder, not 50 percent.

Recorder: Sorry. Thank you for correcting me.

Facilitator: Okay, is the problem clear? Does anyone want to define it further?

Rico: Couldn't it read, "Cut costs by 15 percent or increase production by 18 percent?" An 18 percent increase in production, given present costs, would decrease unit costs by 15 percent, I think.

Facilitator: Is that right, Joe? Are we really talking about unit costs?

Joe, slowly: Well, that's interesting. I hadn't thought of it that way. Of course, if we could increase output by the inverse of .85, that would be the same thing. I don't have a calculator but I think 1.18 is right.

Bill: Why don't we just say, "Decrease unit costs by 15 percent"? That would leave room for a combination of solutions.

Facilitator: Is that all right with everyone? *(Heads nod.)* Okay, the problem now reads, "How to decrease unit costs by 15 percent." Let's go, then. How about starting with a brainstorming session? Is everyone familiar with the rules of brainstorming? Throw out a lot of ideas. Piggyback on other people's ideas, but don't criticize them. We do that later. This can go fast, so make sure the recorder gets them all down. Let's go.

Marta: Reduce quality inspections from every third unit to every fifth.

Rico: Cut down number two line shutdown time—

Facilitator: Okay, next.

Rico: Hey, wait a minute. I'm not finished.

Facilitator: I'm sorry, Rico. Go ahead.

Rico: Cut down number two line shutdown time by developing a portable motor replacement while the main engine gets its daily safety check and service.

Juan and Joe (at the same time): How about—

Facilitator: Okay, one at a time. Juan and then Joe.

Juan: Reduce the number of men at number five station.

Joe: Cut out Sunday overtime.

And so the meeting progressed. At the end they had a long list of suggestions and had given them priorities according to ease of putting them in effect. For each of the top-priority ideas someone was assigned to follow up with a feasibility study and report back at the next meeting. The items and the name of the responsible person were circled on the group memory, and that sheet would be used as a reference at the next meeting.

WHAT HAPPENED THIS TIME

This was certainly a very different meeting from the one we presented in Chapter 2. The changes in your meetings can be just as dramatic with the introduction of the Interaction Method. In this case, Joe, the manager, really hadn't changed his personal style of management very much. He was still gruff and demanding, but he had come to recognize the value of letting his subordinates participate in coping with the problems of their division. Before, Joe dominated the meeting. He didn't get an objective evaluation of his ideas, and he didn't get any good ideas from his staff. Now, with the presence of a strong facilitator, he got some very good new ideas. He utilized the talent and expertise of his staff, and he maintained his managerial power.

Note how the facilitator spent some valuable time with Joe, preparing for the meeting, checking to make sure agenda items were really appropriate to be dealt with in the meeting, and making sure everyone had a copy of the agenda before the meeting. Then, together with the recorder, the facilitator set up the room so the meeting was ready to start on time (see Chapter 14).

At the beginning of the meeting the facilitator made sure everyone was clear about the ground rules—especially that no one was going to make any decisions at that meeting. The constraint of not making decisions at that meeting was one that Joe, as decision maker, could impose legitimately. The facilitator then got the group to develop a clear definition of the problem and protected Joe from Rico's interruption and commentary. Rico wasn't turned off, however, and later used his energy to come up with a much-expanded definition of the problem.

Other important actions of the facilitator included responding nondefensively when Rico felt he was cut off; acting as a traffic coordinator when people were trying to speak at the same time; not answering questions about the meeting's content but instead referring them to the manager; and making sure that everybody knew what was expected of him or her by the next meeting. These are some of the many useful interventions that the facilitator can inject to make a meeting more effective.

While brainstorming was the principal problem-solving method in the PTA and Acme Widget Company examples, it is only one of hundreds of methods available to groups. Problem-solving, planning, and decision-making methods, specific interventions, and discussion and presentation techniques are all part of the bag of tools that make up the Interaction Method. These techniques will be covered in Chapters 6 to 17. Before getting down to these specific techniques we would like to cover some other issues that affect how meetings—and for that matter, groups and organizations—work.

CHAPTER 4

How to Find Win/Win Solutions

The way an organization chooses to make decisions has significant impact on the quality of its decisions and on the group's very survival. Most decision-making techniques produce either win/lose or win/win decisions, and here we want to clarify the differences between the two types.

Let's invent a family of four: mother, father, and two children—a twelve-year-old boy and a girl of nine. The family has been split for years by an argument over where to spend summer vacations. The father and daughter love the sea and want to spend summers by the shore. The son has become a mountaineering and backpacking enthusiast and longs for the mountains. The mother, who ends up making most of the important decisions in the family, doesn't feel strongly one way or the other, but leans toward the mountains to support her son. Both parents are tired of paying high summer rentals for cabins and agree that it's time to invest in their own summer quarters. Now is the time to decide where.

In a win/lose situation the family might decide that the fairest way to settle this question is by majority vote. The father and daughter vote for the shore, the son for the mountains, and the mother abstains. The father and daughter have won; the son has lost an issue he feels strongly about. He could make life miserable for the rest of the family if he is dragged off to the shore every summer.

Another win/lose approach would be to appoint one person to decide. The obvious choice is the mother, who would then be faced by the certainty of alienating at least one member of her family no matter what she decides. If she follows her inclination and sides with her son, her husband and daughter are going to be resentful, and if she goes along with them, the son is going to feel even more left out and ganged up on.

A third possibility is that the family can't make a decision at all. Either the family becomes deadlocked in a two-to-two vote; or a one-to-one argument develops between husband and wife; or the family members can't even agree on a procedure for making the decision. In each case, the outcome is a lose/lose situation. Everybody loses. Family life is made miserable by the unending arguments, and the summer may be spent in the city by default.

"CONSENSUS" DOESN'T MEAN "COMPROMISE"

In a win/win solution everyone feels that he or she has won. Win/win solutions may be available to this family, but to find one the family must agree to work together until they can find a solution that everyone can live with—a solution that does not compromise any strong convictions or needs. That's our definition of consensus: You may not think it's the very best solution, but you can accept it without feeling that you are losing anything important.

In this case the family might sit down together and realize that they are limiting themselves to choosing between two unworkable, win/lose alternatives: buying a cabin in the mountains or buying a cabin by the sea. Renting was another unacceptable solution. If they channel their energies into working collaboratively, they might come up with many new win/win alternatives. Perhaps they could find another family in the same dilemma and arrange to buy and share two cabins, one in the mountains and one by the sea. Or they could buy a camper or motor home, divide the vacation between the two locations, spend less money, and go on more trips to other places. The point is that win/win solutions exist to many problems.

To see how win/lose and win/win decision-making works on a larger scale, let's invent a city of 100,000 in the West. It's a relatively old city which avoided some of the urban problems of the 1960s and is now experiencing signs of rejuvenation: the population is growing again and new construction is starting. However, the city faces a dilemma. While it is fortunate to have a $3 million budget surplus for the last fiscal year, two well-organized and vocal coalitions are vying for these funds.

On one side, there is a coalition of homeowners and members of the fire fighters' union. Because of the age of the fire-fighting facilities and equipment, the city has only an AA fire-insurance rating. If it uses the budget surplus to modernize its equipment, it could get an AAA rating, the insurance rates of homeowners would decrease, and the city would attract more federal funds for housing.

On the other side is a coalition of women's groups. They argue that there is a lack of adequate day-care centers, and this money would go a long way toward providing this much-needed service. Both sides agree that there is not enough money for new fire-fighting equipment and new day-care centers. The city council isn't eager to face this issue. It's an election year, and three members are up for reelection. They know that no matter what side they take, they will meet strong opposition. What should the city council do?

HOW TO SORT THE OPTIONS

One option is to do nothing and postpone the decision indefinitely. This inaction would result in a lose/lose outcome: neither the homeowners nor the women's groups would get anything.

Another option is to take a vote. Then the outcome would be win/lose either way. Regardless of how members voted, they would have to face many organized and disgruntled constituents. In the process of lobbying, both the homeowners and the women's groups would be forced into becoming adversaries and taking extreme positions in order to influence votes.

However, the city council decided on a third option and urged both parties to work collaboratively with representatives of the relevant city departments, state and federal agencies, and experts from the insurance companies. The homeowners and women's groups worked together with a facilitator, using the Interaction Method, and came up with a win/win solution. A portion of the surplus funds was used to convert the five local fire stations to day-care centers, and those facilities were used to attract matching funds from state and federal agencies to operate them. Then the major portion of the surplus funds was employed to build three regional fire stations supplied with the latest equipment, servicing the city more efficiently than the five old local stations and earning the AAA insurance rating. A win/win solution.

But is it worth the time and effort to find win/win solutions? And aren't win/win solutions just compromises?

No, they're not. A compromise would have been to allocate some of the funds for day-care centers and some of the money for fire equipment. A compromise wouldn't have adequately met the needs of either party—a half-baked solution. In this case the objectives of both parties were met. The fire fighters got new firehouses and new equipment without having to remodel antiquated buildings, the homeowners got an AAA rating, and

he day-care advocates got inexpensive, well-located facilities
and the funds to operate them. In general, the quality of solutions reached by group consensus is significantly higher than
the quality of solutions developed by voting or even individual
efforts.

WHY GROUP DECISIONS ARE SUPERIOR

This claim is probably best supported by an extensive research project performed by Jay Hall, a social psychologist. He
designed a test problem which he called "Lost on the Moon"
and studied the results of group decision-making under a variety of conditions. He found that "when a group's final decision
is compared to the independent points of view that the members
held before entering the group, the group's effort is almost
always an improvement over its average individual resource,
and often it is better than even the best individual contribution"
(*Psychology Today,* November 1971, page 51). Hall discovered
that the quality of a group's decisions was significantly higher
if group members followed these simple guidelines:

1. Avoid arguing for your own views. Present your position
as lucidly and logically as possible, but listen to other reactions
and consider them carefully before you press your point.

2. Do not assume that someone must win and someone must
lose when discussion reaches a stalemate. Instead, look for the
next most acceptable alternative for all parties.

3. Do not change your mind simply to avoid conflict and to
reach agreement and harmony. When agreement seems to come
too quickly and easily, be suspicious. Explore the reasons and
be sure everyone accepts the solution for basically similar or
complementary reasons. Yield only to positions that have objective and logically sound foundations.

4. Avoid conflict-reducing techniques such as majority vote,
averages, coin-flips and bargaining. When a dissenting member

finally agrees, don't feel that he must be rewarded by having his own way on some later point.

5. Differences of opinion are natural and expected. Seek them out and try to involve everyone in the decision process. Disagreements can help the group's decision because with a wide range of information and opinions, there is a greater chance that the group will hit upon more adequate solutions.

TRY THE "LOST ON THE MOON" TEST

We suggest you try the "Lost on the Moon" experiment for yourself. (See page 62.) Find four to seven other people and take this test individually, without revealing each other's answers. Then take the test as a group, first voting on the answers and then following the instructions above. The "right" answer, prepared by experts from the National Aeronautics and Space Administration, as well as instructions for scoring your answers, can be found on page 295. Compare the total error score of your individual answers with the scores of the answers you developed in your group by voting and by consensus.

It's obvious that group members will be more committed to a decision reached by consensus than to one settled by majority vote or mandated by one individual. A good decision isn't of much value to a group if few people are willing to accept it.

Americans tend to deal with issues by protests, strikes, and even riots. When frustration and anger get out of control, taking things into one's own hands seems like the only way. Public attention is drawn to issues and sometimes limited gains are won for one side. More often, everyone ends up losing. Regardless of outcome, in a long strike the union depletes its treasury by paying strike benefits; the company loses income and possibly its share of the market. A few years ago, a dock strike between longshoremen and a West Coast city went on for so long that many shipping companies moved to another port. The

DECISION MAKING

ALTERNATIVE DECISION MAKING METHODS & THEIR MOST PROBABLE OUTCOMES	
DECISION MAKING METHODS	**OUTCOMES**
• RIOT • STRIKE • PROTEST	LOSE/LOSE
• MAJORITY VOTE • EXECUTIVE DECISION • ARBITRATION • JURY TRIAL • COLLECTIVE BARGAINING WITH MEDIATION	WIN/LOSE

• COLLABORATIVE PROBLEM
  SOLVING WITH THE
  INTERACTION METHOD
  (CONSENSUS)
	WIN/WIN

city lost revenues and the longshoremen lost their jobs. A win/lose process resulted in a lose/lose outcome.

WHAT'S WRONG WITH VOTING

Our society has institutionalized many other win/lose methods. Obviously, the majority vote is basic to the American way, but it is significant that a growing percentage of the public is becoming disillusioned by the ballot box. Many people don't feel that they have an opportunity to vote on relevant issues.

"LOST ON THE MOON" TEST

Your spaceship has just crash-landed on the moon. You were scheduled to rendezvous with a mother ship 200 miles away on the lighted surface of the moon, but the rough landing has ruined your ship and destroyed all the equipment on board, except for the 15 items listed below.

Your crew's survival depends on reaching the mother ship, so you must choose the most critical items available for the 200-mile trip. Your task is to rank the 15 items in terms of their importance for survival. Place number one by the most important item, number two by the second most important, and so on through number 15, the least important.

_____Box of matches
_____Food concentrate
_____Fifty feet of nylon rope
_____Parachute silk
_____Solar-powered portable heating unit
_____Two .45-caliber pistols
_____One case of dehydrated milk
_____Two 100-pound tanks of oxygen
_____Stellar map (of the moon's constellation)
_____Self-inflating life raft
_____Magnetic compass
_____Five gallons of water
_____Signal flares
_____First-aid kit containing injection needles
_____Solar-powered FM receiver-transmitter

When they do, the alternatives are either too limited (candidates say and do the same things) or are expressed as extremes (the mountains or the shore, fire protection or day-care centers, environmental controls or energy self-sufficiency).

People all through society are demanding more involvement in community decisions. In organizations and businesses, employees are demanding more participation in the decisions that affect their lives. And in families, children are no longer tolerating decisions imposed by parents. So the win/lose alternative of individual or executive decision is becoming increasingly unworkable.

As society becomes more complex and interconnected, no one official or group will be able to dictate what should happen. For an issue of urban renewal the mayor may need approval of the city council or board of supervisors, who in turn may need approval of the planning commission, which may need the support of the construction workers and downtown businessmen, who may all be blocked by local residents of the area who take the issue to court.

There are no longer only two sides to many issues—matters that can be submitted easily to the win/lose mechanisms of arbitration or the courts. As a result of growing demands for involvement and an increasing complexity and interconnectedness of issues, the need for win/win solutions is obvious.

WHAT'S WRONG WITH NEGOTIATING

Here comes a startling realization: Our society has not institutionalized ways to get together people who represent different sides of an issue and put them to work collaboratively toward a win/win solution. Mediation is available for getting two parties to negotiate with each other—but negotiating is bargaining, not collaborative problem solving. The only institutionalized procedure that encourages—in fact, requires—consensus is the jury system. But juries are asked to reach unanimous agreement about yes/no decisions—guilty or not guilty. Juries do not develop win/win solutions; they only pass judgment on pre-structured, win/lose outcomes. Moreover, juries are not instructed in the most successful and efficient methods of reaching consensus. The fact that they do come up with unanimous decisions every day shows that consensus is indeed possible.

The Interaction Method, we are firmly convinced, embodies the fundamentals of one win/win method that can work for communities, organizations, and all kinds of groups.

Fifty years ago people said that mediation and arbitration would never work. They didn't—because they didn't have to. Organized labor did not pose a threat to management. The lose/lose threat of strikes forced the development and acceptance of mediation of new contracts. Because of the threat of work stoppages, binding arbitration provisions are standard in many contracts. But these two mechanisms are not producing the comprehensive solutions that our society needs for survival.

CAN ORGANIZATIONS SURVIVE?

Organizations today are besieged. They are experiencing pressures from the outside: consumerism, worldwide competition, the fast-changing market place, and society's demands for social responsibility. And from inside: the forces of changing technology and an increasingly educated, demanding, and powerful work force. These forces are compelling organizations to make changes. In their book *Managing with People,* Jack Forgee and Raymond Weil comment,

> People don't seem to want what they used to want. The old deal isn't good enough. . . . People don't want to do the same thing over and over. . . . People want greater freedom to do as they wish and with their own bodies. . . . People want their work to

be challenging and interesting. They have for a long time, but more so now. . . . Many people are tired of hearing about political democracy while living in an oligarchy for 40 hours a week and being governed by corporate or institutional rules which were not of their making and which they lack the power to change.

We predict—and there is evidence to support this—that twenty years from now a variety of processes and technologies will exist to involve large numbers of people in effective collaborative problem-solving and decision-making.

NOW FOR THE REALITIES

If consensus cannot be reached, a group can always fall back on some win/lose method like voting or executive decision. However, it is very difficult, if not impossible, to move from a win/lose approach to a more collaborative one. Even if a group has to resort to win/lose decision-making, the experience of searching collaboratively for a win/win solution encourages group members to develop a real understanding of complex issues and gain the satisfaction of having had an opportunity to participate in developing the best possible alternatives.

A key question remains: Assuming that win/win decision-making is a worthwhile objective, how do you put it to work within the realities of our contemporary organizations? Specifically, how do you reconcile the delegation of power and responsibility to a boss with the idea that many other people should participate in problem-solving and decision-making?

To answer this question, we need to return to our distinctions between hierarchical and horizontal organizations. The solution is somewhat different in each case, but since most hierarchical organizations have some horizontal groups within them, we suggest that you read about how to make participation work in both.

WHAT HAPPENS IN HIERARCHICAL ORGANIZATIONS

The critical question that managers ask when faced by the prospect of group participation is: "How can I involve my subordinates in decision-making without giving up my ultimate responsibility and accountability for the final decision?"

The key to this problem lies in our definition of consensus. Remember: Consensus is reached when everyone in the group can buy into (or live with) the decision without feeling compromised in any way. Managers, this means you too. As a member of the group, your approval is necessary for consensus. Your veto blocks consensus. Since voting is not permitted, you can't be outvoted by your subordinates. The group must develop a solution that you can support wholeheartedly. If consensus is impossible, then the decision is placed back in your hands, and you can exercise your right to make an executive win/lose decision. If you and your subordinates clearly comprehend that you will have to make the decision by yourself if a win/win solution cannot be developed within the time constraints you set, your group will work harder at developing realistic solutions, and you yourself will not feel that you are being pressured or losing power. In practice this works by what we call "hierarchy collapsing." When an important problem has to be solved or a decision affecting several individuals in parts of your organization has to be made, and you want to deal with it in a collaborative way, you form a group that may cut through several levels of your organizational chart.

YOU SET THE RULES

Let's assume that the meetings of this group will be run by the Interaction Method. If you're the ranking executive in the group, you play the role of manager/chairperson. At the begin-

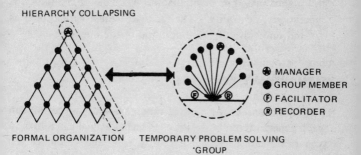

HIERARCHY COLLAPSING

FORMAL ORGANIZATION   TEMPORARY PROBLEM SOLVING GROUP

⊛ MANAGER
● GROUP MEMBER
Ⓕ FACILITATOR
Ⓡ RECORDER

ning of the meeting, you set a clear limit on the time available for the problem to be solved or decision made. You also clarify any other constraints that apply—limitations imposed by you or your superiors, by organizational policy, by financial limitations, or by other internal or external realities. There is a danger in assuming that too many variables cannot be changed and therefore limiting the range of possible solutions too drastically, but there is an equal danger in withholding essential information; you may give your group the feeling that anything is possible and thereby doom the group's efforts to certain failure.

In any event, once the constraints have been clarified, you become an equal working member of the group. You speak up for your ideas, express your feelings clearly, and try to keep your mind open to the ideas of other members of the group.

As we explained earlier, you should not attempt to run the meeting, but find someone to act as facilitator. Ideally, the facilitator should be trained and experienced in the skills of facilitation but have no personal stake in the subject matter of the meeting. The facilitator may come from outside your organization, from another part of your organization, or from your own group. Neutrality is assured by the system of checks and balances we have described. The facilitator, as a servant of the group, must refrain from behavior which any member of the group finds biased or manipulatory. The goal of facilitation is "operational neutrality." The facilitator must be accepted as fair and uninvolved for the duration of the meeting.

EITHER WAY YOU WIN

If, by the end of the allotted time, you and your group can reach consensus on the decisions to be made, you can return to your desk, revert to your executive role, and announce the decision, knowing that it has the support of key people in your organization. (In general, we have found that win/win solutions can be developed in more than half the cases where our method is tried.) If a win/win solution cannot be found, at least your group understands the issues involved, your position, and the difficulties of making the decision. You thank them for their cooperation and input, and make the decision yourself.

Usually, members of your group will tend to be more sympathetic and understanding regardless of what you decide than if you pop the decision on them without giving them the chance of meaningful involvement. You haven't lost very much by the process of seeking a win/win solution, and you may have gained a great deal: valuable information, new ideas, or even a final solution.

What if you don't have days or weeks to develop consensus? Assume that you get a telephone call in the morning from your boss requesting a solution by five o'clock for a problem that has just cropped up. The problem lies completely in the area of your responsibility, but any solution will probably have a direct effect on your staff. You believe that it would be a good idea to involve your immediate staff of ten people in the problem-solving and decision-making. You need their ideas and their backing—fast.

EMERGENCY!

You call a meeting for ten A.M. When everyone is present, you begin, "I'm sorry for calling a meeting on such short notice, but the boss just now told me about a problem and he needs a decision by five this afternoon. I want you all involved in the decision because it will affect all of us. I've got a meeting this afternoon with clients, and I can't get out of it. So, we've got two hours now to see if we can reach a win/win solution. That means coming up with something that you can buy into and I can, too. If we can't reach consensus, I'll have to go ahead and make the decision myself, but even so, you'll have given me a lot of input to help me make my decision. So let's work really hard to come up with something.

"Joan, since you're least involved in this problem and we all know you're a good facilitator, I'm asking you to run this meeting. I'll be a member of the group and I suggest we rotate the role of recorder. Before we begin, I want to lay out a few constraints. I know for a fact that the boss is dead against changing Policy A at this time. Also, any solution we come up with has to be paid for from our existing budget. And finally, I'm personally against hiring any new people now, although I'm willing to stay open on this point. Okay? I'll give you the problem and then turn the meeting over to you, Joan."

Let's assume that by eleven-thirty Joan has been able to facilitate matters so that the group has generated three potentially workable solutions. She now tries to move the group toward consensus. Several techniques are available to her. She decides to try "negative voting."

"All right, we have only half an hour left. Let's turn the corner and see if we can get some consensus. We have three alternatives labled A, B, and C on the group memory. Let's start with A.

"Let's have a show of hands from all those who wouldn't be able to live with Solution A." (Three hands go up, including yours.) "Okay, solution B: Raise your hand if you couldn't accept B." (Two hands go up.) "Solution C." (Six hands go up.)

WORKING TOWARD CONSENSUS

Joan would now probably focus on Solution B, since it had the least opposition, and try to work with the two dissenting individuals. Once they express their reasons for opposing Solution B, their arguments would be written down on the group memory. Then Joan might ask the group as a whole to generate changes that might satisfy one or both of the dissenters:

"Okay, Phyllis said that she wouldn't accept Solution B because it would mean that she would have too much to handle. Can anyone think of a way of dealing with that? . . . Okay, George would be willing to assist you part-time. What do you think, Phyllis, would that make a difference? Can you now accept Solution B? . . . Could everyone else live with this change?"

By trial and error Joan would try to bring the group to consensus. She would protect individuals from being coerced by the rest of the group, always working to turn objections into positive alternatives. Depending on many factors, including the complexity of the issue, the skill of the facilitator, the time available, and the level of trust that prevails within the group, the group will either reach consensus or not. If it does, the rest would be simple. You might praise the group for its hard work and cooperation, let them know that you are going to take the agreed-upon solution to your boss, and adjourn the meeting knowing that you have your staff behind your decision. You might have been able to come up with the same solution by yourself, and faster, but then it would be your solution, not your staff's.

If consensus turned out to be impossible, you might thank the group for its contributions. (For relatively unimportant decisions, consensus may not be necessary.) Then, if you are clear about your decision, you might announce it. Otherwise, return to your office and weigh the alternatives. At least you could draw on three developed solutions and know how your staff feels about each. Your staff would also know what your biases are and have a good sense of what you're going to have to do and why.

Please be sure to note again: We are not talking about doing away with hierarchical organizations and individual responsibility. A hierarchy is very effective for organizing people to accomplish set tasks. For each job, one and only one person is responsible. Questions of authority and accountability are clarified easily.

WHY WORK ALONE?

Our point is that organizational structure does not dictate the process—the sequence of events—by which decisions are made. Just because one person is ultimately accountable, that person does not have to operate alone. A hierarchy can be temporarily reconstituted into a number of horizontal groups strictly for problem-solving and decision-making. It then returns to its original form. An organization, after all, is not a static chart. It is a living organism. It should respond to different challenges in different ways and adapt to different needs.

To summarize: Depending on the nature and importance of a decision, as a manager, you can either make it yourself, delegate the decision to someone else, or form a temporary, collaborative problem-solving group. In the last alternative, you are stepping out of your role in the formal, hierarchical organization and into a role in the temporary, horizontal group for the period of the meeting, and then back to your desk in the hierarchy. In this way, your organization moves between two forms—a formal and permanent authority structure and an informal and temporary process structure. You can enjoy the benefits of both organizational forms. But you will have to bring some flexibility to your management style.

IS IT WORTH THE TROUBLE?

You might ask, "I can see how it's possible to achieve participation in decision-making in hierarchical organizations, but is it really worth the effort? Couldn't I make the decision myself and save time and money? It's nice if my staff feels a greater sense of involvement, but are there any tangible benefits to my company or organization? Will profits or productivity increase?"

We have already given evidence that the quality of decision-making and problem-solving produced by a well-facilitated group can be higher than that generally attainable by an individual working alone. So one answer is that your profits will indeed be affected positively by the increased quality of group problem-solving and decision-making.

HOW GOOD MEETINGS PERK UP MORALE

Not only will more work be accomplished during a meeting, but also more work may be produced by people after meetings. There is no need for the usual recovery time when people hang around the water coolers bitching about how bad a meeting was and trying to calm down enough to go back to work. When people leave meetings feeling good, the transition back to their jobs is easier. And when you feel good about your team and what it can do collaboratively, you tend to work harder on your own. It's a combination of not wanting to let the team down and feeling that your job is meaningful because it is necessary for the group's success.

A different way to gauge the benefits of participation in hierarchical organizations is to contrast productivity and worker absenteeism in similiar companies run by Japanese and by typical American management systems. The Japanese system of management places a high degree of importance on employee participation. Ideas and suggestions are expected to bubble up from the bottom, not trickle down from the top, as in most American companies. The higher you are placed in the Japanese system of management, the more your function is to encourage your subordinates to generate solutions.

HOW IT WORKS IN JAPAN

If an important policy decision is to be made, groups are formed at all levels of the company to discuss the issues and move toward consensus for action. The process of employee involvement and discussion can take a good deal of time. Under the American management system, a few executives might make the decision faster, but then comes a lengthy period when the decision must be sold to countless people up and down the organization. Once a Japanese organization finally comes to a consensus, it can move very fast. The total time between initiation and implementation of policy can therefore be shorter under Japanese management.

A professor at the Stanford School of Business, Richard Johnson, has studied comparable companies in the United States whose only significant difference is the management system. Johnson selected two television manufacturers with almost identical assembly lines. The only difference is that one company is run under a Japanese management system and the other under the traditional American system. In this case, as in every other comparison study conducted by Johnson, the company run by Japanese management principles achieved significantly higher productivity with a dramatically lower rate of absenteeism. Managers attribute this difference to the increased sense of

personal involvement that is produced by the process of participation. Since each section of an assembly line worked and
solved problems as a team, a worker knew that he or she was
letting the team down if he or she didn't turn up for work the
next day. The team would have to cover for any absent worker
because substitute workers are rarely hired.

So a good deal of evidence exists that in hierarchical organizations employee participation and consensual decision-making
is possible and practical. The Interaction Method is one key to
creating the required collaborative environment.

WHAT HAPPENS IN HORIZONTAL ORGANIZATIONS

In the charter of many horizontal organizations, where members have equal power and responsibility and decisions are
usually made by voting, H. M. Robert's *Rules of Order* (1876;
prescribing British parliamentary procedure) is prescribed as
the way to conduct business. This is true of most governmental
bodies such as state and federal legislatures, boards of supervisors, and school boards as well as many boards of directors of
profit-making and nonprofit organizations. As a result, these
organizations are restricted to debate, as opposed to collaborative problem-solving. They are tied to win/lose (as opposed to
win/win) decision-making. Robert's *Rules of Order* makes no
allowance for open investigation and analysis of a problem.
Instead, problems must be raised in the form of suggested solutions and stated as resolutions: resolved that such and such
should happen. The dialogue is restricted to debate, pro and
con, supplemented by amendments to a proposed solution.

This process violates all the principles of collaborative problem-solving we have discussed. Pre-made solutions are presented before there is even agreement that there is a problem
to be solved; members are forced to take sides to discuss the

issues; and the spontaneous flow of ideas is often restricted by clumsy, elaborate procedures. That's why in most formal organizations, including Congress, collaborative problem-solving and support-building is done informally in caucus before formal meetings. A meeting becomes an official debate and a necessary prelude to the final vote. And, as we have shown, the need to report a majority vote produces a win/lose mentality, which inhibits consensual decision-making.

HOW CHAIRPERSONS WORK WITH FACILITATORS

Parliamentary debate is useful as a court of last appeal. Majority vote is a fair way of settling an issue if collaboration breaks down. But the Interaction Method can work well in meetings of horizontal organizations. The exact procedures will be covered in later chapters, but in some cases, the entire meeting is run by the Interaction Method; the chairperson participates actively as a member of the group and returns to the chair to nail down final motions with a formal vote.

In other cases, when "new business" comes up, members can decide by what process they wish to deal with the issue and use the Interaction Method to arrive at consensus. At that point the chairperson can either assume the role of facilitator or turn the meeting over to someone else to facilitate, as did the PTA president in the previous chapter. After the agenda item has been dealt with, the facilitator turns the meeting back to the chairperson, a formal vote is taken, and the meeting proceeds to the next agenda item. Here's how this can work in practice.

At a meeting of the board of directors of a museum of contemporary arts, Ms. Hertzstein, the chairperson of the board, opened the meeting by the traditional procedures of Robert's *Rules of Order*. She called the meeting to order, asked for the minutes of the previous meeting to be read by the secretary, and called for committee reports. The chairperson then moved to old business and called for a vote on two motions tabled from the last meeting. When all the old business had been cleaned up, Ms. Hertzstein moved to new business. The first agenda item involved categories of membership. The board had decided to initiate a new membership drive but now had to decide on how many and what type of membership categories there should be. The chairperson recognized that this was going to be a complex issue. To deal with it by Robert's *Rules of Order* would mean entertaining motions suggesting particular categories before the board had even agreed on whether there should be different memberships and, if so, how many. This would be clumsy and time-consuming. So Ms. Hertzstein suggested switching to problem-solving by the Interaction Method. Since this had produced good results before, the board members agreed.

Ms. Hertzstein, who had strong opinions about the membership issue, joined the semicircle of board members; two members of the museum staff who had been trained in the Interaction Method got up to facilitate and record.

During the next hour the facilitator helped the board to come to agreement that different categories of membership were useful for raising funds for the museum, that there should be no more than four categories, that there should be a student membership rate, and that nonmembers should be allowed to attend most of the museum programs. Then the facilitator asked for specific suggestions for membership categories. All the alternatives were recorded in the group memory and, by adding and eliminating categories, the board reached consensus on four categories that met their specifications.

At that point the facilitator turned to the chairperson and said, "Ms. Hertzstein, would you please take over now to formalize this decision."

Ms. Hertzstein, resuming her position as chairperson: Is there a
    motion from the floor?

Mr. Lutz: I move that we adopt the four membership categories circled on page 25 of the group memory.

Chairperson: Is there a second?

Ms. Vasquelas: I so second.

Chairperson: It has been moved and seconded that we adopt the four membership categories as recorded on page 25 of the group memory. All those in favor say aye. *(Everyone says aye.)* All those opposed say no. *(No one responds.)* The motion has been carried unanimously.

The chairperson then continued on to the next three agenda items, handled them by parliamentary procedure since they involved routine business, and ajourned the meeting.

A CHAIRPERSON CAN ALSO FACILITATE

If you're chairperson and you encounter resistance against the Interaction Method, you can stay in the chairperson role and employ many of the techniques described in this book by simply being aware of the distinction between process and content. Merely by refraining from using the chair to push for your personal views, you can improve the quality of your meetings. It is the underlying concepts behind the Interaction Method that are important.

We believe in choosing and adapting whatever techniques you find useful. For example, we have seen meetings in which the chairperson continued to use a version of Robert's *Rules of Order,* but asked someone else to record, creating a group memory on newsprint attached to the bulletin board of the conference room. Board members found the graphic display very useful and were able to visualize and apply the detailed information easily.

WHY TEMPORARY GROUPS NEED THE INTERACTION METHOD

What about temporary groups that are becoming increasingly popular for dealing with problems inside and outside of organizations? Task forces and committees are springing up everywhere. If there is a problem involving a number of organizations, agencies, or departments, a task force is appointed consisting of representatives from each of the groups.

It has become axiomatic that if someone does not participate in the process of solving a problem and making a decision, he or she is not likely to accept the outcome. Or, another way of saying it, all the people who must ultimately approve, accept, or implement a decision should be involved from the beginning in the process of making the decision.

Granting that for the foreseeable future the win/lose process of representative politics will continue to be a reality of governmental decision-making, let's look at informal organizations as an alternative. As we have seen, it's not enough to bring people together in a group and hold a meeting. The process by which the meeting is run is critical in determining whether the group will become a multi-headed animal or a constructive, collaborative organism. That's why the Interaction Method is a key to making a task force work

WHERE POWER COMES FROM

In some organizations (i.e. city councils or boards of directors) the power to make binding decisions flows from elected representation. The constituency (or membership) elects representatives who are empowered to make decisions that affect those who elected them. In other organizations and temporary groups—citizen goal-setting programs, investigative committees, and interdepartmental task forces—the members can only make recommendations. Their power comes from overlapping membership and the power of consensus.

Suppose a dispute erupts over the hiring of minority teachers. The board of education, the superintendent of schools, two different teachers' unions, and three parents' groups are involved. A task force with members drawn from these organizations, as well as other people with relevant expertise, would have no binding power over any of these organizations. However, the members of the task force can and should have influence in their respective groups.

If the assistant superintendent, officials of the two teachers' unions, and representatives of the three parents' groups are members, the task force gains power through overlapping membership. If it works collaboratively, makes its own decisions by consensus, and does not vote, the issue of numerical representation—the stumbling block of many community task forces—can be avoided. The group won't get bogged down in arguments about whether one organization should have more votes because it represents more people. Since consensus is being used, one vote is enough to block an unacceptable proposal.

HOW TO MAKE A TASK FORCE WORK

To make a task force effective, someone must accurately present each point of view. Members represent typical concerns, not numbers of people. They speak for themselves, but they also represent others who think and feel the same way. The key is that all the main points of view should be included in the task force.

Once a task force can reach consensus and a win/win solution, its members can return to their respective positions in their organizations with a high probability of getting their people to "buy into" the decision. If the task-force proceedings have been open and fair, if there has been plenty of opportunity to hear all sides and for people to contribute, public opinion will strongly influence the parties to accept the consensus of the task force. Once again, the people involved and how they work together will determine success.

If, in the case of the dispute about hiring minority teachers, the task force can reach consensus, the solution would probably be accepted by all. If consensus cannot be attained, then the task force might issue a report including a summary of its deliberations and, in particular, how it defined the problem; an analysis of the present situation; the alternatives that were considered, with the advantages and disadvantages of each; and perhaps a majority and minority position statement.

All this valuable information would be fed back into the existing formal decision-making procedures. The result might be a lengthy legal battle in the courts or a prolonged teacher strike to be resolved in the end by collective bargaining and mediation. However, the prospect of these time-consuming courses of action should be enough to encourage the participants of the task force to keep working for a win/win solution.

The Interaction Method is suited to dealing with such a situation because it is task oriented, nonmanipulative, easy to comprehend, collaborative, and graphic. Because ideas are not labeled with the names of individuals and because no one is permitted to dominate the discussion, so-called experts have less opportunity to dominate and intimidate the less-educated and less-verbal members. Everyone's ideas are recorded on the group memory, regardless of how they are expressed. People who would normally be antagonistic can find themselves working cooperatively.

HOW FACILITATORS DIFFER FROM MEDIATORS

A neutral party contributes greatly to collaborative problem-solving by highly diverse individuals. Mediators and arbitrators have become accepted as neutral third parties, and the role of the facilitator evolves from this tradition, but with a major difference: mediator and arbitrator get involved in the content of a dispute. The mediator acts like a diplomat, running back and forth between the two parties and making suggestions about what the final resolution should be. The arbitrator has power to act like a judge and, after listening to both sides, to make a final decision.

A facilitator remains detached and therefore more unbiased and neutral. He or she does not get involved in the content of the problem but only in making suggestions about ways to reach solutions. Because all parties are meeting together, this neutrality of the facilitator is critical. And the system of checks and balances permits all parties to monitor what happens and be sure that the facilitator does not step out of his or her role. Even though the facilitator may have personal opinions about an issue, these opinions are not expressed (or allowed to interfere), which is why it's much easier to get all parties to agree to a facilitator than to a mediator or arbitrator. We have witnessed the acceptance of good facilitators who held strong and ordinarily vocal views on the subject under discussion—as long as they remained in their neutral roles for the duration of the meeting.

HOW TO GET A COMMUNITY INVOLVED

We also know of many citizen involvement efforts that successfully applied win/win measures after traditional political methods failed.

The Department of Recreation and Parks in Berkeley, California, had been trying for ten years to involve the neighborhood in the planning of a recreational facility. Each time a proposal reached the city council, it was shot down by some group that felt it had been manipulated or had not been involved in developing the proposal. Partly out of frustration, the department hired Ethan Gluck, a planner trained in the In-

teraction Method. His task was not to design the park building
but to design a way for members of the community themselves
to plan the facility in collaboration with the department. Ethan
enlisted the community through open meetings where he used
the Interaction Method. He did not contribute his own ideas or
evaluate those of the participants. His role was to help people
express their views and listen to each other, and to make sure
that everyone had an opportunity to be heard.

Since he was hired by the city, many citizens were suspicious
at first. They had seen too many professional people telling
them what to do. But after a few people had challenged Ethan's
neutrality during meetings, particularly when they felt they had
been cut off unfairly and when Ethan apologized or let them
continue, they became convinced that those meetings were "for
real"—not attempts by the "establishment" to manipulate
them.

Everyone's ideas were put down on the group memory—
children's ideas next to old people's. All ideas had a chance to
be heard, developed, and evaluated in an atmosphere of cooperation. This time all segments of the community were on board.
Ethan helped a representative cross section of the community
move collectively through the planning process—from pro-
gramming to selection of an architectural firm. The plans for
the recreational facility were presented by community leaders
to the city council and passed. The community had accomplished in six months what it had been unable to achieve in the
previous ten years.

The rest of this book offers specific tools and techniques to
put the Interaction Method to work in meetings of all types and
sizes and in all kinds of situations requiring an organization's
best efforts.

CHAPTER 5

A Summary of the Interaction Method

We have covered some of the common problems encountered in all kinds of meetings and groups, and here they are again in summary form to refresh your memory:

Multi-headed animal syndrome. Everybody going off in different directions at the same time.

Confusion between process and content. Are we talking about *how* to discuss the topic or *what* topic to discuss?

Personal attack. Attacking individuals rather than their ideas.

Traffic problem. Difficulty in leaping into the conversational flow and getting a chance to participate.

Unclear roles and responsibilities. Who is supposed to be doing what?

Manipulation by group leader. Rubber-stamp meetings and abuse of process power to achieve personal objectives.

Data overload. Having to hold on to too many ideas in your head at one time.

Repetition and wheelspinning. Going over the same old ideas again and again.

Win/lose approaches to decision-making. Partial solutions, compromises, polarization, and low commitment.

Other common problems include:

Confused objectives and expectations. Why did you call the meeting and what is the group supposed to be doing? Hidden agendas.

Unresolved questions of power and authority. Do we have the power to make this decision?

Problem avoidance. "Everything is fine"; "There are no problems around here."

General negativity and lack of challenge. There is nothing we can do about it, so why try?

Communication problems. Not listening to or understanding what others are saying or making faulty assumptions.

Poor meeting environments. Can't hear, can't see, too stuffy, etc.

Personality conflicts. Lack of openness and trust, underlying tension, racism, and sexism.

The key to the success of any meeting, regardless of how it is run, is planning and preparation. In planning a meeting there are some basic questions you have to answer. Each question concerns a variable that has to be fixed, and in the following chapters we will answer the questions listed above as well as those listed below:

Why have a meeting? What are your *objectives* and *expectations?*

What *type* of meeting do you want to have?

Whom do you want to attend? What should be the *composition* of the group?

What kind of *involvement* and *participation* do you want?

How many people do you want? What *size* of meeting?

Where are you going to meet? What should be the *room arrangement?*

What *roles* and *responsibilities* should individuals have during the meeting?

Who will have the *power* and *authority* to make decisions?

What *methods* and *techniques* of discussing, planning, problem-solving and decision-making are you going to use?

How much *time* are you going to allow?

Will there be an *agenda?*

Will there be *presentations?*

Will there be some kind of *record?*

What are the desired *outcomes* of the meeting?

How are you going to determine *tasks, deadlines,* and *responsibilities?*

This, then, is the how-to part of the book. We like to think of it as a meeting cookbook—it's chock full of recipes to make your meeting cook on all burners. We hope you'll feel free to:

mark up, index, and underline the whole book, especially this part, in any way that will help you to use it;

write notes in the margins;

use and modify our tools or invent your own and jot them down in the front or the back of the book; and

take this book to meetings.

By now you know that the Interaction Method rests on four well-defined roles and responsibilities which collectively form a self-correcting system of checks and balances. All four roles are equally important. Each contributes to the health and productivity of a group. No one person is in the traditional leadership role of having to "save" the group. Instead, everybody has a stake in the outcome and is equally responsible for the group's successes and failures.

To review who our four key people are:

The *facilitator* is a neutral servant of the group and does not evaluate or contribute ideas. The responsibility of the facilitator is to help the group focus its energies on a task by suggesting methods and procedures, protecting all members of the group from attack, and making sure that everyone has an opportunity to participate. The facilitator serves as a combination of tool guide, traffic officer, and meeting chauffeur. He or she is also responsible for all pre-meeting and post-meeting logistics.

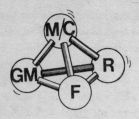

THE INTERACTION METHOD
SELF CORRECTING ROLES:

M/C = MANAGER/CHAIRPERSON   F = FACILITATOR
GM = GROUP MEMBER   R = RECORDER

The *recorder* is also a neutral, nonevaluating servant of the group. The responsibility of the recorder is to write down basic ideas on large sheets of paper in front of the participants. The recorder does not edit or paraphrase, but uses the words of each speaker. The objective is not to record everything that is said but to capture enough so that ideas can be preserved and recalled at any time. In this way, the act of recording does not significantly slow down the progress of the meeting. The record itself is called the group memory and serves as an accepted record of what is happening as it is happening. Participants can relax and let go of ideas in the knowledge that their contributions have been heard and preserved in full view of the group.

The *group member* is an active participant in the meeting. It is the responsibility of the group member to keep the facilitator and recorder in their neutral roles and to make sure that ideas are recorded accurately. As long as the meeting is being run by the Interaction Method, the control of what happens rests in the hands of the group members. They can make procedural suggestions, overrule the suggestions of the facilitator, and generally determine the course of the meeting. Otherwise the group member devotes his or her total energies to the task, knowing that the facilitator is protecting participants from personal attack, keeping individuals from dominating the discussion, and worrying about the best methods and techniques for dealing with the agenda.

The *manager/chairperson,* under the ground rules of the Interaction Method, does not run the meeting but becomes an active participant. Otherwise, he or she retains all other powers and responsibilities. The manager makes all final decisions; has the power to set constraints and regain control if not satisfied by the progress of the meeting; sets the agenda; argues actively for his or her points of view; urges group members to accept tasks and deadlines; represents the group in meetings with other groups; and deals with media and the public at large.

The Interaction Method functions like the automatic pilot on an airplane. If the meeting gets pushed off course the system of roles and relationships can correct itself automatically. If the facilitator steps out of line, the group members and manager/chairperson will push back. If the recorder begins to editorialize, the others will object. If the manager/chairperson attacks a group member of vice versa, the facilitator will intercede. The method is so simple that any group can understand the system and learn to run its own meetings effectively.

CHAPTER 6

How to Be a Good Facilitator

Learning to become a facilitator is like learning to play a game or a sport. You can learn the rules quickly and begin to play. But to become a good player takes considerable practice. You must know something about the theory of the game and about strategies for dealing with different situations as they come up. But most of all, you must develop your skills by using them.

Some people like to start on a new project by getting an overview to understand why something works, why it is necessary. Earlier chapters, especially Chapter 2, answer the "why." (It is very important to understand why a facilitator can do a lot for a meeting and why the role works. It also makes your life easier: If you really understand the theory, you can invent your own techniques.)

Other people like to jump in and try to learn by experience. They just want to be given a few rules and techniques and shove off on their own. We encourage this, too. If everyone knows what a facilitator can and cannot do, your group can help you to learn. Here are some do's, don't's, and specifics on:

1. how to get a group to focus on a common problem and a common process;

2. how to protect group members and ensure that everyone participates; and

3. how to remain neutral and build trust.

Since the role of facilitator is based on flexibility and accommodation to the needs of the group members, it would be hypocritical and impossible to lay out a step-by-step procedure comparable to Robert's *Rules of Order.* Unlike the chairperson who can waltz to the regulated music of Robert's *Rules of Order,* the facilitator has to do a combination tap dance, shuffle, and tango to a syncopated rhythm produced by unpredictable humans.

There is no "right" way to facilitate. Much depends on your personality, the situation, and the nature of the people in your group. You must pick the techniques that seem most appropriate at the time. Remember, your group is a reservoir of knowledge and creativity. With the techniques detailed here, you can tap this resource. Then you and your group can solve almost any problem you face.

HOW TO EXPLAIN THE FACILITATOR'S FUNCTION

It is very important that everyone in the meeting understand exactly what your function is. The first time you facilitate a group, your explanation may help to lower the anxiety for some members. By explicitly defining roles and responsibilities, you create a social contract with your group. You agree to try to remain neutral and not to evaluate or contribute your own ideas, and the members agree to share the responsibility of keeping you in your role.

So here's what you might say as a facilitator when all participants are present:

"Hello, my name is _____, and I'm going to be your facilitator today. Just so that we're all clear, being a facilitator means that I am not going to contribute my own ideas or evaluate yours. My role is to help you focus your energies on the task. I am going to try very hard to remain completely neutral and to defend you from personal attack if necessary. I'll make some suggestions, but only about the process of the meeting—ways to proceed, not matters of substance. I'm your servant and this is your meeting. Being a good facilitator is difficult, so please help me. If you think I'm pushing too hard or manipulating you in any way, please let me know. If you correct me, I'll try not to be defensive. With your help, I'm sure we'll have a good meeting and get a lot done today." (For variations of this introduction, see Chapter 3.)

Then you should make sure that all other roles are clear to the group. The recorder should explain his or her role and the function of the group memory, and you should let the group members know what their responsibilities are. The role of manager or chairperson should also be clearly defined. And, if there are other roles to be played (especially those of observer and expert, which we cover at the end of this chapter), you should define these. When everyone knows the ground rules, you are ready to begin the meeting. (These introductions can be abreviated after you have facilitated the same group a few times.)

HOW TO FOCUS ON THE SAME PROBLEM IN THE SAME WAY AT THE SAME TIME

The facilitator frees group members to focus on their common task. By assuming the responsibility for guiding the group, you offer people a better opportunity to achieve what is called synergy: when the group itself becomes more than the sum of individual members. This potential for a high level of creativity and accomplishment usually lies dormant. It is a large part of your job to try to awaken the sleeping synergy, like an orchestra conductor who gets each musician to play so as to create a sound that no single musician could ever produce.

You'll remember our discussing the multi-headed animal syndrome—the tendency for people in meetings to go off in different directions at the same time. We concluded that in an effective meeting a group must be of one mind, focused on the same problem in the same way at the same time.

The more group members understand the dynamics of meetings, the better they will function together. You may have to start by explaining the difference between content (what the people want to do) and process (how they are going to do it). You have to tell your people to hold their horses until they have agreed on:

1. The first agenda item (the content).

2. The way they are going to deal with it (the process). This second step is rarely taken in meetings. It means that you have to "rein in" your group and not let it go at the problem until the new procedure is understood.

HOW TO BUILD AN AGENDA

Suppose you face a group which doesn't have an agenda and has never been in a meeting run by the Interaction Method. Here is how you might get the group working.

Facilitator: Are there any more questions about why we're here and how the meeting is going to be run? *(No more questions.)* Okay, let's get going. Let's get a list of possible agenda items, and then choose one as a start. Why don't you toss out things that you think need to be done today, and the recorder will get your thoughts down on the group memory. Don't worry which items are most important, and don't evaluate each other's suggestions. Just make sure that your own agenda items get included. Okay, let's go. Who's got an item? *(The group generates a list of issues.)*

Facilitator: Okay, any more items? Remember, we can keep adding to the list as we go along. *(Someone suggests one more item.)* Okay, let's stop here. *(Looks at the group memory.)* Looks like we have a lot of work to do. *(Laughter.)* Obviously, we aren't going to be able to solve all these problems at this meeting. So, we've got to choose a place to begin. Who can think of an item that's really pressing, that we need to take care of first. *(Three people suggest three different items, which the recorder stars on the list.)* Okay, we have three pressing issues. Is there a logical sequence to them? *(Someone suggests an order; several heads nod in agreement.)* We should be able to cover all three items today, so if it's all right with everyone, let's begin with number three, then number five, and then number two. *(No objections are voiced.)* So, now we're going to tackle item three. But before you rush off in different directions, let's agree on how we're going to discuss this issue. There is no one right way to solve this problem. We will have to poke at it from one direction, see how it goes, and then come back from a different direction, just like a boxer. Let's see if we can agree on the first punch. Any suggestions?

Frank: Let's get José to give us a rundown on what he's been doing so far.

Facilitator: Any other process suggestions?

Maria: We could all say what we think should be done.

Paul: I think the answer to this problem is simply—

Facilitator: Wait a minute, Paul, hold your horses! You'll have a chance to give us your solution later. You're trying to solve the problem before the rest of us have decided how we're going to begin. That's what I was talking about before. It may be frustrating at the start, but if we're going to work together we've got to use the same tools at the same time. We've got to agree on the "how." So, Paul, please hold your idea for a moment. Do you have a process suggestion, a way of attacking this problem?

Paul: Well . . . I agree with Maria; we could go around the room and give our solutions.

Facilitator: Good. Any other thoughts?

Elizabeth: Let's see if we can get to understand the problem better.

Facilitator: Any ideas about how, Elizabeth?

Elizabeth: Well, see if we can figure out why it's happening. *(Heads nod.)*

Facilitator: How about this as a way of getting going? Why don't we begin by asking José to give us a short analysis of the problem, since he's been closest to it. Then, as a group, let's continue to analyze the problem by building on José's presentation and come up with a list of possible causes of the problem. We'll see if we can agree on some of the most probable factors and then try to think up ways of taking care of them. If this approach doesn't work, we'll try attacking the problem head on as Maria suggested. Is everybody willing to try this approach? *(Heads nod.)* Okay, José, why don't you give us about a five-minute overview of the problem and what you've been doing about it.

To start this way takes more time than just leaping in and having a free-for-all. But the payoffs are worth it.

Many meetings don't start from such a rudimentary base. Perhaps an agenda has been prepared and some participants have had previous experience with the Interaction Method. Then the group could begin right away with the first item and would only have to agree on the methodology. Sometimes a tentative "process agenda" can be developed.

WHO "OWNS" THE AGENDA?

Particularly in meetings of task forces and community groups the first part of the meeting has to be devoted to shaping the agenda so the group will feel it "owns" a common list. If you, as facilitator, make up an agenda and start the meeting by telling the participants what they are going to do, some people are likely to object and start challenging your right to be so directing. A group will naturally resist having an agenda laid on it without an opportunity to add items of their own or to decide which items to deal with first. Agreeing on a working method is also critically important. After you have started to build trust with your group, you will get permission to be more directive about which approach to use.

Notice that at the very beginning of the above example, the facilitator had to suggest a method (process) just to build up a list of agenda items: he asked each member to toss out what he thought had to be done, without evaluating others' suggestions. Obviously the process of agreeing on a process could become ludicrous—an endless regression. You've got to begin someplace.

If one or two people want to disrupt the meeting entirely, they could refuse to agree to any process. Then, as facilitator, you might have to confront them directly: "It seems you don't want this group to get anything done; what's the matter? Are you concerned about something?" If it turns out that some participants are committed to a lose/lose strategy of disruption, then collaborative problem-solving is impossible. You should step down as facilitator and a win/lose procedure will have to be adopted.

KEEP THE REINS LOOSE AT FIRST

When you facilitate a new group, it's a good rule to let the group begin by struggling with the decision of where it wants to begin and how. Give as few directions as possible, especially at first. Wait until people are convinced you are there to help them and that they need your help. Soon participants may start to complain that the meeting is moving too slowly and ask you to take more control. Then you can start being more emphatic, but still without stepping out of your role. You can give such directions as "I think we should stop and move on to the next alternative and make a list of the advantages and disadvantages. John, can you think of an advantage of this alternative?"

You can tell by your group's faces whether the members are with you or not. Their expressions will let you know if you are pushing too hard.

In the previous example, the facilitator got the group to generate a list of ways to tackle the first problem, while keeping Paul from leaping in. The final process suggestion from the facilitator was actually a combination of the two most popular suggestions. Later in the meeting, you, as facilitator, might be able to skip this and simply tell the group what you think should be the next process.

Keep on making sure that all group members are constantly clear about what's "what" and what's "how." If there is confusion, stop and clear it up. Underline the transition from one process to the next: "Okay, now we'll stop brainstorming and start evaluating." "We're now moving on to item three." "John, have you finished?" "Okay, now it's your turn."

All these little jumps are simple and unconscious for the mind of an individual, but infinitely more complex for a group of minds to grapple with. They need to be explicit and conscious.

WHEN TO MOVE ON OR SLOW DOWN

Because you are not trying to solve a problem or make a decision yourself, you can diagnose more easily when your group is getting hung up or fixated—when it's time to try something else, to move on. As facilitator you must ask yourself and your group: Are we getting anywhere? Is it time to move on to a different topic or try a different point of view?

You are in a good place to make such process suggestions and decisions. You must try to slow the group down when it picks up too much speed, starts to bypass important issues, and makes hasty decisions. It's easy to flag the group down. Try saying, "Hey, we have plenty of time left! Let's make sure we're all together. You don't want to rush into something you may regret later."

When the energy of the group is getting low, when people lose interest or show signs of frustration because they are not getting anywhere, it's your job to become an energizer. You can pump up the group with your own energy. Move around the room. Show enthusiasm. You don't have to sound like a cheerleader, but you can say, "You've been doing well! Let's not get bogged down. We've just a little more to do. Let's really push. Maybe it's time to move on to the next point."

Sometimes you can get people to become aware of their sluggishness. Try "Hey, you all look dead this morning. What's going on?" Or try a little humor: "You all look as if you had too good a time last night." Laughter and smiles, along with honesty and acceptance, help tremendously. So does a physical change; get people to stand up and stretch. Open windows. Take a short break.

Be aware of the group's many possible moods. Stay in contact with their happiness or sadness, exhilaration or frustration, friendliness or hostility, peacefulness or anxiety. Empathize with your group and try to stay on the same wavelength.

WHEN THE GROUP GETS STUCK

Here's how the facilitator can use a group memory to focus the attention of the group. When nothing cohesive emerges from a meeting, move up close to the group until you have everyone's attention. Then walk back to the proper place of the group memory, point, and say, "Okay, here's where we are. We just finished talking about criteria. Is there an eighth item, or can we move on and test what we've now got against the alternatives over there?"

The last line on the group memory becomes a marker to return to after a digression.

Remember, you're in a powerful position when you facilitate; you command the attention of the group. Don't abuse this power. You should become a lens through which the attention of the group becomes focused on the problem. You can help to sharpen and direct the attention of the group, but don't block it. Don't be seduced into basking in the limelight. Whenever possible, step aside and let the group move at its own speed. When the meeting is going well, you may only have to say something every few minutes. Some groups can go for long stretches facilitating themselves. You can sit down and wait until you are needed.

It's a great temptation to be a ham and get pumped up by the group. However, the group came to work, not to listen to you. The participants should do 95 percent of the talking. Become aware of how often you talk. Do you speak after each contribution of the group, or every second or third? This is a measure of the degree to which you are controlling the flow and monopolizing the attention of your group. Talk only when you have to, and then be short and concise.

HOW TO HANDLE SILENCES

Silences produce some of the most difficult times for facilitators. There you are in front of a group and nothing is happening —nobody is talking. It is a great temptation to start talking yourself—just out of sheer nervousness.

Different kinds of silences convey different meanings. Check out what is happening. Is the group just pondering a point and making a natural pause? Or the silence could be the result of confusion, fatigue, or boredom. Find out what's happening— don't assume too much. Try "Hey, is everyone asleep or are you thinking?" "Everything all right?" Or "Is everyone lost or do you just want some time to reflect?"

If you ask a question and don't get an immediate response, don't say anything; just wait awhile. If you answer your own questions, people will get lazy and let you do the work for them. Wait them out.

If you really want some suggestions on what to do next, say, "I need some help. What do you think we should do next?" But then be quiet! Don't start offering possibilities until people have come to grips with the question for a while. If, after a minute or two, nobody comes up with anything, you can prime them by suggesting some examples: "For example, we could move on to the next agenda item or take a break or try coming at this problem from a different point of view—what do you think?" If no useful suggestions are forthcoming, you can offer a menu of alternatives and see if you can get some commitment around one.

Finally, if you feel some movement is better than no movement, you can take the proverbial bull by the horns and say, "Well, since there doesn't seem to be any strong feeling one way or another, I suggest we try . . ." But keep in mind that while there are times when it is appropriate to be forceful and even dictatorial, if you assume too much control, your group will revolt and tell you to stop being so pushy, or worse, become totally dependent on you and relinquish a sense of responsibility for the success of the meeting.

HOW TO ENSURE PARTICIPATION

You'll recall two problems that limit effective participation: (1) difficulty in getting a chance to speak, and (2) fear of personal attack (the group-rape syndrome). It's your role as facilitator to prevent these problems.

By consent of the group, a facilitator is empowered to act as a gallant police officer. A good facilitator promises to make sure that every group member has an equal opportunity to be heard and is protected from personal attack. (This includes group members who are absent from the meeting.) You don't have to be an experienced group leader to keep these promises. By handling yourself like a fair and friendly traffic cop you can go a long way to promoting participation.

Start the meeting on a positive note. It's hard for people to be creative and productive in a negative atmosphere. Most people relinquish their creativity when they are confronted with "Yes, but . . ." or with put-downs: "That's silly." "That's impractical." "That'll never work."

Your role is to be positive and encouraging. Help the group along. Let them know when they're doing a good job: "Good idea! We're really moving along. We're really beginning to work together now. You're doing fine! Let's keep it up." By establishing a positive, nonthreatening atmosphere, you'll help people in the group express themselves—especially the shy or naturally quiet ones. They'll be more open and responsive. When they don't feel so tentative and cautious, they'll feel freer to contribute what they might otherwise consider an outrageous idea (often the most creative). You'll hear them saying, "This is pretty far out, but maybe . . ."

LYING DOESN'T HELP

It's important to compliment the group, but don't exaggerate. Be sincere. The group will sense when it's not doing a good job, and if you lie to them about it you'll only reduce your credibility. Instead, when things go wrong, say so—but state it so as to encourage the group to recognize that the situation can be changed:

"Well, it looks as if we're getting bogged down. We were doing fine a while ago, but we got distracted. Some of you look as if you've tuned out. How are you feeling? Let's do a little backtracking and review the group memory to see how we got off the track. I think we can still head back in the right direction. Come on, anyone remember what we were trying to do?"

By all means do accept incomplete ideas. People don't always think in well-formed prose. Group members may offer ideas that sound strange, incomplete, fragmented. Accept them anyway. Don't tell somebody to rethink a notion before offering it. If an idea is impossible for you to decipher, ask him or her to help you rephrase it. If it sounds like the tip of an iceberg, you might say something like: "Fine, if you want to add more later, we can always come back to it. Maybe the group will want to work more on that idea, too. Okay?"

Try to move along with the energies of the individuals and the group as a whole; flow with your people. If they're thinking in disorganized fragments, let them do that for a while. See whether they're able to pull themselves and their thoughts together.

Protect the group from anyone's domination. In a hetero-geneous group there are bound to be many social and profes-sional types. And there is almost always one person who loves to do all the talking. As facilitator, you can try to take the focus and the floor away from that individual by deftly interrupting, "Thanks, Bob. Now, what do you think, Ruth?"

HOW TO PUNCTURE A FILIBUSTER

To handle this kind of situation, you have to move quickly and discipline your body language. Move toward the person who does all the talking. When he or she looks at you or stops to take a breath, leap in and turn to someone else (you may even have to resort to turning your back on the marathon talker). If you do this a few times and the person still doesn't get the hint, you may have to be blunt: "Bob, you're sure doing a lot of talking. Let's hear from some of the other people." The secret is obvious—be gentle but firm.

Sometimes individuals in groups get left out. Their feelings get hurt and they become alienated. For a variety of reasons they may have trouble articulating their views. Quiet members can get run over by the highly verbal and aggressive people in the group. Some people feel no one listens to them anyway, or that their views are "too different" and therefore won't be respected. They clam up and withdraw.

In community gatherings the "expectation theory" often sa-botages participation. That is, the poor and uneducated go to meetings with the expectation that professionals (teachers, principals, city planners, government officials) and other well-educated people will naturally display their verbal prowess and dominate the meeting. Likewise, the latter will expect the mi-nority group to be passive and listen. It becomes a self-fulfilling prophecy. The same thing can happen when people from differ-ent levels of a hierarchical organization get together.

Skillful facilitation can greatly broaden the participation in these situations. As the process guide, you can hold back the highly verbal and aggressive people while you encourage responses from the rest. At first, it's like pulling teeth, but after a while people will feel more at ease and less shy. What's more important, as their self-confidence increases, people get used to the reality of participating. Then they begin to expect and demand it.

HOW TO AVOID REPETITION

Nothing saps a group's energy like being bored by people who constantly repeat themselves or by long-winded discussions. The group memory can help you get the group off the merry-go-round. You can remind people that they've already said something. Pointing to his words on the group memory, you can look at Richard and say, "You've already said that. See, Richard, we've got it written down. Is there anything new you'd like to add? If not, let's go on."

If people get off the subject, you can refer to the group memory and say, "Here, we said we were going to talk about this. I'm not sure that's the problem you're addressing now. If you want, we can put that down too, and tag it for later." Or if someone is just talking too much about the topic at hand, gently nudge her: "Gloria, could you try to be more concise?" Be prepared to deal with people who come to meetings with the intention of using the group as a captive audience to air their personal philosophy or gripes.

There is a difference between creative conflict and interpersonal confrontation. Creative conflict occurs when people are actively stating and listening to opposing points of view. Any agitation that results is directed at the *ideas,* not at the people voicing them. But interpersonal confrontations can bottle up creative resolutions: when two or more people begin to focus on each other's personalities rather than their ideas, when they begin to detour into petty bickering, someone has to intervene before the entire group's energy is distracted.

HOLD YOUR FIRE!

When destructive arguments start, try to get the combatants to focus their energy on solving problems rather than on attacking each other. Maybe this will work: "That's one idea. Let's not evaluate it yet. The recorder will just write that down for now. How about some other ideas? What do you think? Let's keep it positive and constructive." Whenever possible, try to get participants to deal with their interpersonal conflicts outside the meeting room.

To ensure a positive environment (especially if you anticipate that there will be personal confrontations), ask everyone to say what he/she likes about an idea before stating a negative concern. This often prevents potential solutions from strangulation in their infancy.

Some individuals particularly need to be protected from being interrupted or having words stuffed in their mouths by other group members. It's your job to guard the rights of the not-so-articulate. Be patient yourself and hold the reins on impatient group members: "Take your time! We'll wait for you. Hold on; let Martin try to say it in his own words. If he wants help, he'll ask for it." Sometimes the group will want to rush; certain members will try to steamroll over the less articulate and aggressive people. Slow them down: "Take your time. Don't rush; we've got enough time. Let's hear from Joan."

Don't let group members bully others. Don't let people criticize or insult each other. If someone says, "That's a dumb idea —boy, are you stupid," you should counter with, "Hold on! Barry's ideas are just as important as everyone else's." Group members will appreciate this and feel more comfortable about participating and sharing their personal ideas if they know they won't be jumped on.

SEE YOURSELF AS OTHERS SEE YOU

Being in front of the group and having the members focused on you as a leader is a mixed blessing. As facilitator, you should become aware of the nonverbal messages your body posture and movements send to the group members. You may think you are projecting a pleasant and positive visage, when in reality you are shaking your head negatively. Try to watch yourself sometime on videotape or practice in front of a mirror. Become aware of how you use your body to bear down, to exert power or to back away from a situation. Often, out of sheer exhaustion or dire frustration, your body will relay a negative message to the group. And since we've already discussed the importance of setting and maintaining a positive tone, it's obvious that a wilted facilitator can be detrimental to a group.

Be aware of your "space language." That is, carefully arrange the meeting environment to make it the most comfortable and efficient space possible. To project a sense of openness, closeness, and receptivity, don't put anything (such as a table, podium, or desk) between yourself and the group. It may be difficult enough to establish rapport without purposefully building a fence to separate yourself from the group.

In other words, be sensitive to your environment. Since you are facing the group directly, you can make eye contact with everyone easily and see when someone wants to talk or when several people want to say something at the same time. By nodding, pointing, moving toward someone, or addressing someone by name, you can gently control the flow of conversation. In a small group you may not have to do much signaling, but when a group consists of seven or more people, your traffic functions become very important.

HOW TO REGULATE TRAFFIC

Your objective is to get those people who want to talk to line up and go to bat one at a time—and to prevent anyone from barging to the head of the line. You can accomplish this in a variety of ways. When several people start talking at the same time, you can say, "Hold on! Let's go one at a time. Why don't you go first, Mary, and then Phil and Harry." And when someone is talking and a few others signal that they want to speak, you can recognize them in the order you want them to talk by pointing to them in sequence. ("You, you, and then you.") If someone butts in, say, "Wait a minute, Frank! Phil and Harry have been waiting to talk, and then you go." Members of your group then see that you are firm but fair. They'll relax and be content to catch your eye because they know they will get a chance to be heard. In large meetings (over fifteen people) you may have to insist on the raising of hands.

Sometimes as you stand in front of an energetic group, you can feel as if you are standing in the middle of a jungle path with all kinds of animals rushing to a water hole. Loud, assertive beasts are pushing their way past others; sleek, speedy animals dart back and forth; timid animals wait with watchful eyes for a chance to move without being crushed. And then there are the fierce animals, more hungry than thirsty, ready to leap upon an unsuspecting fellow traveler. It is your job to tame these beasts and get them to move along peacefully together.

HOW TO DEAL WITH PROBLEM PEOPLE

In almost every meeting one or two people cause problems for the rest. Dealing with these problem people is like walking a tightrope. You must maintain a delicate balance between protecting the group from the dominance of individual members while protecting individuals from being attacked by the group. As always, you should try ways for everyone to win before resorting to interventions which will produce win/lose solutions.

Here is a method we have found helpful. While each situation is a little different, the following sequence of responses usually works.

Accept. When a problem person disrupts a meeting, begin by accepting what the person is doing, rather than simply ignoring the interruption. You can acknowledge the individual's action by describing it without evaluating. When a Doubting Thomas makes a loud noise in disapproval of a particular suggestion, you might say, "Thomas, looks like you don't believe that we'll be able to reach consensus on this. Am I correct?" Always check out your perceptions. Don't rush off to assumptions. You may be wrong.

Legitimize. Once you have let a problem person know that you have heard him or her correctly, legitimize the validity of the feelings behind the behavior. "Thomas, I know you're concerned. The process of coming to consensus can be frustrating. And you may be right." You don't have to agree with the problem person; just acknowledge that it is legitimate to feel that way. Point out that he or she may be helping the group by raising doubts or introducing different points of view.

Defer. Suppose you have reached a decision point: You can either deal with the issue right away or try to get agreement to defer until later. Let's take the latter option first. In many situations it's better not to try to resolve an issue in the middle of a meeting, or it's just more appropriate to address it later. Make sure that the concern is recorded in the group memory so it will not be forgotten; then explain to the problem person why you prefer to defer. In the case of the Doubting Thomas: "We won't know if we can reach consensus until we try. Are you willing to give it a chance? If we can't reach consensus we can always fall back and settle the matter by a win/lose approach." If the problem person agrees to defer, quickly refocus the meeting and continue with what you were doing before the interruption. If the problem person insists on continuing the disruption, go on to the following step.

Graduated response. In dealing with problem people, always begin with the most subtle and least threatening interventions. If a low-key approach doesn't seem to work, then you may have to escalate, saving direct confrontation as a last resort. Move gradually from win/win to win/lose techniques. In the case of a loudmouth, begin by looking directly at the person, thanking the individual for his or her contribution, and then calling on someone else. "Thank you, Harry. Okay, Elizabeth, you're next." If this doesn't work, move to Harry's side of the room and finally step up very close to Harry, making him feel uncomfortable by your physical proximity, by your invasion of his private space. Look him in the eye and say, "We've got that, Harry!" Still remaining close, turn away from Harry and call on someone else. If that doesn't work, confront Harry outside the meeting! "What's going on, Harry? Why are you dominating the meeting and not letting other people have a chance to talk?" Finally, you may have to confront Harry in front of the group: "Hold on, Harry. It's my opinion that you're dominating this meeting and not giving other people a chance to talk. I'd like to check my perceptions out with the rest of you. Do you feel the same way?" This is the most threatening approach and should be reserved for last.

MEET THE PROBLEM PEOPLE

Problem people fall into certain basic types. Here's how you can handle some of those types.

The latecomer always comes to meetings late, making a big commotion, stopping the meeting and wanting to be caught up. As a general rule, don't confront the chronic latecomer in the meeting in front of the group. It won't help and will just lead to embarrassment. There are any number of reasons why a latecomer doesn't come on time: he or she doesn't think the meeting is very important, doesn't believe it will start on time, tries to schedule too much, or is always behind. Wait until after the meeting and then simply ask the latecomer why he or she is late for the meeting so frequently. Don't lecture! Ask the latecomer what would make the meeting important enough to want to be on time. Perhaps you might ask the latecomer to be the facilitator or recorder for the next meeting.

The only way meetings are going to start on time is by starting them on time. Waiting five minutes at one meeting will lead to a ten-minute delay the next. And pretty soon everybody will be timing their arrival according to their personal estimate of when the meeting really will begin. If you start meetings on time, people will get the idea that when you say ten-thirty, you mean ten-thirty and not ten-forty-five. (If it's ten-thirty and only a few people have arrived, let *them* decide when to begin the meeting. Maybe they will think it's a waste of time to begin before certain other members are present.)

Every group member is going to be late sometime. To keep disruptions to a minimum, focus the meeting away from the door. When someone comes in late, acknowledge his or her presence: "Hi, Rita, glad you could come. Sit down here and catch up by reading the group memory." Don't stop the meeting to review. Let the latecomer sit quietly without participating for a while to get a feeling for what has been happening. If the latecomer is a critical person and a detailed review is required, take a short break and review the group memory without wasting other people's time.

The early leaver drains the energy of the meeting by leaving before it ends. Like the latecomer, this individual shouldn't be confronted before the group. Find out later why this disruptive behavior continues. Maybe your meetings are too long or too loose. Maybe there is something you can learn from the early leaver.

At the beginning of the meeting, check to see if everyone can stay until the end. If all the participants commit themselves to staying, a potential early leaver is less likely to sneak out. If one or more people announce they are going to leave early, find out when and decide at the beginning of the meeting whether you will continue in the absence of these members. There is nothing worse than continuing a meeting with people slowly wandering out. It's like sitting in a bathtub and watching the warm water drain out around you.

The broken record keeps bringing up the same point over and over again. Use the group memory to acknowledge that the point is important to the individual. Demonstrate that it has been heard and recorded several times. "Yes, Alice, I know this idea is really important to you. We have written it down on page three and on page six of the group memory. We won't lose it. We will have a chance to evaluate it later with all the other ideas when we are finished generating alternatives. Is there something else that you want to add? If not, can you let go of it now?" If the individual is worked up over the issue and looks as if he or she needs an opportunity to talk it out, you could suggest, "Why don't we take three minutes now to hear what you've got to say, so you can let go of it. We want you to be able to free your mind so that you can move along with us through the rest of the meeting."

The Doubting Thomas constantly puts down everything: "That will never work"; "That'll never happen"; "I don't like that." This Thomas is always negative; you're wrong until you prove yourself to be right. While it's healthy to have a skeptic in any group, aggressive negativism is a damper on creative effort. As a facilitator you can use mental judo to cope with the doubting Thomas. Get the whole group to agree to a process of not evaluating ideas for a set period of time, then use this agreement to correct anyone who violates it, especially the doubting Thomas: "Wait a minute, Harry! You and the rest of the group agreed not to evaluate ideas for a while. You just jumped on Joe's suggestion. Hold on! You'll get a chance to evaluate ideas later."

The headshaker nonverbally disagrees in a dramatic and disruptive manner. Headshakers shake heads, roll eyes, cross and uncross legs, slam books shut, push chairs back, or madly scribble notes after someone has said something. These nonverbal gestures can interrupt a meeting as effectively as words. Perhaps more insidious for you as a facilitator, the headshaker can grab your attention and get you to lose your temper at him or her. You begin to find yourself reacting to whatever the headshaker does, since you're the only one in the group who is directly facing this person.

The first strategy to try is to ignore the headshaker and focus your attention on the person who is talking. Often the habitual headshaker is unaware of his or her behavior. You can turn to the individual and say something: "Frank, I see you're shaking your head. Looks like you disagree with what has just been said. Do you want to share your reactions with the rest of the group?" Sometimes if you treat these gestures like any other negative comment, Frank will become more aware of what he is doing and tend to control his body language. But if the headshaker becomes disruptive or extremely annoying, wait until a break and share your perceptions. "Frank, every time you start shaking your head, you interrupt the meeting just as much as if you had cut somebody off verbally. What's bothering you?" Perhaps he has a legitimate gripe. Eventually you may have to say, "I think you're being unfair to the others, and I personally find it really annoying! Please try to control your body language!"

The dropout sits at the back of the room, doesn't say anything or reads a book or doodles. The dropout tends to be more disturbing to the facilitator than the rest of the group. You're trying to run an energetic, creative meeting and Carl is sitting there, yawning and reading a magazine. There is an almost irresistible urge to catch the dropout in the act by asking,

"What do you think about that, Carl?" And then watch him squirm. Gotcha! But sometimes the doodler hasn't really dropped out. Some people think better with a pencil in their hands. Or the real dropout may have a good justification; perhaps there is no reason for him to be at the meeting at all. Sometimes just walking up near the dropout is enough to wake him or her up. Or wait until you have eye contact, ask a question, and then take the dropout off the hook by turning to someone else: "What's your idea on this, Carl? I'll give you a moment to think. How about you, Jennifer?" During the break, ask the dropout why he or she isn't participating. Sometimes this behavior is an indication the meeting is not very effective, that a topic is irrelevant, or that the dropout is more or less understandably preoccupied with something else for the time being.

The whisperer is constantly whispering to a neighbor and is one of the most irritating of the problem people. It is very hard to concentrate with two people whispering and giggling near you. But many group members don't have enough courage to object. As facilitator, try walking up close to the whisperers. Often this low-key intervention will work. If there is a lot of whispering going on, you can say, looking around the room, "Hey, let's keep a single focus here! We won't get anything done if people are going off in different directions." If two cronies are really going at it, you can stop the meeting and say, "Do you want to share what you're talking about with the rest of the group? If not, why don't you go outside the room to talk? We still have a lot of work to do here." At a break, ask them what's going on. A very subtle technique is to find a way to get chronic whisperers to sit apart from each other.

The loudmouth talks too much and too loud, dominates the meeting, and is seemingly impossible to shut up. Loudmouths are a common breed, gravitating naturally to meetings of all kinds. Often the loudmouth is the senior person or decision-maker in a meeting—a fact which makes dealing with the loud-

mouth more difficult for the facilitator. The most subtle techniques for coping with loudmouths involve your physical position in relation to them. Try moving closer and closer to them
while they are talking and maintain eye contact until you are
standing right in front of them. Your physical presence—you
standing, they sitting—will often make them aware of their
behavior and they will stop talking. Then, immediately shift
your focus and call on someone else. Otherwise, deal with
loudmouths outside the meeting. Often loudmouths are people
who have to blurt out ideas as soon as they come into their
heads. Give them a pad of paper and ask them to create their
individual memory, or get them to serve as recorder. That will
keep them busy and keep them from talking. Point out that they
are dominating the meeting and preventing others from participating. If nothing else works, you may have to confront
them directly in the meeting.

The attacker launches personal attacks on another group
member or on you as facilitator. If two group members are
going at it, try to interrupt the fight by physically moving
between them, getting them to talk to you rather than to each
other. Ask, "What's all this about? What's the problem?" Remind them that everyone is at the meeting to work on a task,
not to watch them work out their personal problems. "That's
fine if you want to work out your differences, but why don't you
do that after the meeting?" Use the group memory to refocus
on ideas rather than individuals. Walk up close to the recorder
and get the attacker to focus on what is being written. "Make
sure we are capturing your criticisms. You feel that this suggestion over there is unrealistic and unworkable?" Also, you might
try the techniques of deferred evaluation (see the Doubting
Thomas, above).

If it's you who is being attacked, try to resist the natural
instinct to deny the charges and defend yourself. If it's your
facilitation that's being criticized, take a step backward, give
yourself a moment to collect yourself, thank the attacker for his

or her criticism, and then use the boomerang technique by turning the issue back to the attacker for positive suggestions. "You feel that I am not giving you and Louise enough opportunity to state your case. What do you think I should do to correct the imbalance?" If the attack is in defense of other group members, check out the accusation with them. "Louise, do you feel the same way? Do you feel that I've not been giving you enough time to state your case?" This technique can be a way of getting the group as a whole involved in correcting the situation, but don't let the group attack the attacker.

The interpreter always speaks for other people. "What Alberto is trying to say is . . ." If Alberto is in the middle of talking, jump in quickly and say, "Hold on a minute, George, let Alberto speak for himself. Go on, Alberto, finish what you were saying." Or if Alberto has already finished, check out the interpreter's interpretation with him. "Alberto, do you think George understood what you said? Is that an accurate representation of what you were saying?" This technique gives group members an opportunity to tell George they don't need him to be their mouthpiece.

The gossiper introduces hearsay and gossip into the meeting: "Well, I overheard them talking about . . ."; "I remember the regulations saying something about . . ." Hours of valuable meeting time are wasted arguing over whether something is true or not when five minutes and a telephone call would answer the questions definitively. When you see potentially important information being introduced with vague qualifiers ("Somebody mentioned that . . ."; "If I remember correctly . . ."), check it out immediately: "Do you know that for a fact?" "Are you sure?" "Can anyone else verify that?" If the responses are weak, ask, "How could we find out the answer to that question? Who would know?" Then, either defer the issue until after the information can be obtained or take a short break to make a telephone call, look up the information, or invite an expert to your next meeting.

The know-it-all uses credentials, age, length of service, or professional status to argue a point: "Well, I'm the one who has a Ph.D. in physics, and I know it doesn't work that way"; "I've been working in this business longer than anyone else here, and I know that will never fly." Acknowledge the know-it-all's expertise once, but emphasize why this issue is being considered by the group. "Yes, we all recognize and respect your experience in this area, but the decision has to be made by the group as a whole after weighing all the alternatives." "Yes, we know this is your specialty and you may be right, but one reason why we're tackling the problem as a group is to come up with some new insights and solutions. Your knowledge may actually be blinding you to new ways of looking at the problem. Will you indulge us for a while even though some of the suggestions may seem crazy to you?" Or try, "That's your opinion, but there may be equally valid other points of view."

The backseat driver keeps telling you what you should be doing: "I would have let people discuss the issue more before brainstorming"; "I would move on to the next issue if I were you"; "Tell him to shut up." As a servant to the group, the facilitator should request process suggestions from the group and generally follow them. When a backseat driver starts criticizing your facilitation, ask him or her to suggest a procedure and then check it out with the rest of the group. If the other group members concur, act on the suggestion immediately. The backseat driver will be satisfied and defused for a while. If the group disagrees, the backseat driver's argument will be with other group members, not with you. Occasionally you will encounter a backseat driver who thinks that he or she is a more sensitive, skillful facilitator and will disagree with everything you do. This can be really annoying and slow up the meeting. Point out that there are different styles of facilitation and many ways of approaching problems. There is no one right way, but you have to start someplace. Ask the backseat driver politely to bear with you and try your approach. If it doesn't work, the group can always try something else. In extreme cases, you may have to challenge the backseat driver openly: "Do you want to facilitate? That's fine if you do, but if you don't, please do me the courtesy of withholding your criticisms until after the meeting." The backseat driver will usually back down, but if your offer is taken up, step down gracefully. The backseat driver will either do a better job, which is okay, or do a worse job, in which case the group will come to respect the difficulties of the position, appreciate your facilitation, and ask you to step back into your role. But don't say, "I told you so."

The busybody is always ducking in and out of the meeting, constantly receiving messages or rushing out to take a phone call or deal with a crisis. What's worse, the busybody is often the manager or senior person in the meeting. That's why he or she feels so free to come and go, but by doing so the busybody ends up wasting his or her time and the time of the rest of the participants. During each departure the meeting may come to a standstill or the busybody has to be briefed upon reentry. Often there is no point in continuing a meeting if a key person is absent. As a facilitator, it is almost impossible to deal with a busybody during the meeting. Only group members or the manager/chairperson can exert any real pressure on the busybody to stop the interruptions and remain in the meeting. You can recommend that the meeting be recessed or adjourned until the busybody can attend. without interruptions. At least this preserves the time and energy of the other participants and helps to demonstrate to the busybody that his or her actions are disruptive.

The best time to deal with a chronic busybody is before the meeting. Point out how maddening and inefficient this behavior is and see if you can get the busybody to agree to hold all calls for the duration of the meeting; or you can meet away from the busybody's office where there can be no interruptions. Another possibility is to schedule the meeting before or after normal business hours to minimize distractions. In any case, if you can get the busybody before the meeting to make a commitment to remain in the meeting for a given time without interruptions, you will have some leverage you can use if the individual resumes busybody behavior: "Hey, just a minute! I thought you promised to hold all calls for the next hour."

The interrupter starts talking before others are finished. Often the interrupter doesn't mean to be rude, but becomes impatient and overly excited. Like the loudmouth, the interrupter is afraid that a new, red-hot idea will be lost if it isn't blurted out immediately. As a facilitator you should deal with an interrupter immediately. Remember: One of your major functions is to be a traffic cop and let everyone have a chance to be heard without being cut off. This may be one of the first tests of your neutrality and service to the group. People will be watching to see if you will really protect them. They want to see if you will stop the interrupter, even if he or she is a VIP. You should jump in immediately, saying something like, "Hold on, Irving, let Charlene finish what she was saying." You must be impartial and fair in your interventions. Don't play favorites. Between meetings you can point out to the chronic interrupter how irritating his behavior is to other group members and suggest that the interrupter bring a pad of paper to write down ideas until there is an appropriate time to express them—a personal group memory. Or make the interrupter the recorder—recording is a good exercise in listening. Some interrupters and loudmouths have become excellent recorders and have made dramatic changes in their behavior.

The teacher's pet spends more energy looking for approval from the facilitator than focusing on the content of the meeting. The teacher's pet can be very distracting to you as a facilitator and can hook you into paying too much attention to one individual. You are supposed to serve the group, not pass judgment on how well it's performing. You can be encouraging, but don't let the group or an individual become dependent on you and use you as a crutch. If a teacher's pet keeps talking to you rather than other group members, walk over to one side of the group and break eye contact. The idea is to get people to talk to each other, not to you. If the teacher's pet tries to trap you into an evaluation, boomerang the question back. "I don't know, Ruth. How do *you* think the meeting's going?" The responsibility for the success or failure of a meeting must be shared by all participants.

HOW TO REMAIN NEUTRAL AND BUILD TRUST

One reason why the Interaction Method works so well is that it insists on the neutrality of the person who runs the meeting. Running a meeting is like driving a car; it's easy to steer in any direction you want. If you are personally affected by the outcome of a meeting, it's almost impossible not to maneuver the meeting (consciously or subconsciously) toward results that you favor. As we have pointed out, being a manager/chairperson of a group and running your own meeting is like trying to be captain, quarterback, referee, and record keeper at the same time. That's too many roles to play at one time.

And yet, let's face it: no one is really neutral; everyone has personal preferences and values. So the practical objective is to maintain "operational neutrality." That means that as far as the participants of a meeting are concerned, you, the facilitator, are not letting your own ideas affect the course of the proceedings. It is part of the social contract that you make with your group: that each member has a responsibility of letting you know if you exhibit a bias toward one point of view. If no one objects to your behavior during the meeting, you have achieved operational neutrality.

In most meetings the role of facilitator can be rotated in your group. Periodically, someone (other than the manager/chairperson) can be chosen to plan and conduct the meeting, so each participant only has to facilitate every few weeks or months.

For very critical meetings, when everyone is emotionally involved, it may be important to find someone from outside your group to facilitate, someone from another department or division or from outside your organization.

If you follow the guidelines here, you can achieve operational neutrality even if you have a strong investment in a meeting. If you refrain from arguing for a particular point of view, you may be able to assist others to work creatively together and reach a win/win solution. You will find that many (if not all) your "great" ideas will come up naturally.

KEEP QUIET!

Don't answer questions about a meeting's substantive content. One of the biggest traps for a beginning facilitator looms when someone in the group asks about your thoughts about the subject: "Weren't profits at an all-time low last quarter?" "Do you know what the executive vice president thinks about that?" "What do you think about that?"

It is a great temptation to respond to such questions, particularly during an argument, because people are used to getting answers from a person who stands in front of a group. The trick is to boomerang the questions back to the group: "That's a good question. Who knows the answer?" "Carlos, you're the manager of this group. Do you know the answer to that question." "I don't know. How can we find out?" "What do you think?"

Sometimes, but not often, a member of the group may try to pin you down: "Hey, man, what do you think? Don't you have any feelings about this? You're a part of this effort."

Then the thing to do is to remind the individual of your function in the meeting and why it's important that you don't get involved in issues. Like this: "I've been asked to facilitate this meeting. To do a good job and to make sure that I don't manipulate anyone I promised to try to remain neutral, to stay out of the issues. Sure, I have feelings about the issues; any person would, and I'll be happy to share them with you after the meeting. But as long as I'm in my role as facilitator, I am not supposed to answer that sort of question. If I take sides, I'll lose my credibility." If you believe you know something that no one else in the meeting does and this piece of information is essential for dealing with the problem at hand, then you can step briefly out of your role and offer your contribution.

SUCCESS DOESN'T DEPEND ON YOU

Don't assume the responsibility for saving your group. In your enthusiasm and desire to make a meeting work, you might begin to think that success totally depends on you. It doesn't. Remember, you're a servant of your group; you're doing what the group members want you to do. If they make a decision and it proves to be a poor one, it's not your fault. It's always easier to find someone else to blame for poor meetings, and you, as facilitator, are a likely target. Remind your group, particularly if things start breaking down and fingers start pointing, that it's their meeting; if they don't like what's happening they can change it.

This is not to say that you have no responsibility for what happens. The perceptiveness and appropriateness of your suggestions about the group's methods are important to the success of a meeting. Just don't let yourself get saddled with all the responsibility.

Remember that one of the best ways to achieve neutrality is to ask the group for help: "It's really going to be hard to remain neutral in matters as important as these, so please help me. Let me know if I cut you off too soon or push you in a direction where you don't want to go." If you let people know that you're trying your best and seek their assistance, they will be more tolerant of your mistakes and feel more responsible for what happens. But you have to be sincere in your request and nondefensive when you are criticized—and you almost always will be!

Toward the beginning of a meeting, in particular, you will be tested. Someone will say, "Hey, you evaluated my idea." Or "You didn't listen to what I said." Or "I think you're forcing things too much." When that happens, you must thank the person for his or her criticisms and back off. Like this: "Thank you for letting me know. I'll try not to do that again. Tell me if I do." Don't let your hackles get up, even if you think that what you were doing is appropriate. Once people accept that they do have control over how the meeting is run, that you're not a henchman for the boss, they will relax and be less aggressive.

WHEN TO STEP DOWN

In extreme cases, when emotions are high and the level of trust low, you may have to offer to step down as facilitator. In community meetings where people may be suspicious of this new meeting technique, you may have to add after defining your role, "Let's try operating this way for an hour or so. If it's not getting anywhere, or you feel you can do better without my assistance, I'll be glad to step down."

Very rarely have we seen a group ask the facilitator to leave. One case involved a militant group of students at a conference. Then, after an hour of meeting without a facilitator, the chaos was so extreme that some students started to say, "Hey, who's running this meeting, anyway? What we need is facilitation or whatever you call it. Where is that guy? We need him back." In the end the entire group asked for the facilitator to return and showed a deeper understanding and appreciation for his function.

It is acceptable to step out of your role as facilitator and contribute your own ideas and evaluations when:

1. the level of trust in a group is high and there is a genuine interest in your participation;

2. the meeting is very small (three or four people) and you are an essential part of the team;

3. you have such a great idea that you can't hold it any longer; or

4. the problem with which the group is dealing lies in an area of your own special expertise and you are asked for advice.

When you step out of your role as facilitator, make sure that the transitions are clear, both out and back. Ask permission of the group: "Is it all right with you if I take off my facilitator hat and toss in an idea on the subject?" (Wait for heads to nod.) "Okay, what I think is . . ." (Followed by a brief discussion.) "Okay, now I'm putting on my facilitator hat again. Are there any more thoughts on the subject?"

Don't do this too often. You group will get used to you as a facilitator and depend on your neutrality and process suggestions. Every time you step out of your role, people will have to relate to you in a different way. It can feel to them as if an outsider had just joined the group. Don't be surprised if your "brilliant" idea falls on deaf ears. We recall a facilitator who took off his hat to make a suggestion and it was dropped like a hot potato, but twenty minutes later a similiar idea was volunteered in a slightly different form by a group member—and adopted with great enthusiasm. If you are patient, you will be surprised how many times someone else will come with with "your" ideas.

ADMIT YOUR MISTAKES

If you acknowledge from the outset that you're not infallible, the group will empathize with you. Being honest and good-humored about not having all the answers builds up your credibility with the group. If you make a mistake, be the first to admit and correct it: "Wait a minute—I forgot something. We should make sure everyone agrees there's really a problem concerning this issue before we spend time trying to solve it." Try to beat your critics to the punch. Demonstrate that you're wide awake—even to the point of being the first to criticize yourself if you do something dumb.

Although your role demands some acting from you (that you be vibrant, mobile, positive, energetic, etc.), by all means admit it whenever all those roles put too much strain on you. Tell the group if you're hung over, upset, tired, sick, or distracted. Elicit more than the usual support from them. Frankly admit how much you're going to have to depend on them.

When in deep doubt about how to handle a difficult situation, be honest about your predicament: "Look, I don't know quite how to handle this. Frankly, I'm lost. Does anyone have any suggestions about how we can get out of this jam?"

Never forget that you're not alone. As long as you maintain your honesty, people will stay by your side and sail through the meeting with you.

HOW TO BE AN OBSERVER

Sometime, someone may ask to observe one of your meetings. That's fine, as long as your group approves and the role of observer is clearly defined. Observers are nonparticipants. They should sit in the back of the room, be silent, and not influence the course of the meeting either verbally or nonverbally (no head-shaking, nodding, frowning, etc.). It's the function of the facilitator to strictly enforce these ground rules. If they are constantly broken, the facilitator can ask the observer to leave. If an observer wants to begin participating in the meeting, this change must be approved by all group members; then the individual should physically join the group by moving forward and sitting in the semicircle of chairs.

HOW TO BE AN EXPERT

At times your group may want to invite someone to make a presentation, answer some questions, give some advice, but not participate in the meeting. That's a legitimate request. It can be very disrupting to introduce a new person into an ongoing group, and many people have had bad experiences with experts coming to meetings and bossing everyone around.

As we have said before, people can accept almost any role for a time as long as the role is made clear and agreed upon in advance. The role of expert (or resource person) is to offer a service to the group—to be a consultant. The expert is to remain silent and observe unless called upon. If resource people understand what they are being asked to do ahead of the meeting, they won't be surprised and offended when they are not invited to join in the proceedings. It is the responsibility of the facilitator to explain the role of expert in advance, to keep the expert from dominating the meeting, and to ask him or her to leave if ground rules are violated.

THE FACILITATOR

FACILITATOR
- IS A NEUTRAL SERVANT OF THE GROUP
- DOES NOT EVALUATE OR CONTRIBUTE IDEAS
- FOCUSES ENERGY OF GROUP ON A COMMON TASK
- SUGGESTS ALTERNATIVE METHODS & PROCEDURES
- PROTECTS INDIVIDUALS AND THEIR IDEAS FROM ATTACK
- ENCOURAGES TO PARTICIPATE
- HELPS THE GROUP FIND WIN/WIN SOLUTIONS
- COORDINATES PRE- AND POST-MEETING LOGISTICS

SPECIFIC TECHNIQUES:
- CLEARLY DEFINE YOUR ROLE
- GET AGREEMENT ON A COMMON PROBLEM & PROCESS BEFORE BEGINNING
- BOOMERANG QUESTIONS BACK TO GROUP MEMBERS
- BE POSITIVE—COMPLIMENT THE GROUP
- DON'T TALK TOO MUCH
- SUPPORT THE RECORDER
- DON'T BE AFRAID TO MAKE MISTAKES
- HELP TO EDUCATE THE GROUP

CHAPTER 7

How to Be a Good Recorder

You can't talk about the recorder without discussing the group memory, and vice versa. We have already explained why a group, like an individual, needs a short-term and a long-term memory and how the group memory serves this crucial function. It's essential that you understand the rationale for a group memory as well as the specific techniques of recording.

The group memory is extremely useful as a work-in-progress and as a finished product. As a meeting unfolds, the recorder creates the group memory from what participants are saying; it becomes a powerful visual tool, a readymade instant replay, that helps members concentrate and see what is going on. The group memory also increases the productivity of meetings after they are over by serving as a readily accessible record of what happened. Because the flow of events has been captured by the recorder under the watchful eyes of all participants (with the clear understanding that it is the responsibility of the group members and manager/chairperson to see that their ideas are accurately portrayed by the recorder), the group memory becomes an *agreement* of what was decided or accomplished by the group.

The group memory also:

1. helps a group to focus on a task by providing a physical point of attention;

2. is an instant record of a meeting's content and process; it keeps meeting participants informed not only about *what* they decided but *how* they reached their decisions;

3. guards against data overload by providing a short-term memory (you can only juggle about seven pieces of information in your head—the group memory can keep track of hundreds);

4. "remembers" your ideas (you experience a psychic release because you don't have to hold on to them in your head);

5. frees you from taking notes;

6. assures you that when your idea has been recorded, it has been "heard" by the rest of the group;

7. enables you to check to be sure that ideas are being recorded accurately;

8. helps prevent endless repetition (you can point to an item whenever an idea has already been recorded);

9. provides a graphic display, which is essential for presenting visual information, drawing diagrams, and working with spatial relationships;

10. makes sophisticated problem-solving methods possible by holding on to information developed in one step of a method for use in a later step (for example, it holds on to ideas during a brainstorming session so they can be evaluated later);

11. encourages participation because it respects individuals (anyone can see that everyone's idea is important enough to be written down);

12. records an idea without the name of the contributor, which depersonalizes it and transfers "ownership" to the group, and thus the original owner can let go of it, get a better perspec-

tive on its value and validity, and other group members can view it divorced from a personality or vested interest;

13. increases your sense of accomplishment because you can see all the work you have done on the walls surrounding you.

14. offers continuity to a meeting (you can pick up where you left off before a break);

15. makes it easy to catch up latecomers or people who could not attend a meeting—they can review conclusions as well as the process by which the conclusions were reached;

16. reduces accountability problems: names, action items, and deadlines can be recorded during a meeting to avoid later confusion and ambiguity about tasks or responsibilities;

17. is low-cost, easy to use, and available to any group that wants to increase its effectiveness.

WHAT THE RECORDER DOES

Like the facilitator, the recorder is a neutral servant of the group, capturing the ideas of members on large pieces of paper in everybody's full view. Do not edit or paraphrase; use the words of the speaker, but don't record his or her name. You may lag behind what is being said; that's normal. If you get too far behind, ask the group to slow down until you have a chance to catch up. Each group member shares the responsibility of letting you know if you have missed something important or if you have not heard correctly. (If group participants want to talk "off the record" or are concerned about confidentiality, they can ask you not to record a comment or discussion.)

Remember: this is the social contract you make with your group. In the beginning of the meeting you should introduce yourself and define your role: "Hi, my name is _____; I've been asked to be your recorder. I'm new at this, so please help me out. I'm going to try to make a record of this meeting called the group memory. It'll all go on the paper taped to the wall. Obviously, I can't write down everything, so I'll try to catch key ideas, using your own words. Please let me know if I miss something that you think is important or if I start to editorialize or paraphrase. It's hard not to make my own interpretations, so keep me honest. If I get too far behind I'll ask you to wait a moment until I catch up. If you can't read my writing, please let me know."

WHO CAN BE A RECORDER

Almost anyone can learn to be an adequate recorder. There are only two qualifications. First, your handwriting must be fairly legible. You don't have to print; that's often too slow. But you do have to be able to write quickly in a large, clear hand while standing up. For some people this is very difficult. If this applies to you, politely decline the job.

Secondly, you do have to understand the technical language of the group sufficiently to abstract and write down what is important. If you know nothing about computers and you're asked to record a meeting of systems analysts, you will quickly find yourself over your head in IO's and CPU's, and you'll end up frustrating the participants with interruptions for corrections and explanations.

Take turns recording or train a secretary to record. In general, it's best to record for a whole meeting, although in very long meetings you can rotate the role.

DON'T BE DEFENSIVE!

When you first record for a group and define your role as its nonjudgmental and nonmanipulative servant, human nature may lead certain people to test you. For no particular reason, a participant may challenge you: "That's not what I said! Will you put it in *my* words, please? Change that word!" However you feel, even if you know you're right, don't argue. Don't be defensive or irritated at having to modify what you have written. Be accepting of modifications and corrections. If you become defensive, you might cause a confrontation that would divert the group from its task. This would contradict your goal as a recorder—to remove blockages and help the group's energy flow more freely. Also, by being defensive, you risk discouraging people. They may hesitate to give you honest, critical feedback that could benefit your performance.

Concentrate, listen closely, do your best to write down the key words of the group. Discipline yourself to tune out other phenomena. To get totally into "acoustic space," don't look at the group. Face your writing and try to fade into the background. You'll be able to hear better and people will feel less intimidated than if you watch them, hang on every word, and then turn around to write down what they said.

Focus your attention and energy on the group memory. Remember: If you fall too far behind, interrupt, stop the group, and try: "Is this what you said? Hold on a minute till I catch up." Or: "Sorry, I didn't catch that. Wait a minute." Or: "Could you repeat that, please?"

SILENCE OFTEN WORKS

Some group members will have trouble expressing themselves. Don't try to help them by putting words into their mouths. Be quiet; talk as little as possible. If nothing is being said, just stand quietly facing the wall until the silence is broken. (Don't turn around and stare at the person who is talking —this can make people extremely self-conscious.)

If you try to record too much, you will quickly fall behind, and the group memory will look too much like a page of dense text. If you record too little, your record will appear overly abbreviated, and it will be difficult to reconstruct what was said over the course of an entire session. The trick is to listen for *key words and phrases.* Try to capture basic ideas and the essence of what the speaker is saying. Experiment. You will find your own style of recording and your own appropriate abbreviations.

A good recorder needs stamina. You have to write fast. You have to keep a great deal of information in your head and continue to digest it. Your arm can get very tired from having to write so much. It's quite common to fall into the "wallpaper syndrome"—and then the group memory becomes a repetitious mass of unreadable material, a seen-but-yet unseen background that stretches monotonously like the wallpaper in your bedroom. The same is true of a sheet of group memory that is written in the same color in letters of unvarying size and in the same format. Then it's hard to separate and distinguish individual entries. One page looks so much like another. In fact, it's the idiosyncrasies—the blobs, misspellings, diagrams, smudges —that help you remember particular sheets of group memory. When you see a word that has been enlarged in a funny way for emphasis, the whole incident comes back to you. So, break up the monotony of your recording. Here are some hints to help you avoid the wallpaper syndrome.

HOW TO BREAK THINGS UP

Listen for key words
Try to capture basic ideas, the essence.
Don't write down every word.
Write legibly. Print or write an inch or an inch and a half high.
Don't be afraid to misspell.
Abbreviate words.
Circle key ideas, statements, or decisions.

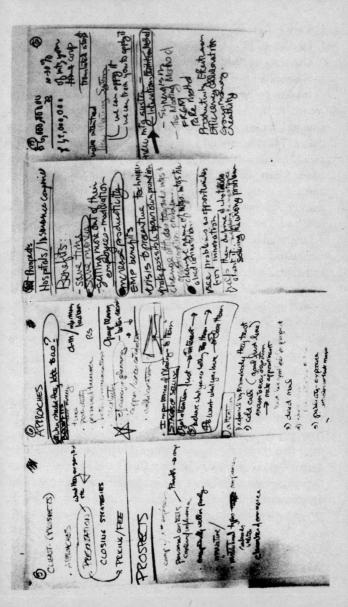

Vary colors: use colors to highlight and divide ideas.

Underline.

Use stars, arrows, numbers, etc.

Number all the sheets.

It takes a while to get the hang of changing colors while you record. At first you may feel as if you don't have enough hands. One technique is to choose four markers of bright, contrasting colors. Take the caps off all four. Place three in one hand (three should be comfortable) and write with the fourth in your other hand. When you have finished recording one idea or concept and are pausing to listen to another, get used to returning the marker you have just used to your other hand and grabbing a new one. This exchange will become automatic after a while.

One of the biggest fears of recorders is the possibility of misspelling in public. When you hear an unfamiliar word, you'll be tempted to hesitate. Don't! You'll fall too far behind if you worry about spelling specific words. Clear yourself beforehand; explain to the group that your spelling won't be perfect. When you write big and fast, it's hard to spell correctly. Admit your fallibility. When you make a mistake, members of your group will tend to empathize and identify with you.

You should feel free to ask for help. When ideas flow fast, as in a brainstorming session, ask for another recorder to take a separate sheet and alternate the task of recording after each speaker. Coordinate by saying, "I got that, you take the next." If someone wants to express an idea with a diagram or drawing, hand that person the magic markers. People generally feel that they have communicated better if they have a chance to draw their ideas themselves on the group memory, and you are demonstrating that the group memory really belongs to the group—not you.

HOW TO HELP THE FACILITATOR

A recorder is in a unique position to get perspective on what is happening. Group members are involved in their subject. The facilitator is mainly concerned with the meeting's process. When you are not bogged down in recording, you have a good opportunity to observe the dynamics of the group and perceive patterns that may not be evident to the facilitator. If you see something that might help the meeting, an alternative strategy or different way of approaching the information in the group memory, you should share your idea with the facilitator during a lull or break in the meeting. Don't make comments or process suggestions directly to the group. That will split the focus of attention. Your role is to *support the facilitator,* to learn to work together as a team, assisting each other with constructive criticism and positive reinforcement. If there is a dispute between the two of you, the facilitator has the right to decide. Otherwise, during breaks you can discuss what has been happening and what can be done to improve the meeting.

When the group gets off track, the facilitator may turn to you and ask you to review the last portions of the group memory. People then become reoriented and see where they got off on a tangent. In general, being a recorder can be a good stepping stone to becoming a facilitator. You get a chance to feel what it's like to be in front of a group and observe how the facilitator deals with problems.

HOW TO CHANGE HATS

Standing in front of a group is a powerful position. It's hard not to abuse this power if you are very involved in the subject of the meeting. If you are dying to leap into the fray of the meeting (and you are a legitimate member of the group), ask someone else to record and sit down.

If you are burning with the desire to toss in an idea of your own, you can step out of your role under the same conditions we discussed in the previous chapter. Ask for the permission of the group: "Is it all right if I take off my hat as recorder and share an idea with you? . . . Well, then, my idea is . . . Okay, now my hat is back on as recorder."

To re-emphasize: Most groups resent it when a recorder does this too often and will express dissatisfaction in direct and indirect ways. Don't be surprised if someone says, "No," only partly in jest, or if an idea of yours falls on deaf ears.

Whatever tools you use to create a group memory, you must be able to display a lot of information simultaneously during a meeting and then be able to store the information afterward. Flip charts aren't suited to this function because one page of a chart doesn't display enough information to be useful and, when filled, it's flipped back and out of view. Blackboards don't work well either. When the blackboard is filled or the meeting is over, there is no way of preserving what has been recorded. Furthermore, chalk tends to make an annoying squeak, is hard to read (low contrast), and doesn't come in many strong, bright colors.

After extensive experimentation, we have found that the best tools for making a group memory are magic markers and large sheets of paper taped or pinned to the walls.

IT'S CHEAPER BY THE YARD

The best, least-expensive paper is 24-inch rolls of white meat-wrap or butcher paper. (Look up "Paper Dealers" in your yellow pages.) A portable paper cutter offers the easiest way to cut and store the rolls of butcher paper. You can also use precut sheets of paper (rip up a flip chart) or the unused side of wide computer printout sheets. If you belong to a nonprofit organization, sometimes you can obtain end rolls of newsprint free from a local newspaper or publishing house.

Colored marking pens are good writing tools. They are brilliant and crisp. Watercolor markers are best; they don't bleed and can be washed out of clothes. (We recommend El Marco Watercolor Markers by Flair.) Beware of permanent-color markers, which often bleed through and stain the wall behind the paper and emit noxious odors (they have a petroleum base).

To mount the paper to the wall, use drafting tape (3M brand). It won't pull off plaster or rip paper and it's easy to tear by hand. If you are lucky enough to find a tackboard or fiberboard wall, use push pins. Pins are much neater and quicker than tape, and there won't be any sticky pieces of tape on the sheets when you roll them up after a meeting. You can get these materials at an art supply, stationery, or drug store.

You need at least eight, preferably sixteen, linear feet of flat, unbroken wall area in front of your group. Cut the paper into three-to-four-foot lengths and mount the sheets side by side so that they form a continuous expanse of paper. Also pre-cut some extra sheets for handy spares. If it's going to be a long meeting mount two layers of sheets, so when you remove one that is filled, there will be another blank sheet ready to be used.

KEEP MOVING!

Do everything you can to minimize interruptions to the flow of the meeting. When you stop recording to put up some fresh paper, participants will tend to stop talking until you are ready to continue. Therefore, it's a good idea to enlist an aide, someone to take the completed sheets off the front wall, place them on the side walls of the meeting room, and put up blank sheets while you continue to record. The two of you should function like a pit crew at the Indianapolis 500, working as quickly and efficiently (and as unobtrusively) as you can to get the meeting back on the track.

The recorder is responsible for taking down and organizing the sheets of the group memory after a meeting. Each sheet should bear its number. The date, the group's name, and the meeting place should be clearly printed on the first page. As a rule, each group memory should be preserved at least until the conclusion of the following meeting, so that it will be available for reference in its original form.

Storing sheets of butcher paper is awkward. The best system is to roll the sheets together, tape them closed, label the outside, and store the rolls loosely or, preferably, in the type of tubes used for architectural drawings. A wine carton can substitute as a rack to store the rolled sheets standing up.

If group members want individual copies of the group memory, you will have to have it transcribed. We have discovered no simple, cheap way of reducing and duplicating the large sheets of paper. The process of transcription goes quite quickly, especially if you bring a typewriter into the meeting room and leave the group memory on the walls or mount the sheets on a stand (or partition) in front of the desk of the typist. A good typist can type twenty sheets of group memory an hour. Try to tape each page pretty much as the words appear on the original page. Charts and diagrams should be reproduced by hand in spaces left between the typewritten material. If only one copy is needed, a Polaroid picture of the graphics is often faster and more accurate.

TELL THEM WHY!

A word of caution: Head off secretarial rebellions by explaining to the typist why he or she is being asked to transcribe these funny sheets of paper. Spend some time describing the group memory and why it is helping your group to improve problem-solving and decision-making. Invite the typist to a meeting to observe the Interaction Method in action; perhaps he or she

3/25/76 ①

Acme experiencing serious financial difficulty

material/labor cost too much

⇒ must produce less expensively

President:
⭐
- cut costs by 15%
- maintain current prod. levels

- How to cut costs by 50% 15%?
  or increase productivity by 18%?

unit cost = $\frac{output (1.18)}{cost (.85)}$ $\frac{cost (.85)}{output (1.18)}$

HOW TO CUT UNIT COST BY 15%

Brainstorm:

priority		Feasibility study
②	Reduce quality inspection every 5th item	Marta 4/1
	cut down #2 line shut-down time – portable motor replacement	
③	reduce #men at #5 station	Juan 4/1
①	cut out sunday overtime	Joe 4/1
← priority	Action Items: who/what/when	

might want to learn how to record. If your typist or secretary understands the entire meeting process and why the transcripts of the group memory are important, he or she will be less likely to balk at the new typing job.

The group memory works well as a long-term record of a meeting for a group of people who generally attend meetings and don't have to communicate the results of each meeting to others. If someone misses a meeting, that person can be caught up by being "walked through" the group memory by someone else who attended the meeting (the recorder). Today's group memory can be placed on the back wall of the meeting room for easy reference during the next meeting, offering a sense of continuity from one meeting to the next.

If a lot of important information ends up spread over many sheets of the group memory, the recorder should prepare a summary sheet for the next meeting. This is another aspect of the recorder's role: although you are a silent secretary during

---

MEETING   GROUP MEMORY   3/25/76

Product Division: Rico, Juan, Marta, Bill, Tom, Mary, Joe

Acme experiencing serious financial difficulty

material/labor cost too much

➤   must produce less expensively

President: cut costs by 15%
                    ·maintain current production levels

　How to cut costs by 15%   or increase productivity by 18%
                                   unit cost: cost (.85)/output (1.18)

HOW TO CUT UNIT COST BY 15%

(Brainstorm): Priority List		Feasibility study
2.	Reduce quality inspection every fifth item	Marta 4/1
	Cut down #2 line shutdown time—portable motor replacement	
3.	Reduce the number of men at #5 station	Juan 4/1
1.	Cut out Sunday overtime	Joe 4/1

ACTION ITEMS: who/what/when   ——————⤴

a meeting, you also have a responsibility to look constantly for new ways of making the group's work more accessible and comprehensible to group members. During breaks and between meetings you should be thinking about how information can be presented to be most useful for accomplishing the task of the group. Since you are reorganizing information that has already been recorded and since you are not adding your own ideas or interpretations, you are not violating the neutrality of your role.

THE GROUP MEMO

The group memory of a meeting, by itself, is too abbreviated and condensed to be understood easily by someone who is not familiar with the day-by-day workings of a group. Therefore, if you need to communicate what happens in your meetings to nonmembers or members who get together with the group infrequently, the recorder should prepare a written summary of the group memory—a "group memo." The group memo is similar to traditional minutes but with two important differences. First, the group memo is based on a previously accepted record of the meeting, the group memory. The group memo contains only information and decisions which have been recorded in the group memory in front of the group; it should hold no surprises. (Even so, a group memo should be submitted for approval at the following meeting.) And secondly, the group memo communicates the process and content of a meeting—not just final results.

The group memo should be written so that someone who didn't attend a meeting could understand what happened. A group memo does not have to be very long or formal, but it should communicate how your group reached its conclusions: Here's how we defined the problem; this is the way we analyzed it; here are some of the alternatives we considered; we used the following criteria to make our decision; and this is what we

GROUP MEMO

NAME: _____ TITLE: _____ DATE: _____

What Happened & How:

_____

Decisions/Action Items:

_____

Next Steps:

_____

This group memo is my interpretation of what happened at this meeting. If you would like to correct an error, make an addition, consult the original group memory, or receive a transcribed copy of the group memory, please call _____. For more information concerning the objectives of the meeting and who attended it, see the attached agenda.

Recorder _____

GROUP MEMO

Problem Solving Session on

NAME: Product Division   TITLE: Cost Reduction   DATE: 3/25/76

What Happened & How:

Joe met with the supervisors to develop ways of reducing production costs. After briefly reviewing the background of the current financial situation of Acme Widget Company and answering questions, the group brainstormed a list of suggestions and then prioritized them according to ease of implementation. The three most promising ideas were assigned to individuals to make feasibility studies and report at the next meeting.

Decisions/Action Items:

(Person responsible for feasibility study)

Possible Ways to Reduce Costs by 15%

		Who	When
1.	Cut Sunday overtime.	Joe	4/1/76
2.	Reduce quality inspections from every third unit to every fifth.	Marta	4/1/76
3.	Reduce number two line shift down-time by developing a portable motor replacement to be used while the main engine is checked and serviced.	Rico	4/1/76

Next Steps:

The group will meet at 10:00 AM next Monday, April 1st to review the feasibility studies and try to agree by consensus on which approaches to implement. If consensus cannot be reached, Joe will make the decision himself by 5:00 PM that day.

This group memo is my interpretation of what happened at this meeting. If you would like to correct an error, make an addition, consult the original group memory, or receive a transcribed copy of the group memory, please call ___Mary___. For more information concerning the objectives of the meeting and who attended it, see the attached agenda.

Recorder _Mary Towners_

decided. Follow the phases of problem-solving in Chapter 16. Make sure to include tasks and deadlines. With some practice, you should be able to prepare a memo of a two-hour meeting in less than an hour, particularly if you do so while the meeting is still fresh in your mind.

Particularly for a group that is responsible to a larger organization or membership, the group memo is well worth time and energy because it greatly improves communication. Group memos keep people up to date on the actions of the group while providing group members with readable, accessible documentation of their work. Group members may even take their work more seriously if they know that what they do is being communicated to others.

It should be clear by now that the recorder performs essential functions before and after a meeting.

Before a meeting, the recorder is responsible for coming early to the meeting room, cutting and mounting fresh sheets of paper for the group memory, and working with the facilitator to make sure the room is set for the meeting.

After the meeting, the recorder takes down the group memory, labels it, and stores it or gives it to the typist to be transcribed. The recorder is also responsible for preparing a summary sheet and/or writing a group memo and seeing that it is typed, approved, and sent out to the appropriate people.

The job of the recorder is as important as that of the facilitator. Since it entails so much work, we recommend that you rotate the role within your group and reward and praise those who contribute this valuable service.

CHAPTER 8

How to Be a Good Group Member

As a member of your group, you play a vital role. After all, it's your group and your meeting. You and your fellow group members are responsible for what happens; the facilitator and recorder exist only to serve you. It is you, the group members (along with the manager or chairperson), who meet, work, solve problems, and make decisions. You are the team; it's your game. It helps to have a referee and scorekeeper, but without players there is no action.

Traditionally, group leaders have been treated as an elite. They are told how important they are, how they and only they should be educated in leadership skills. They read books on leadership, they attend training programs, and like the quarterback on a football team, they get all the glory—or blame.

The Interaction Method changes that. The facilitator is not a leader in the traditional sense; the facilitator doesn't lead, but assists. He or she is more like a coach than a quarterback. It is the group collectively that must lead itself. During a meeting the group members must decide where they are going to go and how they are going to get there. So, in the last analysis, the quality of the meeting depends on the quality of the participants.

Surely you have been in enough meetings to recognize that there are effective and ineffective group members. Being an effective group member takes knowledge and skill. Almost all the techniques we described in the chapter on the role of the facilitator can be used by group members, because they can make suggestions about process as well as content. As a group member with process skills, you can be a great resource to your facilitator. Or, if the meeting is being poorly run or if there isn't any leader, you can facilitate from your seat as a participant, using most of the facilitator techniques we have already described. If you never plan to run meetings but find yourself in them anyway, we still recommend that you read this book in its entirety, because it will enable you to come up with suggestions that will make your time in meetings more enjoyable and productive.

Assuming your meetings are going to be run by the Interaction Method, the following are responsibilities you assume as a group member—and techniques you can use to improve your meetings.

HOW TO KEEP THE FACILITATOR NEUTRAL

Your first major responsibility under the Interaction Method system of checks and balances is to monitor the facilitator to make sure that he or she remains neutral and doesn't contribute ideas about content or evaluate those of any group member. As we said before, being a facilitator is hard and depends on your help.

As a watchdog, don't bark indiscriminately. Don't spend

your energy lying in wait to pounce on the facilitator at the first sign of a positive or negative expression of sentiment. Be reasonable. Most of the time your facilitator won't even be aware of minor transgressions. Be pragmatic. If what the facilitator is doing seems to be helping and you and your group feel good about what is happening, don't be a stickler for the rules. Rules are only helpful guidelines.

If you believe that your facilitator is consciously manipulating the group, being unfair to certain individuals, or using his or her power over a meeting's process to achieve some personal objective, by all means speak out. Try positive, nonthreatening approaches first: "Facilitator, you may not be aware of this, but I think you cut off Theresa before she had a chance to finish." Or, "Facilitator, I feel you're pushing too hard. I don't think we've finished with this issue yet." Talk to your facilitator during a break. Point out what you think can be done to improve the meeting. Then, if the low-key protests don't seem to work, you and your fellow group members have a right to stop the meeting and confront the facilitator. It may be that the facilitator is too intimately involved in the issues to be unbiased, and it may be better to rotate the role or fire the facilitator and find a new one. Whatever the problem is, if the meeting isn't working, it's time to try something else.

KEEP AN EYE ON THE MEMORY

Your second major responsibility as group member is to check on the recorder to make sure that he or she is recording accurately what you and others are saying. All conditions mentioned above apply here. Recording is difficult, and an inexperienced recorder will leave out some key items or misrepresent you unintentionally. All you have to do is to say, "Recorder, I said 50 percent, not 15." Or, "What George said was important, and I think you missed it." Usually your recorder will be grateful for your assistance, and a few words of encouragement and praise wouldn't hurt either.

YOU'RE FREED TO PITCH IN

Being a group member in a meeting run by the Interaction Method can be a liberating, positive experience. Other than the two monitoring responsibilities, you don't have to worry about the normal problems: being heard, being attacked, being cut off, being too talkative, etc. You can drop many of your protective guards. You know that your facilitator is watching out for these things, so you can, and should, throw yourself totally into the subject matter of the meeting.

Concentrate on the content and don't worry too much about process. Don't try to backseat-drive a meeting. Remember: There is no one right way to solve a problem or one right process to facilitate a meeting. Particularly if you're a trained group leader or facilitator, it's easy to fall into the trap of showing off your expertise and proving the facilitator wrong: "If I were you, I wouldn't have done such and such." Focus on the problem, not the facilitator, and don't kibitz unless you're asked for your advice or the facilitator clearly needs it.

LISTEN, LISTEN, LISTEN!

Respect your fellow group members. Be a good listener. When others speak, give them full attention. Don't cut them off or distract the attention of the group with unnecessary movements or snide remarks. Keep a common focus. There is nothing worse than two people whispering to each other while you explain your brilliant idea.

WHERE TO SIT

Be aware of where you sit. Don't always sit in the same place with the same people. By changing your position, you can help to shake up the seating pattern and keep a group from becoming physically polarized—cliques that favor one alternative sitting next to each other.

DON'T BE NEGATIVE

Keep an open mind. Don't evaluate an idea before it has a chance to be developed. Negativism is one of the major problems of meetings. As a group member you can help greatly to set a positive tone. Look for the worth in an idea. Don't jump on its faults. Try the little trick of saying what you like about an idea before you express your concerns: "What I like about your suggestion is that it could solve the employment problem, but my concern is that the unions wouldn't accept it."

DON'T BE DEFENSIVE

Conversely, don't be too defensive if your idea is criticized. Try not to take it as a personal attack. Stay open to criticism and use it to develop your ideas further, not to drive yourself into positions that may become untenable. Once your idea is recorded on the group memory, it belongs to the group. Let it survive on its own merits. What is important is that your group collectively find its own solution to its problems. The more personally you identify yourself with your idea, the harder it may be for the group to accept it.

CHAPTER 9

How the Boss Stays Boss

The role of boss (manager/chairperson) depends on whether your group or organization is hierarchical or horizontal. Remember our definitions: at each level in a hierarchical organization, the authority to make decisions rests with one individual; in a horizontal organization, every group member has equal authority (one vote). The boss role is a link to the traditional system of decision-making; it recognizes and respects the realities and necessities of your organization and the special role that you play in it.

YOU'RE TOO VALUABLE TO RUN MEETINGS

Designing and conducting effective meetings is time-consuming work. A productive meeting requires pre-meeting planning and post-meeting follow-up. Like staging a play, a lot of preparation goes into making the one- or two-hour event a success. As a manager, your time is too valuable to spend on logistics. But the time of your staff is also too valuable to waste in meetings that are poorly planned and conducted. If a meeting blows up, your staff will waste even more time cooling off and complaining to others about what happened (the meeting recovery syndrome). So delegate the task of planning and conducting meetings to your staff. You can increase the productivity of your meetings while developing the skills of your people by getting them to share the responsibility for making meetings successful.

When we analyzed typical meeting problems we came to the conclusion that some of them occur because managers try to play too many roles. Remember: It's almost impossible to play the "heavy," the decision-maker, and still run a fair, non-manipulatory meeting. You can't be captain as well as referee and record keeper. Since you can't give away the power and responsibility of your position, you should give up trying to be a benevolent meeting leader. You can't be neutral, so why try? Your team needs you to participate fully in the meeting. It's a better use of your time and energies to turn running the meeting over to someone else: a facilitator.

But if you let someone else facilitate your meetings, what's your role? You're not just another member of the group. You're still in command. Here are your specific responsibilities before, during, and after a meeting.

WHAT TO DO BEFORE A MEETING

Even though you aren't going to be running the meeting, it's still your meeting. You are bringing together your people as the most effective way of using them to carry out your responsibilities.

First, why are you holding a meeting? What do you want to

accomplish? You have to figure out what type of meeting you want (see Chapter 11). You should work with the facilitator to develop a tentative agenda and determine whether you want your staff to suggest additional agenda items. Or you can establish a procedure so that you and members of your group can call in agenda items to your secretary.

For each agenda item you should decide a reasonable process for accomplishing it. In other words, you develop both a process and content agenda. Your secretary should send out the agenda to the other participants at least a day in advance so that they will come to the meeting with a clear set of expectations, and those who have to give reports will be prepared. Last-minute agenda items can always be added at the beginning of the meeting.

You must decide who should attend the meeting, what roles you want people to play (facilitator, recorder, group member, resource person, observer), and when and where the meeting is to take place. The facilitator or recorder should be responsible for setting up the meeting room in advance and making sure all the necessary materials are there.

Probably the most important decision you have to make before a meeting is to determine how much participation you really want from your staff. Do you want people only to feed you information? Or do you want to involve staff members in solving certain problems? If you want to involve your people in making decisions, what are these decisions, and how do you want to involve people in making them? Do you want to poll people individually, or do you want to try to work for consensus in the meeting? There is no "right" answer to these questions. A lot depends on your own management style. Just be clear in your own mind ahead of time and communicate your decisions so that your staff doesn't develop unrealistic expectations.

WHAT TO DO DURING THE MEETING

At all times during a meeting, you, as manager and decision-maker, retain the power to stop what's happening and change the format. If you have been working with your staff to reach consensus without success and time is running out, you have the right to say, "Thank you very much for your input. We're running out of time. I'll have to make a decision myself. I'll let you know tomorrow what I have decided."

You can't give away your power and responsibility even if you want to, so don't pretend to. But watch out; don't give with one hand and take away with the other. If you say you want to work collaboratively with your staff on a problem, don't set unrealistic time limits that doom the attempt to failure before it begins. Your staff will get wise to you and stop participating altogether.

At the beginning of collaborative problem-solving and decision-making sessions, lay out any constraints or essential information that you know, and then participate as a regular group member. It's vital that you be open and straightforward about your feelings and ideas. Don't hold back and try to be neutral. To be acceptable, any solution or decision must incorporate your views. It is up to the facilitator to keep you from dominating the meeting. Your staff will respect you for being clear about the views you bring to a meeting. If you ask as much from them, the level of trust in your group will grow naturally.

Support your facilitator. If he or she is a member of your staff, it's particularly hard to tell the boss to keep quiet and to stop interrupting. Encourage the facilitator to perform the role. Thank and reinforce him or her when you are called down for stepping out of line. This will demonstrate your seriousness about running your meetings in this way and help the facilitator gain self-confidence. Don't backseat-drive; let the facilitator have a chance to do things his or her own way. Don't try to make the facilitator wrong. Don't throw your weight around.

You will only create a split focus in the meeting; people won't know who is running the meeting.

Generally, try to talk less and listen more. Don't retreat, but don't feel that you have to talk twice as much as anyone else. The lower your profile in the meeting, the more others will participate and contribute. And isn't that the purpose of the meeting?

It's your responsibility to keep pushing for accountability. Make sure that action items are clearly stated and recorded in the group memory. Keep pushing until you are satisfied that everyone knows who is supposed to do what and by when. Don't let the facilitator go on to the next agenda item until enough is done (closure) on the present one.

During a meeting held strictly for reporting, it's all right for you to play the role of facilitator, too, since all you have to do is to recognize the next presenter and handle the question-and-answer sessions after each report. However, if a report flushes up a problem that you want to deal with collaboratively, step down as facilitator and into your role as manager. Appoint someone else to facilitate and continue under the usual Interaction Method procedures.

WHAT TO DO AFTER THE MEETING

After the meeting you return to your normal function as manager. If decisions were reached by consensus, it's up to you to make them official and act on them. If you renege on a decision to which you and your staff agreed, you will quickly lose credibility and make a sham out of participation. Continue to monitor progress on tasks and represent your group at meetings with your associate managers and senior executives.

WHAT THE "HORIZONTAL" BOSS DOES

As chairperson of a horizontal group or organization, you probably have to perform the following functions:

1. You are responsible for seeing that your group performs its duties.

2. You're held accountable to the larger organization, the board of directors, or the membership for the nature and quality of the decisions of your group.

3. You often have to play a public-relations and ceremonial role, representing your group in meetings of other groups and to the media and public at large.

4. It's up to you to give your group direction and assist it in setting goals and objectives.

5. Your group may look to you as an expert in its field.

6. You assign tasks and responsibilities to members of your group and follow up to see that these tasks are performed (a kind of manager).

7. You are responsible for knowing what all of the committees that report to your group are doing.

8. You may attend the meetings of these committees as an ad hoc member.

9. Part of your job as chairperson is to develop future leaders for your group or organization.

10. You set the agenda for the meetings of your group.

11. You conduct its meetings.

That's a lot to do. Because of your knowledge, experience, and respected opinion, you have been made chairperson. Yet, under Robert's *Rules of Order* the chairperson is not supposed to offer opinions while in the chair. According to the rules, the chairperson is not allowed to get involved with the content of the meeting.

KEEP TEN JOBS, GIVE UP ONE

But you've got too much to contribute. You can't be neutral. Your group needs your expertise. It needs you to participate fully in meetings. We have shown that you can't be involved in the content of a meeting and also run a fair, nonmanipulatory meeting. You're in a double bind. Keep the first ten important functions we have listed above and give up the eleventh. Most of the time it will get in your way.

If your group wants to work collaboratively and develop win/win solutions, we have explained why Robert's *Rules of Order* won't work very well—in fact, it will usually inhibit what you want to do. So we suggest that you can perform as chairperson more effectively by employing the Interaction Method and letting someone else facilitate your meeting. Your group can conduct all of its meetings the Interaction way or use it only for those portions which involve collaborative problem-solving and decision-making. Both will work.

Here are some minor changes and additions to your functions as chairperson when you use the Interaction Method as an alternative or supplement to Robert's *Rules of Order*.

WHAT TO DO BEFORE THE MEETING

You are responsible for planning and designing the meetings of your group. You probably have the best overview of what is happening and know what critical decisions need to be made. Therefore, you have to determine what issues need to be brought up at the next meeting and figure out the best way of dealing with them.

Then you must prepare the agenda. You may receive assistance and input from others in your organization, but it is up to you to send out a clear agenda to group members well before the meeting or to delegate that responsibility to the facilitator.

You must choose a facilitator and recorder and make sure they understand their roles before the meeting. Unless you have delegated the job, you are responsible for all other pre-meeting logistics.

WHAT TO DO DURING THE MEETING

Even if someone else facilitates the meeting, you still call the meeting to order and take care of all the opening procedures. You can review the agenda (with the option of asking for additions), and then call on people to give reports. It doesn't make much difference if you continue to run your meetings in the traditional way through reports and the "old business."

It's when a problem surfaces, either as a result of a report or as part of "new business," that you (and your group) have a critical choice to make. Either you can attempt to solve the problem by Robert's *Rules of Order,* or you can turn the meeting over to a facilitator and recorder.

Once a meeting is operating by the Interaction Method, you should participate actively as a group member; move physically out of the focus of attention and join the semicircle of group members facing the group memory. Don't compete with the facilitator; let him or her run the meeting. Concentrate on the task. Consistent with your managerial functions, you have a responsibility of pushing for closure on issues and clarity on action items.

If, for some reason, the facilitation process breaks down or consensus cannot be reached, you can return to your normal role as chairperson and resolve the dispute by the win/lose method of majority vote.

When a problem has been solved (or consensus attained), thank the facilitator and resume the chair under parliamentary procedure. You move into "new business," "entertain a motion from the floor" that reflects the decision of the group, and conduct an official vote (see the example in Chapter 4). At that point, you can turn the meeting back to the facilitator to address the next item on the agenda, or adjourn the meeting. (This procedure of returning to parliamentary procedure is necessary only if your by-laws require you to record an official vote on all major decisions.)

WHAT TO DO AFTER THE MEETING

You resume all normal functions of chairperson. You represent your organization at meetings with other organizations or the press, you see that decisions reached in the meeting are followed through and conveyed to the appropriate individuals, and you continue with your other normal managerial jobs.

CHAPTER 10

How to Plan Your Meeting

A meeting is just a tool. Obviously, group members can work by themselves as well. It's good for certain kinds of things, bad for others. Meetings are good for generating lots of ideas, sharing information, and making collective decisions. Meetings aren't generally good for organizing information, doing detailed analysis and research, translating ideas into coherent words or drawings, and thousands of other tasks more easily done by individuals alone.

WHEN TO HAVE A MEETING

Specifically, if you are a manager or chairperson, calling a meeting may be a good idea when:

1. you want information or advice from your group;
2. you want to involve your group in solving a problem or making a decision;

3. there is an issue that needs to be clarified;

4. you have concerns you want to share with your group as a whole;

5. the group itself wants a meeting;

6. there is a problem that involves people from different groups; or

7. there is a problem and it's not clear what it is or who is responsible for dealing with it.

WHEN NOT TO HAVE A MEETING

A meeting is generally not a good idea when:

1. you have to deal with personnel issues like hiring, firing, and negotiating salaries;

2. there is inadequate data or poor preparation;

3. something could be communicated better by telephone, memo, or a one-to-one discussion;

4. the subject matter is so confidential or secret that it can't be shared with some group members;

5. your mind is made up and you have already made your decision;

6. the subject is trivial; or

7. there is too much anger and hostility in the group and people need time to calm down before they begin to work collaboratively.

You must come to see meetings as important gatherings in the work of your group or organization. After all, most meetings are a means to an end. You can't tell whether a meeting was ultimately successful until you have seen what happened (or didn't happen) afterward. Were its decisions carried out? Did people do what they said they were going to do? If nothing happens as a result of meetings, no one will take them seriously and they will be a waste of valuable time.

CHAPTER 11

What Type of Meeting Are You Going to Hold?

A meeting is not just a meeting; there are different types. You can meet to solve a problem or make a decision, you can gather to share information or hear a presentation, or you can get together just to rap. It's not enough to say, "Let's have a meeting." You must know why. What do you want to accomplish? What is the purpose of your meeting?

There is a big difference between meeting to make a decision and meeting to share information. So why should both meetings be run the same way? Different types of meetings need different roles and procedures to be effective. Some meetings should be kept small. Some can be large. Others require that certain individuals be present. This chapter focuses on why you are meeting and what you are trying to do.

If people arrive at a meeting with different sets of expectations, you'll hear, "I thought this was going to be a reporting session. I didn't think we were going to have to make a decision." Or, "I didn't know I was expected to give a presentation. I'm not prepared." Or, "Why are we here anyway? Who called this meeting?" Obviously, it's much easier to be clear about the purpose of your meeting in advance than to clear up differing expectations once the meeting begins.

One way to clarify expectations is to state specifically in an agenda, handed out in advance, the type of meeting to be held. But to do this, you need to use consistent terms. When you say, "We're going to have a problem-solving meeting," everyone should know what that means. It doesn't make much difference what words you choose as long as everyone understands them.

WHEN YOU SHOULD HOLD PROBLEM-SOLVING MEETINGS

The phrase "problem-solving" means different things to different people. In our work, we define a problem as a situation you want to change. A problem could be a state of confusion over a new set of regulations, not having a name for a product, or having to fill a job vacancy. What's important is that you (or somebody) wants to change the status quo. For example, if you see your children tussling together and you don't mind, it's not a problem for you (although it may be one for the younger child). For a problem to exist, there has to be an agent and a desire for change.

This leads to one of the reasons why meetings often fail: There is no energy in the meeting because no one recognizes a problem or wants to deal with it. Maybe a lot of things could be changed, but if everyone is content, there may be no reason for a meeting. A problem-solving meeting can work only if there are people in the meeting who are able to (and want to) change something—to solve a problem—and who know how to go about doing it in a group. The Interaction Method is ideal for this type of meeting.

WHEN YOU SHOULD HOLD DECISION-MAKING MEETINGS

A problem-solving meeting is a meeting to attack a problem but not necessarily to make a decision. A decision-making meeting is one in which there is pressure to make a final decision by choosing from previously developed alternatives.

If you are trying to make a decision by consensus, then the Interaction Method is essential. If your organization is hierarchical, the meeting must include the ultimate decision-maker or your efforts will be wasted. The size of the group should be less than fifteen, although if the basic elements of the decision have been sorted out ahead of time, working with up to thirty people is possible.

If your group or organization is horizontal, like a board of directors, you may be required to take a formal vote. But, as we have explained elsewhere, it is possible and effective to try for consensus using the Interaction Method and then turn the meeting back to the chairperson and Robert's *Rules of Order* for a final ratification or majority vote if consensus cannot be reached.

In any case, before the meeting be sure that everyone understands and accepts how the decision is going to be made and who is going to make it. That way, people will come prepared and will not feel steamrolled by a process they did not expect. If you are a manager and made up your mind before a meeting, don't fake a decision-making meeting. Your people will almost always know when they are being used as a rubber stamp. That's bogus participation and will sour your group to meaningful involvement. Simply call an information-sharing meeting and announce your decision. It's more honest and is not likely to backfire.

WHEN YOU SHOULD HOLD PLANNING MEETINGS

Planning is future-oriented problem-solving. When you plan a trip, you are figuring out how you are going to solve the problem of getting from here to there. When you plan a meeting, you are deciding how to deal with a problem as a group. So the requirements for a problem-solving meeting hold for a planning meeting as well. It's useful to make a distinction between short-term logistical planning and long-term policy-making and goal-setting. For short-term logistics it is often not necessary to involve many people, and the smaller your group, the quicker you will be able to get through the details. For long-term plans, you may want to include many people in order to win commitment to organization goals. If you want to include more than thirty people, you must design a participatory planning process, which is beyond the scope of this book.

WHEN TO HOLD REPORTING AND PRESENTING (FEEDFORWARD) MEETINGS

A large percentage of regular staff meetings are information-sharing or reporting sessions. They are one of the most misused types of meetings. Much of the reporting could be done on a one-to-one basis or in writing. Often the purpose of the meeting is for the manager to check up on whether the staff is doing its work. As we have pointed out in Chapter 1, on the average, 7 to 15 percent of personnel budgets is spent on person/time in meetings. And a major fraction of this time is wasted in listening to someone else give a routine report. It is a great waste of valuable human resources.

As long as reporting meetings are just lecturing to the rest, there isn't much need for rules, and there really is no limit to the size of the group. You can lecture to five or 5,000; it doesn't make much difference. If, on the other hand, reporting is used to spot problems to be dealt with collaboratively by the group, the subsequent problem-solving sessions should be run by the Interaction Method.

Sometimes facilitation is needed during the question-and-answer period after a report. These discussions can become heated, and the meeting can get off the track easily. In this case, the manager could facilitate and someone else should record the problems so that they can be worked on later. Many managers make the mistake of leaping into these post-reporting sessions and make snap decisions, thereby cutting off collaboration and involvement by the staff.

Be aware that just because you have said something to a group, it doesn't mean they have heard or understood what you said. Allowing time for questions is one way to increase the value of a report.

WHEN TO HOLD REACTING AND EVALUATING (FEEDBACK) MEETINGS

The dynamics of a "feedback" meeting are very different from those of a "feedforward" meeting. Here you have many people expressing their opinions or suggestions to one (or several) individuals, usually an executive or public official. Such a meeting can be valuable because everyone has a chance to participate as well as listen to other people's opinions. It is a way of tapping the feelings and ideas of a group—a form of participation.

Unlike the reporting meeting, feedback sessions should be thoroughly organized and programmed. The Interaction Method can work well. The facilitator makes sure that everyone has a chance to participate and protects the executive or official from personal attack. Decision-makers should not try to run this kind of meeting. It is difficult to stay open to negative criticism and not become defensive, even hostile. A skillful facilitator can maintain a positive tone and save the decision-maker from getting into a heated encounter.

The role of recorder becomes important here, because the group memory can capture and preserve ideas as they are expressed, as well as give the participants some assurance that their ideas are registering. This assurance can be further strengthened after the meeting by feeding back to the participants their recommendations in the form of a group memo.

HOW ABOUT LEADERLESS MEETINGS?

For some gatherings, structure may be inappropriate: cocktail parties, open houses, informal rap sessions. And at some meetings leadership is rejected on principle: in some men and women's consciousness-raising groups, communes, encounter groups, and certain membership organizations. But just because you don't impose a structure on a meeting doesn't mean that no structuring will occur. Before long, the common meeting problems we have discussed are bound to appear. The more forceful individuals will begin to dominate the less outspoken, and the multi-headed animal will emerge.

In *Radical Feminism,* a book about the women's liberation movement, Ms. Jo Freeman describes the shortcomings of the "structureless" group:

> The basic problems didn't appear until individual rap groups exhausted the virtues of conscousness-raising and decided they wanted to do something more specific. At this point they usually floundered because most groups were unwilling to change their structure when they changed their tasks. Women had thoroughly accepted the idea of "structurelessness" without realizing the limitations of its uses. People would try to use the "structureless" group and the informal conference for purposes for which they were unsuitable out of a blind belief that no other

means could possibly be anything but oppressive.

. . . Contrary to what we would like to believe, there is no such thing as a structureless group. Any group of people of whatever nature that comes together for any length of time for any purpose will inevitably structure itself in some fashion.

. . . For everyone to have the opportunity to be involved in a given group and to participate in its activities, the structure must be explicit, not implicit. The rules of decision-making must be open and available to everyone, and this can happen only if they are formalized.

For fun, observe your next cocktail party or after-dinner discussion. Watch how an unspoken set of ground rules will appear spontaneously. If the visiting professor speaks, he may demand total attention and not hesitate to interrupt others. The hostess, on the other hand, may be the only one allowed to change the subject abruptly—the dynamics will change, but they won't go away.

If you're trying to do something collectively, to make some decisions, the organically grown structure may not be consistent with your basic philosophies. The Interaction Method's explicit contracts of neutrality and nonmanipulation provide safeguards that structurelessness does not.

HOW TO HANDLE COMBINATION MEETINGS

Many meetings contain some reporting and some problem-solving and decision-making. That can work out okay as long as the roles and procedures change as you switch from one type to another. Meetings get into trouble when the transitions are sloppy—if in the middle of a report someone asks a question, which surfaces a problem, which leads to other problems, which lead to an argument, which results in the manager imposing a decision. People may leave the meeting stunned, wondering how things went from a report to a unilateral decision by the boss.

If you think that a meeting may switch from reporting to problem-solving, make sure that a facilitator and a recorder are available and that everyone is agreed to tackle the problem. Later, if there is a jump from problem-solving to decision-making, check out whether it is possible to make a decision, and if so, who is going to make it and how. The old "one thing leading to another" can get you in trouble.

CHAPTER 12

Who Should Attend Your Meeting?

When you decide whom to invite to a meeting, you may be making a more important decision than you think. It will have a significant effect on what happens, because there is, of course, a direct connection between who attends the meeting and the content and quality of the decisions that will flow from it.

If you hold a meeting to decide between alternatives A and B, and you invite only people who you know are sympathetic to A, what's going to happen? Obviously, your group will choose A. Or what if a local law-enforcement department investigates itself? Or if a group of big businessmen gets together to develop solutions to the escalation of inflation? Aren't they likely to see the problem as "labor asking for unreasonable wage increases"? And if labor gets together, won't they see the problem as "big business"?

The same goes for administration versus teachers, industrialists versus ecologists, sales versus production. If you have only the same kind of people with the same kind of views, you are going to get only predictable solutions. This sameness (or homogeneity) of meeting membership is a principal cause of many ineffective (and sometimes inhuman) decisions made today.

Even if you appoint a committee of brilliant people with somewhat different sets of expertise and background, there is still a danger that their desire to support each other and reach a common agreement will override their independent, critical thinking and their investigation of several alternatives. Psychologist Irving L. Janis has labeled this tendency of groups to think alike. He calls it "groupthink." Here are some of the reasons why he thinks groupthink happens.

NINE ROADS TO GROUPTHINK

1. There is some truth in the old line that "power can go to your head." If you have ever been around a high elected official or the president of a large, prestigious organization, the individual can seem to radiate a sense of self-importance, a glitter of power. This is particularly true of members of important policy-making groups. Whether in the boardroom at the top of a skyscraper or in the White House, it is easy to feel a sense of collective power and importance—that we can do anything we want because we believe in the "right" things; and because we all are good people and well-meaning, our decisions will be "right." This is a very seductive and dangerous attitude, and has led to some of the most disastrous decisions our businesses and governments have made.

2. The higher you are promoted in an organization, the more insulated you can become from the realities of people at lower levels and on the outside. Because the prevailing values of the organization affect who is promoted and who isn't, a natural screening process takes place so that only the same kind of

people make it to the top. There you are far away from the action and in daily contact with very limited (and usually similar) points of view. You might think that the higher you rise in an organization, the more accurate information and more varied kinds of expert advice you receive. After all, your decisions affect many people. Ironically, because of filtering—the "tell 'em what they want to hear" attitude—reality is sometimes just the opposite.

3. When groups are homogeneous, it is hard to avoid stereotyping the "opposition." Since the "other guys" are not represented at the meeting, it's easy to project all sorts of evil motives on them, to speak for them in their absence. This fosters inaccurate and dangerous assumptions as well as a "we/them" mentality.

4. You might think that the more a group develops mutual trust and a sense of togetherness, the more individual members would feel free to voice disapproval openly. This is true up to a point. But some groups swing to a point where members don't want to rock the boat by disagreeing because this might ruin the feeling of oneness. People who harbor genuine doubts will put a lid on them; they rationalize that if they raise objections this would only complicate the group's work. And for some people the feeling of belonging, of membership, has more personal importance than the desire to see the group make the best decision.

5. As a group grows together, it develops a common set of beliefs. Anyone who challenges these beliefs may be regarded as a disrupter, and pressure will be placed on him or her to step into line. Rather than encouraging different views, members push for conformity, and thereby negate a most important reason for meeting as a group. This leads to groupthink and the development and consideration of a very limited number of alternatives.

6. When the membership of a group involves a senior executive and staff, loyalty and support sometimes are offered as

another reason for not criticizing the prevailing views. The argument goes something like this: These are hard times; everyone is after the leader's head; the last thing he or she needs is more criticism.

7. Where there is great eagerness for concurrence in a group, indications of disagreement may be ignored. If a group member is silent on an issue, this is often taken by the rest of the group as a sign of agreement. No effort is made to probe for what the individual really thinks and feels.

8. Groupthink often develops when a group is under great pressure to make a decision. "The chips are down; we've got to make a decision by five o'clock this afternoon; this is not time to bicker; we've got to pull together." Normal standards and procedures may be dropped. In the panic to reach closure, important steps and considerations are left out. The result may be a decision that does not reflect the intelligence and common sense of the group members.

9. Finally, once a decision has been made by groupthink, there seems to be an unspoken pact not to challenge the leader or the decision, even if there are warnings that the decision is not working. People say, "If there is a problem, it's just that we haven't gone far enough." The response is often, "Let's do more of the same." More bombing, more taxes, more incentive, more supervisors, etc. No one questions whether the original plan was correct to begin with, and no contingency plans are developed.

While groupthink is most obvious and most disastrous at high-level meetings, it can occur in any homogeneous group that works together over a long period. This chapter is devoted to ways of avoiding groupthink and homogeneity in important policy-making, planning, and decision-making meetings. It will explain how to select meeting members, what to do during a meeting to avoid groupthink, and how to protect against groupthink between meetings.

WHO SHOULD BE THERE

Obviously, the best way to avoid the consequences of a homogeneous group is to make sure that your group and your meetings are as heterogeneous as possible. Make sure you have as many possible points of view included in your problem-solving and decision-making. Ideally, participants should include all who have relevant expertise, who are affected by the problem, and who must make the final decision. That's the key to successful participatory process. Here are some specific things you can do.

A large percentage of meetings in predominantly hierarchical organizations maintain a fixed membership—the manager and his or her staff. When all group members come from the same division, often with similiar backgrounds and expertise, this works all right for information-sharing and reporting meetings; but when problems arise, these usually have repercussions way beyond the confines of the group. That is the point when you should consider involving other people in your meeting. Ask yourself, "Who has relevant expertise? Who must be in on this decision? Who will be crucial to the implementation of whatever solution is reached?" If you ask yourself these questions, you most likely will hit upon several other key individuals. The purpose is not only to avoid the pitfalls of groupthink, but also to take full advantage of the benefits of collaboration and participation. You can save a great deal of time and energy by involving someone in a decision rather than having to sell the decision after the meeting. If you let the problem dictate the membership of the group, you will arrive at a heterogeneous group naturally.

When we described hierarchy collapsing, we were talking about equalizing the difference between manager and immediate staff; in fact, many times an organizational problem calls for a problem-solving group drawn from a cross section of the whole organization. The design of a new product may require a horizontal section of people from different divisions: marketing, production, sales, and research and development. A problem concerning employee benefits demands a vertical cross section from top management through supervisors to hourly workers. We are convinced that these cross-sectional groups should be used more—and not just at the top levels of management.

If you begin to think about who is most affected by various problems, you will identify what are sometimes called "natural work groups"—people who are naturally connected by their tasks. In a hospital a natural work group would be the floor nursing team, the registered nurses, nurses aides, and orderlies assigned to care for a certain number of patients. On an assembly line the group might represent all skills needed to manufacture a component. In a school it might be all the teachers and aides responsible for a grade level. Instead of always meeting as a homogeneous group (all the English teachers, all machinists, all nurses) there are many benefits to meeting in natural work groups. These groups are oriented toward problems shared by all the members; they are heterogeneous and have a common responsibility. For them, meeting together develops teamwork and improves morale.

PICK A STRATEGY

The membership of a formal horizontal group is fixed. The members have been either elected or appointed. If members are elected, it's likely that some differences of opinion are represented; but many board members are chosen because they are much alike, which increases the risks of groupthink. Because final decision-making is restricted to official members, the option of holding *informal meetings* is rarely pursued. Not only can boards invite a wide variety of people to testify (a win/lose approach), they can also meet in collaborative problem-solving sessions with extended membership. A school board can meet in a work session with teachers and administrators, a corporate board of directors can meet with middle management, a board of supervisors can meet with citizen groups. At least, these sessions will expose group members to other points of view and promote dialogue and understanding. At best, win/win solutions can be hammered out.

HOW TO MAKE A GROUP CREDIBLE

The effectiveness of a temporary horizontal group like a task force is almost entirely dependent on the selection of members. Since a task force has no final decision-making power, its strength comes from the process of inclusion. If the right people aren't involved, the product will have little impact. If you create a task force to develop an urban-renewal plan for a neighborhood and don't involve representatives of the neighborhood organizations, you're headed for trouble. Most likely the plan will not reflect citizens' needs, and its implementation is bound to be blocked by lengthy legal battles.

As a rule, don't let a task force start working until you are convinced that its membership reflects all viewpoints on the issue. If the membership is not credible to the relevant communities and organizations, the results will not be credible. Just as important, make sure you have involved individuals who can either make decisions themselves or can speak for (or influence) institutions that have the power to make decisions. A group of students may go off by themselves and develop a plan for changing their school, but then find themselves in a we/them adversary relationship to the administration. If the students involve administrators and faculty in their deliberations, they may have a greater chance of convincing others who have the needed power.

HOW TO FLUSH PROBLEMS OUT OF HIDING

If you are going to hold a problem-solving meeting to address a particular problem, make sure that most, if not all, participants recognize the problem and want to do something about it as a group.

Check out how problems are usually solved in your organization or group. Sometimes staff members have a tacit agreement not to expose troublesome situations in front of their manager; they deal with the problems quietly between meetings. If you are a manager and your people are "sitting" on their problems, maybe it's because they think you hold meetings only to check up on them and criticize them for having problems. They get rewarded for hiding their problems—not for surfacing and solving them. You will have to convince your people by your actions that you want them to bring problems to the surface, that you want to operate as a member of a team, and that more creative and workable solutions can be found through collaborative problem-solving.

BRING IN SOMEONE NEW

Occasionally, bring in new people to your meetings, depending on the agenda for the day: experts, people from other divisions or groups, members of the next larger rings of involvement. Not only do new people tend to inject new life into groups and put everyone on good behavior; they also help to break down communication barriers and prevent the formation of subgroups.

IS EVERYBODY REPRESENTED?

If you have trouble assembling a representative cross section for a committee, make a checkerboard. List all the possible qualifications of participants across the top: age, sex, race, geographical distribution, organizational affiliation, level of education, expertise, etc. Then list the potential candidates vertically on the left and check off their qualifications. One person can meet several qualifications, i.e. a black woman under thirty from organization X and background Y. By examining the pattern of qualifications, you can spot glaring gaps or the beginnings of homogeneity.

Many of the following ideas have been discussed elsewhere. Here we apply them to the groupthink problem.

HOW DIVERSITY HELPS

The more heterogeneous a group becomes, the more you need to clarify and organize its roles and processes. A great deal of energy can be generated by a bunch of people with different views. This energy can be destructive or creative, depending on how the meeting is run. That is why the Interaction Method is so vital—it is designed to channel the creative energies of a diverse group toward a common task. The role and skill of the facilitator become more important the larger and more complex the group. In fact, as you become more experienced as a facilitator, you will welcome some conflicts because you can use the energy as a constructive force to break open the problem and push for innovative solutions. It's much more challenging and fun to work with a lively group than a complacent one.

Even if you are stuck with relative homogeneity of membership, a facilitator can do much to point out the dangers of groupthink and encourage the group to develop several alternatives before making an important decision.

HOLD BACK THE BIG GUN

Whether you are a facilitator or a group member, do urge the senior manager or decision-maker to hold back on his or her opinions until other group members have had a chance to be heard. This makes it less likely that valuable ideas will be overshadowed by the forcefulness and magnetism of the leader. But don't let the leader drop out entirely; particularly if it's a collaborative problem-solving and decision-making meeting, the decision-maker must truly participate for consensus to be attained.

SPEAK OUT!

Encourage group members to speak out. By doing so, they are helping to develop more comprehensive solutions. Reinforce and protect minority opinions. Don't let individuals give in to the majority view until their reservations are gone—or at least clearly understood by the rest.

APPOINT A DEVIL'S ADVOCATE

Sometimes a useful device to encourage people to be critical is to assign somebody to play the role of devil's advocate. The devil's advocate agrees to be a Doubting Thomas, to point out every flaw and possible objection. This specialized role sounds phony after a while, but it can demonstrate the importance of looking at the opposing side of an issue. Ultimately, every group member should share the responsibility of offering constructive criticism.

VOTING IS A LAST RESORT

Don't ask for votes unless consensus proves impossible. As we have shown, voting usually produces lower-quality win/lose solutions than consensus. But don't assume you have reached consensus until you have checked with everyone in the group. Don't take silence as agreement. Find out what the silent, thoughtful people are thinking. The quiet ones are often nursing valuable ideas or insights.

BEWARE OF PREMATURE DECISIONS

Don't push too hard for decisions. Don't panic. Double-check to see whether a decision really has to be made by a certain time. If not, sometimes delaying a decision until more information can be gathered may be a better alternative than making a poor decision that everyone will regret later.

BETTER "SLEEP ON IT"

For critical decisions, try to separate the development of alternatives from the final decision-making. Schedule one meeting for problem-solving and another for decision-making. Give people a chance to "sleep on it" to gain perspective. It's easy to get caught up in the enthusiasm of the moment and become blind to serious flaws in an idea.

CONFRONT THE "OTHER GUYS"

Guard against making assumptions about the "other guys." Whenever feasible, involve the other side (or parties) in your deliberations. The discomfort of confronting and working with someone in meetings may be offset by the danger of escalation when a decision is based on a misunderstanding.

HOW TO PROTECT AGAINST GROUPTHINK BETWEEN MEETINGS

The accomplishments of one meeting may be enhanced—or made worthless—by what happens before the next meeting. Here is a list of what you can do between meetings to prevent your group from becoming isolated and falling prey to groupthink.

1. Between meetings, encourage everyone to consult with other members of their department, organization, or constituency. Where secrecy or security is not an issue, get them to share what has been happening in your meetings and to bring back suggestions or criticisms of others.

2. It's a good principle of involvement and participation to keep your problem-solving and decision-making as visible as possible. Give everyone an opportunity to see what's happening and to contribute after a meeting; post the group memory in the hallway outside the conference room. That way you won't later encounter the objections, "If only you had consulted us! If only we had known!"

3. If your group needs the support of a larger organization or constituency, don't move from one phase of problem-solving to the next before getting input and agreement from the larger body. If others have not agreed to your definition of the problem, they will never accept your solutions.

4. If your group needs the final approval of a decision-maker who can't or won't attend your meetings, keep that person up to date on what's happening. Don't work for weeks and deliver a final report. Provide him or her with a group memory or memo of your meeting, and ask for comments and input as your meetings progress.

5. If you deal with issues that entail weighty consequences, you can validate the work of your group in a number of ways. You can break into subgroups and go over your problem again. Sometimes a smaller group will highlight differences of opinion

and come up with a new insight into the issue. Or you can create one or more parallel groups to work simultaneously but independently on the problem. The ensuing competition—and even the redundancy—may help expose blind spots that result from earlier groupthink. And if you are having trouble deciding between alternatives, you can invite independent evaluators, experts who have not participated in your problem solving process; they may bring valuable new perspectives.

CHAPTER 13

How Many People Should Attend?

After you have determined *why* to have a meeting, *what* you want to accomplish, *who* should be there, and *when* and *where* the meeting is going to be held, you must decide *how many*. You have to stop and check to see if it is feasible to achieve your goals with the given number of participants, and if so, how.

Obviously, the dynamics of a meeting become more complex the larger the group. Most meetings are just too large. This chapter examines the advantages and limitations of different-size meetings, and tries to establish some guidelines about what you can hope to do and what roles and processes you will need. We have selected four arbitrary divisions (2–7, 7–15, 15–30, and above 30). Somewhere around the boundary of each of these divisions, the dynamics of meetings seem to change.

WORKING WITH 2–7 PARTICIPANTS

Many meetings fall into this category, particularly staff meetings of a manager and his or her immediate subordinates.

The group size may seem to be determined by the number of people at the next level in the hierarchy, so the question of how many people should attend a staff meeting is rarely raised. If most of the meetings you attend are staff meetings, be sure to read the previous chapter. It may be that other people in your organization should be included in a particular meeting, depending on the issue.

One question that is raised often about using the Interaction Method for staff meetings is, "How can we use these techniques? Our meetings are too small. We can't afford to have a member of our staff facilitate or bring in somebody from outside our group."

First, all the dynamics and problems we have discussed so far occur whenever two or more people get together. The same principles of how to run effective meetings still apply; the Interaction Method just makes them explicit. If you are aware of the important distinction between process issues (the how) and content issues (the what) and if you deal with them separately, you will improve the effectiveness of your meetings.

If there are four or fewer people in your group and if each understands the concepts of facilitation, your group can facilitate itself. You will find the facilitator hat being passed around naturally. If two members get into an argument, a third will become the neutral third party and begin to facilitate. If the group gets bogged down, someone can make a process suggestion like "Why don't we back off this issue and move onto the next?" or "Let's defer judgment for now." If issues get emotionally charged, some form of third-party facilitation and some form of recording may become essential.

When there are only two or three people in your group, it still helps to sit facing some sheets of butcher paper mounted on the wall. When the meeting process involves the generating of lists (beginning with a list of agenda items), someone can reach for the markers and record the items. When someone is making a presentation, he or she can build a group memory by recording the main points. When decisions are made, you can avoid misunderstandings by writing them down. Your small group can record itself and facilitate itself, thereby improving the effectiveness of even informal meetings.

If your meetings are in the range of four to seven participants, you have a variety of options. For really critical meetings where everyone is intimately involved, it may be worthwhile to get a trained facilitator from somewhere else in your organization or outside. You can solve the recorder problem by training an assistant or secretary; you will increase the skill level of this subordinate and provide a means for him or her to observe your meetings while also serving a useful function. Having your secretary understand what is happening in your group can be a great advantage.

Remember that your meetings are costing your organization a lot of money and the decisions you make affect performance directly. The expense of bringing in a facilitator or recorder may be more than justified by the increased effectiveness of your meetings. Some organizations maintain a pool of trained facilitators. As part of their jobs, they are on call two to ten hours a month to facilitate or record important meetings throughout the organization.

The larger the group, the more structure your meetings will need. When there are only two or three participants, everyone plays multiple roles. For six or seven, do separate the process from the content roles. One person (not the manager) can become a combination facilitator/recorder. It's hard to play both roles, but it may be better than having no facilitator at all. The role can be rotated during a meeting depending on who is least involved with the issue at hand. Or one person can agree to be neutral for the duration of the meeting.

Once you've become aware of these concepts, it will become obvious when a meeting is breaking down and what has to be done. You will know when it is time to volunteer to facilitate or, if you are a manager, to request that someone else facilitate. The sudden burst of motion, the sense that you're getting someplace now, will more than reward you for your efforts.

The advantages of a meeting with only two to seven participants are obvious: It's easy to assemble participants quickly; the meeting can be informal and flexible; all types of meetings are possible; it's efficient for dealing with detailed technical and logistical problems; and the group dynamics are relatively simple to manage. But with few participants only a few points of view can be represented, and so the resulting decisions may not have the same quality and impact as a meeting of seven to fifteen participants. More important, there may not be enough people to achieve the critical mass required for the best creative problem-solving.

WORKING WITH 7–15 PARTICIPANTS

Seven to fifteen people is an ideal size for a problem-solving, decision-making meeting. The advantages are: Everyone can participate easily; everyone gets to know everyone else's ways of thinking; it's small enough to maintain informality and spontaneity, but big enough to allocate two members to facilitate and record; and it seems to be the size most conducive for creative synergy. ("Synergy" is the phenomenon of the whole becoming greater than the sum of its parts.) The only disadvantages are that the meetings are complex enough so that they need to be clearly structured; you definitely need a facilitator and recorder. And because of the person-time tied up in the meeting, it may be a waste of creative energies to spend too much time on routine reporting.

For a group of this size, all concepts and techniques of the

Interaction Method apply, and all types of meetings can be held. It is only when meetings begin to exceed fifteen participants that they become clumsy and ineffective as a management tool.

WORKING WITH 15–30 PARTICIPANTS

Most meetings should not have more than fifteen participants. In larger groups the dynamics get extremely complex, often to the point where professional facilitation is required. Unfortunately, many large meetings are held every day, and the results are generally disappointing. As long as there aren't any expectations for collaborative problem-solving and lots of participation at these sessions, and as long as they are used only for information-sharing, they can serve some purpose. But it takes an experienced facilitator to achieve constructive involvement in a meeting of this size. Just the job of making sure everyone has a chance to be heard without being interrupted becomes overwhelming. You have to impose a lot of rules. Hands have to be raised, and the meeting becomes more formal and less spontaneous.

The multi-headed animal looms like a giant octopus at large gatherings, and you have to be a combination entertainer/animal tamer to get all heads to point in the same direction. As a meeting gets larger, members feel less responsible for making it work. Subgroups take shape with hidden agendas; people stop acting as individuals and more as members of a political caucus. The resulting win/lose mentality and the freezing of viewpoints can make collaboration and consensus difficult.

You can involve more than thirty people in problem-solving and decision-making, but you have to break up the crowd into subgroups of less than fifteen. You can create a feeling of being part of a large team, rather than a small group, if you keep shuffling the membership of the subgroups, sometimes according to interest and problem areas and at other times so that there is a representative cross section in each group. The subgroups can meet as a whole for reporting, information-sharing, and formal adoption of decisions hammered out in committee.

WORKING WITH MORE THAN 30 PARTICIPANTS

A New York City official once shared with us his secret for disarming the effect of public participation. "When citizens begin clamoring for involvement, I appoint an advisory committee with a minimum of fifty members, and then sit back and watch the chaos. A year later the committee is still struggling to get itself together, and the issue has been resolved by other means."

Large groups are fine for lectures, panel discussions, formal debates, and voting. Much beyond thirty, it doesn't make much difference how many people you have. Any kind of participation has to be subject to a clear set of rules, and for this purpose parliamentary procedure is well suited. So if you are on the board of a membership organization, keep your meetings small and bring out the troops only when you need them.

It is possible to involve large numbers of people in the planning process. There are many successful examples of citizen involvement projects, from the neighborhood level up to the scale of a whole state. We ourselves have designed and managed conferences and institutional planning processes that have provided opportunities for hundreds of individuals to have a say in the decisions that affected their lives. While the techniques for citizen involvement are beyond the scope of this book, all the principles of collaborative problem-solving in small groups apply as well for large-scale projects. Sooner or later any kind of involvement program requires people meeting together, and the quality and success of these meetings will affect the program as a whole.

CHAPTER 14

How to Make Meeting Rooms Work

Where you meet can affect the way a meeting will work. A good meeting room won't guarantee a good meeting, but a bad meeting room can contribute to a bad meeting. You probably have attended meetings where the room was too large, or you couldn't hear what was being said, or you couldn't see who was talking, or the room was too stuffy or too noisy or too dark. And you certainly have been to meetings where there wasn't adequate preparation, where there weren't enough seats or enough papers, or the slide projector didn't work. These logistical problems can start a meeting off on the wrong foot. Most of these environmental problems can be avoided by preparation.

HOW TO CHOOSE THE RIGHT ROOM

When you choose a room for a meeting, it's like choosing a box for a present. You don't want too big a box because the present will rattle around inside. If the box is too small, the present might be crushed. The same is true of a meeting. Twenty people in an auditorium will feel intimidated by the huge surrounding empty space. Sounds will echo. People won't be able to hear one another because there is nothing to contain and reflect their voices. But in a small office twenty people will feel crowded and crushed—almost claustrophobic. The room will get hot and stuffy, people will have to sit on top of each other, and there will be no room to stretch or get in and out.

One of the first things you should do when deciding where to meet is to make a high and low estimate of the number of people expected, and then choose a room that fits the group. If the estimate changes, be sure to change the room.

It's often hard to visualize how much space a certain number of people will need, so it's worthwhile to rehearse by arranging chairs, tables, and other equipment ahead of time to see how they look. If the seats can be sensibly arranged and there's enough room to move around, then you're all set. If the chairs seem lost in the space or too crowded, then try to find an alternative room.

Often you will have to make tradeoffs. Only certain rooms are available for the times you want to meet. A room that might be the right size may come equipped with fixed chairs, or you may just be stuck with having to meet in a less-than-desirable room. If you are forced to make a choice, think about the effect you want. Crowding a lot of people in a small space sometimes creates a feeling of community and excitement. To meet in such a spot can make members of the group feel that this is the place to be. The hardships of the space can help to break the ice. That's why the British designed the House of Commons to seat only about two-thirds of the members. That's about all that

turn up for most of the meetings, so the room doesn't feel
empty. For the occasional crisis session, the crowded effect of
members standing in the back only heightens the sense of urgency.

There are also ways to make a large room seem smaller (the
reverse is almost impossible). If you're holding an evening
meeting in a school cafeteria, you can set up chairs in a corner,
and then surround the corner with little walls by stacking tables
or turning them on end, or surrounding the space with movable
partitions. The remaining meeting area can feel quite cozy.

THE BEST SHAPE FOR A MEETING ROOM

Generally, the shape of the meeting space is not as important
as its size. Obviously, most rooms are rectangles of reasonable
proportions. The real test is whether you can arrange the necessary number of seats in an appropriate configuration. Recently
many rooms have been designed for specific purposes. And
usually these are worse than everyday rooms. Often the seating
is fixed—usually in a pattern that doesn't work for the Interaction Method. And the shape of the room dictates what kind of
meeting can take place in it.

Sloped floors may be great for viewing lectures, films, or
debates, but they are terrible if you want people to be able to
see each other. Elevated platforms can render a perfectly good
room inflexible by limiting where the meeting has to take place
as well as creating unnecessary formality, distance, and self-
consciousness. So check out the shape of the room. When possible, choose a room with flexibility so you can custom-design
your meeting space.

HOW TO ARRANGE SEATS AND TABLES

The arrangement of seats and tables sets the stage for a meeting and can influence in many ways what will happen. For meetings of five to thirty people, two basic configurations of seats are circular and semicircular. All others are really variations of one or the other. The circular arrangement is conventional. We will discuss its limitations. The semicircular is best suited for Interaction Method meetings.

The seating pattern does make a tremendous difference. A human being is a source of energy, and most of it radiates in the direction he or she is facing. We know from physics that if you distribute several sources of energy evenly around a circle facing inward, the forces will cancel themselves out. So, if you place ten people around a circular table, their energy is directed back at each other. It's locked in. It doesn't add up to anything. If the circle gets squeezed into a long oval, one person's energy is focused on the person opposite and is thereby critically restricted. When everyone faces toward the person at the end of the table, the collective energy is aimed at one individual, not at a common problem. It's true that many managers or chairpersons enjoy being the focus of attention, and even demand it. That's fine for a formal presentation or information session, but collaboration is inhibited if everyone is focused on one individual instead of the task.

The circular seating pattern is fine for meandering discussions or informal gatherings, like sitting around a table after dinner. The closed form encourages a sense of warmth and togetherness. It is easy to make direct eye contact with everyone else. Whatever the mood of a group, it will be heightened by the circle. If anger or aggression are in the air, this negative energy will be aimed directly at individuals and can lead to heavy encounters. Sometimes, when you break off eye contact and look in a common direction, communication will become less emotionally charged and more suited to problem-solving.

So, once again, much depends on what you want. If you want an intense face-to-face exchange, the circle is ideal. If you want a problem-focused meeting, sitting around the table doesn't work very well.

WHAT'S GOOD ABOUT THE SEMICIRCLE

It may sound like a minor matter, but one of the most effective ways to get a group to focus on a task is to seat the participants in a semicircle facing a group memory. The pent-up energy of the group is now released and directed toward the common problem as it unfolds on the large sheets of paper in front of the group. Since all participants must see the group memory as well as each other, the semicircle is an integral part of the Interaction Method.

The way the semicircle is placed within a room is also important. Two factors govern: (1) the location of the doors to the room; and (2) the location of a wall suitable for taping the paper for the group memory.

Ideally, the semicircle should face away from the entrance so that people coming in or going out will not disrupt the flow of the meeting. It's a reality of meetings that some people will arrive late, and others will have to leave and return for biological reasons. Messages will be brought in, participants will slip out early, etc. If the door is in the line of vision of the participants, all eyes will turn instinctively toward each interruption. Some chairpersons and managers purposely arrange the room so that any entry or exit is a noticeable and intimidating act. Participants become prisoners of the meeting. This practice usually backfires. The meeting is likely to be disrupted so often that nothing gets accomplished.

If you run effective meetings, people will usually come and leave on time unless they have conflicting engagements. If people start coming late or ducking out early or not coming at all, it's an indication that your meetings are not as effective, enjoyable, or productive as they could be. Find out the cause. Ask participants to help you make your meetings better. Don't keep people prisoners in your meetings by making it difficult to come late or leave early. It's not the way to build an effective and committed group. Focus a meeting away from the door whenever possible.

HOW TO PLACE THE GROUP MEMORY

The second requirement, directing the semicircle of seats toward the wall suitable for mounting the group memory, sometimes conflicts with the first. The walls should be smooth and long enough to tape at least four—even better, six—two-foot-wide sheets of butcher paper side by side. So you need eight to sixteen feet of smooth wall surface. Many rooms have three sides made unusable by windows, paneling, cabinets, and doors, so that you are forced into using a wall next to or between two doors. Sometimes the situation can be corrected by placing movable partitions or blackboards against an otherwise unusable wall or taping the group memory on the window. Use your ingenuity.

The diameter of the semicircle will be determined naturally by the number of participants, but try to keep it within fifteen feet. If it's larger than that, eye contact, normal conversation, and reading the group memory become difficult. If the group is larger than fifteen, you'll need to create a second row to keep the semicircle tight.

Many people feel uncomfortable without a table in front of them; it becomes a protective barrier as well as a place to put papers, drinks, and personal belongings. We feel quite strongly that it's best to get rid of tables whenever possible. They tend to keep participants away from each other, forcing the size of the semicircle to become larger and decreasing the sense of closeness and compactness of the group. Tables also form a barrier between the group and its facilitator, who sometimes needs to walk up close to participants to get their attention or break up an argument. If participants have a lot of written materials in front of them on the table, they can easily get engrossed in reading and doodling and can drop out from the discussion for periods of time. Since the group memory makes most note-taking unnecessary, the need for a writing surface is diminished.

If tables become a necessity for one reason or another, see if you can find narrow ones that can be arranged in a splayed U-shape with the participants sitting around the outside. Then the semicircle shape can be retained somewhat, and the facilitator still has room to roam about near the participants.

HOW TO CHANGE THE GROUP'S BODY LANGUAGE

Much has been written about body language and nonverbal communication—how your facial expression and the way you move, sit, and cross your arms and legs convey nonverbal messages that often express more than your words. Crossed arms, tension lines in the face, and a slouched seating position can indicate frustration and withdrawal. Strong eye contact, feet on the floor, and a forward posture may mean interest and involvement. When you become aware of these nonverbal clues in others, you can learn to read people more accurately and communicate more effectively with them.

A group has its own group body language. The way people position themselves toward each other can tell you a lot about the interpersonal dynamics and the level of involvement in the group. Pecking orders develop as they do among seagulls on a wharf. If you can read your group's body language, there are steps you can take, either as a facilitator or as a group member, that will improve the effectiveness of your meetings.

If you notice that certain people always sit together or isolate themselves by leaving an empty seat (which creates a we/them situation), you can point this out and suggest mixing up the seating pattern at the next meeting. As a group member, you can break up seating patterns by changing where you sit at each meeting. Sometimes you might try sitting in the middle of a clique on purpose. It is important for the group to become a coherent unit made up of independent individuals, not a conglomeration of subgroups.

An individual can also disrupt the focus of a meeting by sitting outside the semicircle toward the back of the room. It's actually a position of power, because the person can hold back for a while, pretending not to be there—and then suddenly toss out a cryptic contribution. All heads have to swivel around and the individual has monopolized the attention of the group. A we/them pattern is then set up and it can change the meeting to encourage a win/lose outcome.

When you're a facilitator it is *imperative* that you persuade all group members to sit in a semicircle. If one person starts scooting his chair back, you might say, "Hey, Joe, would you mind coming back and joining the group?" It's a good idea to establish a rule that anyone sitting in the back of the room is an observer and cannot participate in the meeting. If an observer wants to contribute, he or she must push a chair up and join the semicircle.

Watch out for an empty chair! It's more than a vacant seat. It's an energy leak—a hole in the meeting—an escape hatch where the group's energy can drain out. Getting a group to start moving on a problem is like boiling water. The smaller the pot, the quicker it will come to a boil. A small, compact group is easier to facilitate than a large, spread-out one. Get rid of empty chairs and get people to move in as close together as possible. When someone leaves a meeting, remove the chair and reduce the size of the semicircle. Physical togetherness increases a sense of mental togetherness. A group will get "cooking" much faster if its seating pattern is tight.

HOW TO CREATE THE RIGHT ATMOSPHERE

The physical environment has a significant effect on the psychological environment of a meeting. Formal settings—baronial boardrooms, long, shiny conference tables, and huge, heavy chairs—can create a formal atmosphere, whether intended or not. There are times when formality and ceremony are appropriate: the announcing of an important decision, the signing of a contract, the installation of an official. But formal meeting rooms are not conducive to rolling up your sleeves and working together. For work sessions, you need an informal space where you can push chairs together and pin things to the walls and where a spilled cup of coffee is not a disaster.

Several recent studies show that a special state of mind and body is most conducive to creativity. If you want to solve a problem or accomplish a task, you can try too hard, you can be too tense or uptight. On the other hand, if you are too relaxed and sloppy, nothing is likely to happen. There is a special in-between state—not too relaxed and not too tense—when ideas begin to pop and lots of work gets accomplished. It's a state of "relaxed concentration."

This principle holds true for groups. If the atmosphere is too formal and rigid, if the facilitator is pushing too hard, if the time limits are excessively tight for the work to be done, then the meeting will be tense and filled with a great deal of wasted motion. If the feeling is too casual, if people are lounging around and not paying attention, not much will happen.

We get best results when people feel comfortable, ties and jackets are removed, and everyone is on a first-name basis. The atmosphere of informality must be balanced by a focus, an organized meeting environment, and no interruptions. When you become aware of this balance, you will know when it's time to get people to sit up and re-focus, or when it's time for a joke and a stretch. It's a special state, this relaxed concentration, and a good facilitator can help a group to attain it.

RIGHT TEMPERATURE, LIGHT, AND NOISE

Temperature, light, and noise are important (if mundane) factors in a meeting environment. You don't think about them until they bother you, and by then there may not be anything you can do about them.

Check temperature controls before the meeting. Remember, bodies give off heat, so the room will be warmer with people in it. Aim for about 68°F., a good temperature for working and saving energy. There is nothing worse than a stuffy, hot, smoke-filled meeting room. A lack of oxygen can drain mind and body. Really! So the janitor is an important ally. Make friends with him or her, and find out how to adjust heat, light, and the P.A. system (you might be surprised how many meetings in hotels get interrupted by a blast of Muzak). If you are holding an evening meeting, remember that in some buildings the heat is turned down automatically.

Remember that the Interaction Method is graphic as well as verbal. Good, even lighting on the group memory is essential —without heavy shadows. Make sure there is adequate light, not too glaring but not too dim and murky. The combination of indirect incandescent and overhead fluorescent light works well.

The point is to keep interruptions to a minimum. You want to keep the momentum going, not start and stop all the time. It's always hard to get back to full speed after an unexpected interruption. You want to get your group rolling and keep it on the freeway of effectiveness until the task is completed.

So get rid of distractions: Face chairs away from windows,

shut doors, hold calls and messages, and make sure you have all the tools and data you need before you start the meeting. Check to be sure there are no plans for a noisy office party or remodeling job next door. Try to find a room that is as isolated and soundproof as possible.

YOU CAN'T PREPARE TOO MUCH

Everything we have talked about in this chapter has had to do with preparation—things you can and should take care of before people arrive for meetings. In the Interaction Method scheme of things, it is the responsibility of the facilitator to get everything set up before the meeting. Even if someone else is taking care of the physical logistics, the facilitator should dou-ble-check. Remember: Most meeting planners do not yet worry about the kinds of problems and solutions we have been talking about. It's up to you to make sure you won't hear one of them saying, "Well, I got you a room to meet in. It's a perfectly good room. What's the matter? You didn't want tables? No place to put butcher paper? Well, you should have told me."

Some inexpensive tools are essential for the Interaction Method: paper, markers, and pins or tape—the components of the group memory. They are not to be found in the conventional conference room. If any other equipment is going to be used, check it out ahead of time. Make sure tape recorders are hooked up right and can pick up voices from any place in the room and that there is extra tape. Check slide projectors, over-head projectors, or computer terminals. Remember: If anything mechanical can go wrong, it will—generally at the moment it becomes indispensable.

So far, we have mainly talked about making changes in the social and psychological factors that affect meetings and about some simple, though powerful, tools—the display system in-volved in the group memory. Clearly, interpersonal problems that emerge in meetings are more critical than problems of physical space. But once you have improved the basics for groups to solve problems and make decisions together, it is time to consider what advanced technologies would further increase the effectiveness of groups. Surely, in this space age, we could invent more sophisticated technologies than magic markers and butcher paper to support collaborative problem solving.

COMING: THE "PROBLEM-SOLVING CENTER"

Since we believe so strongly in institutionalizing new ways to find win/win solutions to complex problems and since a new social institution often gives form to a new physical institution (the way cars led to shopping centers), we predict there will be new kinds of buildings. They may be called "problem-solving centers" and will exist inside large organizations as well as in major urban areas at large.

Ideally, the problem-solving center should support group problem-solving and decision-making in three ways: (1) It should offer a place where people of different or rival interests and affiliations can meet. "Where to meet" can become an issue of territoriality. ("Do you come to my office or do I have to go to yours?") Holding a meeting in your office can give you a psychological advantage. Meeting on neutral territory helps to put people at ease and to create a positive atmosphere conducive to collaboration. (2) A problem-solving center should offer new kinds of meeting rooms and technologies to augment and improve group problem-solving and decision-making. (3) It should be staffed by professionals who can offer third-party facilitation of meetings and assist in the design and coordination of large-scale planning and policy-making programs. This combination of services we call "process management."

In some large organizations the beginnings of internal problem-solving centers already exist. While some companies are experimenting with "decision rooms"—which allow managers access by computer to up-to-date information from all parts of their organization—most organizational problem-solving centers today are physically little different from conventional conference facilities.

Eventually some training and development departments will staff and maintain these centers. In addition to training managers in problem-solving and decision-making skills, these training and development departments will help organizational planning and decision-making by serving as neutral, task-oriented facilitators for important meetings held every day throughout their organizations.

THE MEETING OF TOMORROW

Let's fantasize for a moment. The year is 2000. You are a concerned citizen of a city of 500,000. You have volunteered to be a member of a task force charged with developing a preliminary master plan for an urban area. On the task force are people in business, education, government, and architecture and planning, and local residents—about twenty-five in all. The task force has been underway a month or so. There is a meeting at the Metropolitan Problem-Solving Center, a nonprofit organization that offers its services and facilities to civic groups.

The center looks like an ordinary building as you approach it from the street. But once inside, you have entered another world. The lobby is quiet and comfortable. Along one side there are several futuristic-looking chairs. The people in them are watching meetings on small TV screens. There is no sound; only the occupants of the chairs can hear the speakers mounted in the headrests.

The receptionist asks which group you are with and then ushers you directly to Situation Room B. As you pass through the padded doors, you are reminded of pictures of the mission control center in Houston that you saw on TV during the moon launchings, except everything here seems more human and relaxed. You are the last to arrive. The rest of the members of the task force are already seated in a semicircle in specially designed swivel chairs. On the arm of each chair there is a panel with various buttons. A small TV screen can be drawn around the front of each chair. You can write on these TV's with special light pens. One of the businessmen is using a light pen to edit a page of a planning document displayed on his monitor.

Once you take your seat, the meeting begins. The room is octagonal. Each of the eight walls that surround the group is divided into three large screens. They look like movie screens and information can be projected onto them from the rear. In fact, three of the screens are displaying a summary of the group memory from the previous meeting to bring everyone up to speed.

Your facilitator, a staff member of the center, is asking for reactions to the tentative plan the task force developed in the last meeting. As people talk, key phrases appear in large type of different colors on one of the screens in front of the group. The recorder is sitting at a console to one side, typing on a keyboard and also drawing with a light pen. The record is simultaneously displayed on the large screens as well as on the small TV screens mounted to each of the chairs.

An argument is shaping up between one of the local citizens and the city planner about whether a proposed medical center should be a tall building or a low, two-story structure. The residents are afraid that a tall building would dominate the neighborhood. The planner disagrees. The facilitator suggests that the group take a look at how both structures might appear if you were walking down the street. He speaks quietly into a microphone and suddenly there is a computer simulation of the street scene projected on the panel in front of the group. It's actually a movie of what a twenty-story building would look like as you walk down the street. Then another movie is projected and the building is replaced by a two-story structure. An architect suggests the tower might be set back behind a two-story structure, and promptly that design appears.

The facilitator now wants to get a quick feeling of the opinions of the group. Members push one of three buttons on the panels on their seats, and the results of the poll are instantaneously displayed in front of them. It becomes clear that everyone prefers either the low building or the tall building that is set back, not the tower by itself.

Later the task force is trying to reword an important paragraph of its planning document. The facilitator suggests that everyone take a crack at it individually, so for a few minutes you type on a keyboard attached to your own TV. The words appear on your screen, but you can erase them and move them about easily. When you want to take a look at an old version, that too can be "called up" on your TV. When everyone is finished, all the versions are displayed on a large screen. The group combines the best part of several versions, and the final paragraph is then automatically inserted into the working proposal. The facilitator announces that paper copies of the updated document will be available at the end of the meeting.

The task force works intensively for three hours and then takes an hour and a half break. Some members have a light luncheon in the Center restaurant; others use the sauna, hot tubs, and swimming pools. One member has a sandwich brought in and uses his computer terminal to connect with a nationwide information service to review the latest federal regulations and funding opportunities.

Does all that sound improbable? Every one of the technologies we have described exists today. Some of them are expensive and still experimental, but once there is a recognized need for such centers, they could be built within the next few years at a cost consistent with their usefulness.

CHAPTER 15

How to Put It All Together: The Agenda

We can't emphasize enough: Everyone should know what to expect before coming to a meeting. You must be explicit about what's going to happen, how the meeting is going to be run, who is going to play what roles, and the answers to the rest of the issues we have raised so far. If all participants receive a detailed agenda at least a day (preferably a week) before the meeting, they will come prepared, and most of the common causes of confusion at the beginning of meetings will be avoided. Because most of the procedural questions will have been settled in advance, your meetings will be shorter and more effective.

When you are very busy and rushed, writing up an agenda for a future meeting can seem like a waste of time. It's not—but to make it easier, we have designed a simple agenda form. We have found that filling out a form is quick (you can fill it out in five minutes), and the form itself reminds you of things you might have forgotten. A standard form is easy to read at a glance, and anyone can be trained to fill it out.

Our form includes most of the critical information people should know ahead of time, but you may want to tailor it to fit your particular needs. If your group has a fixed membership and meets regularly, you can design and print a form that includes all the information that doesn't change from meeting to meeting. That means even less to do when you prepare your agendas.

Now let's "walk through" the agenda form and see how to fill out each item. This will also be a good way to review and concretize some of the planning issues we have been discussing.

Name of group

Most groups have a name: Cloverdale PTA, executive committee, task force of long-range planning, board of directors of Acme Widget Co., etc. If your group doesn't have a name, you might consider giving it one. A name can help build a sense of identity and importance.

Title of meeting

Most meetings have a name or description: annual budget review, weekly staff meeting, Project Alpha progress report, emergency meeting on busing, etc. Usually the title conveys the general topic of the meeting. In conversations with other group members it helps you to distinguish between different meetings that your group may be planning to hold.

Meeting called by

It's important to identify who convened the meeting, because participants will want to know who felt the meeting was necessary and whom to contact for questions, additions to the agenda, and directions to the meeting place, as well as whom

AGENDA

NAME
OF GROUP: _____

DATE: _____

STARTING TIME: _____

TITLE
OF MEETING: _____

ENDING TIME: _____

MEETING
CALLED BY: _____

PLACE: _____

MEETING
TYPE: _____

BACKGROUND
MATERIALS: _____
_____

DESIRED
OUTCOMES: _____
_____
_____
_____

PLEASE
BRING: _____

MANAGER/
CHAIRPERSON: _____

MEETING
METHOD: _____

DECISION
MAKING METHOD: _____

FACILITATOR: _____

FINAL DECISION
MAKER: _____

RECORDER: _____

GROUP MEMBERS: _____
_____
_____

SPECIAL NOTES: _____
_____
_____

OBSERVERS: _____

RESOURCE PERSONS: _____

ORDER OF AGENDA ITEMS	PERSONS RESPONSIBLE	PROCESS	TIME ALLOCATED

to notify if they can't attend. So include a telephone number. A meeting could be called by a group member, a manager/ chairperson, or some other individual or group either inside or outside your organization.

Date, starting time, and place

Obviously, when and where the meeting is going to be held are essential pieces of information. Make sure to include the number or name of the meeting room. If participants are unfamiliar with the location, send along a map with directions.

Ending time

Meetings tend to drag on forever, if you let them. People begin to wander out, the meeting dribbles to an end, and everyone leaves feeling dissatisfied and annoyed at spending more time than they had anticipated. Principally, meetings so frequently run over because groups try to accomplish too much in too short a time. We discuss this problem below under "Order of agenda items." The point is to set realistic time limits and keep to them. Begin and end the meeting on time; if you finish the agenda early, end the meeting early. Participants will appreciate that you respect their time and will take meetings more seriously. In general, meetings should be from one to two and a half hours long. Shorter than that, too much time is wasted getting started and building momentum; and if people sit in their chairs for more than two and a half hours without a break, they get restless and stale.

Meeting type

We have described five basic types of meetings—problem-solving, decision-making, planning, reporting, and reacting (feedback)—and we have shown how meetings can be combinations of these types. Each type may require different roles, numbers of people, and meeting methods. You should be clear about what type of meeting you want and plan it accordingly. For example, is it a meeting to make decisions or just to share information? Let everyone know what type of meeting it is going to be so they can arrive with a common set of expectations.

Desired outcomes

It's even clearer if specific outcomes are stated. This should be done by the group as a whole at the end of the previous meeting or by whoever is convening the present meeting. If it's the first gathering of a group, everyone should participate in sharing expectations at the beginning of the meeting. Imagine in advance that the meeting has just finished and that it was successful. Ask yourself: What would success look like? What would have been accomplished? What problems solved, what decisions made? What other kinds of sharing and learning would have made the meeting successful? If everybody is explicit about their desired outcomes, unrealistic expectations can be dealt with in advance or at least before the meeting gets under way.

Background materials

If there are presentations or issues that require the participants to do homework, list the background materials that are being sent out with the agenda or that participants are expected to have and review beforehand. Be realistic: Most people aren't very conscientious about reading handouts, so keep them short. Usually they are read at the last moment, so don't send them out more than a week or so in advance.

Please bring

If you expect participants to bring something to the meeting, let them know. This might include edited documents, filled-out forms, lists of names—even box lunches. There's nothing worse than finding everyone settled down to a meeting and then one by one dashing out to find some piece of paper left in an office.

Manager/chairperson, facilitator, recorder, and group members

These are the four basic roles of the Interaction Method. By having to list names on the form, you will be reminded if you have forgotten to line up a facilitator or recorder, and everyone will know in advance who is supposed to be doing what. It's essential for the facilitator and recorder to be informed of their roles because they have the responsibility for coming early and setting up the meeting room. If you list the names of all the group members that are expected to attend, it gives people an opportunity to get a sense of the size and flavor of the meeting and to see what interests will be represented.

Observers and resource persons

We have already defined these temporary and occasional roles. Observers and resource persons should understand and agree to their roles before the meeting, and the rest of the participants should be aware of who else is going to be attending the meeting and in what capacity.

Meeting method

Everyone should know how the meeting is going to be run —what the ground rules are going to be. We have pointed out the dangers of the so-called "structureless" meeting when you want to accomplish a task. To avoid the multi-headed animal syndrome and all the other common meeting problems, you need some structure. What's it going to be? Robert's *Rules of Order*? The Interaction Method? Some combination of the two?

Decision-making method and final decision-maker

If decisions are going to be made, it's essential that everybody understand how they are going to be made and by whom. Who has the final say? The group as a whole, the manager, or some other (senior) group or individual? Don't play games with people. If group members don't have the power to make decisions, don't let them wait to find out. It will almost always backfire.

If it's a decision-making meeting, be clear about the procedures. If you are working for a win/win solution, list the decision-making method as "consensus." But be clear about the fallback, win/lose approach, if any. If the group can't reach consensus, what will happen? Will there be a vote, and if so, does it take a simple or two-thirds majority to win? How will ties be broken? Or if there is no consensus, will the manager decide? Almost any procedure can work if everyone understands and agrees to it ahead of time.

Special notes

This is the place for any special communications: a plea to group members to attend the meeting, a comment about the importance of the meeting, or an announcement about some special guest.

Order of agenda items, persons responsible, process, and time allocated

Here is the place to list individual agenda items. Be as specific as possible. The more you can define items that involve problems, the more effectively you will be able to use the creative power of the group. Try stating them as questions (see the next chapter).

For each agenda item, list the person who is responsible for introducing the subject (that is, who is making the presentation, who is submitting the problem to the group, who is responsible for this area of concern, etc.). The person responsible for each item should figure out with the facilitator and/or manager/chairperson a good way to handle the issue. In a sense, each agenda item is like a mini-meeting. You have to decide what type of meeting to have: what you want to do and how you are going to do it—a content and process agenda. In most cases, you won't be able to give a specific problem-solving method or technique, but you do want to communicate whether you expect the group simply to listen to a report or to become involved in solving a particular problem or making a decision.

Then you should make a realistic estimate of time necessary to deal with the agenda item. After doing this a few times, you will get a feel for whether an item is likely to be a ten-minute or half-hour issue. Things always seem to take longer than you think, so it's a good idea to be generous in your time allocations. An example of a completed agenda item: "Progress report on the career development program: Do we need an extension of deadline?/Richard/presentation and decision-making/20 minutes."

Suggestion: make a first pass at listing all the agenda items, working out a process for each one and making time estimates, but not worrying about the order of agenda items. Then add up all the time allocations to see if they exceed the total amount of time set aside for the meeting. Often you will find that you have more items than available time, but it's better to discover this before rather than during the meeting. Many meetings are damned as failures because the group had unrealistic expectations: it tried to deal with fifteen items and managed to cover only ten. If it had set out to handle eight issues, and ended up with the same outcome (taking care of ten), the meeting would have been regarded as a great success. Plan your meeting to be a success, not a failure.

Now it's time to order the agenda items. Philosophies about the ordering of agendas conflict. Some people feel the most difficult and challenging item should be first so the participants can deal with it while they are fresh. Others feel it should be last to build excitement or even to tire out participants so no one will have energy left to fight about the issue. In general, we favor putting reports on action items first and then dealing with issues in order of urgency and general concern. If you don't get to cover all the items, then at least you have taken care of the most critical ones.

In actuality, meetings can get totally filled with putting out little (but immediate) organizational fires while larger, long-range issues, which are equally important to the functioning of the group, remain untouched. To counter this tendency, plan special problem-centered meetings to focus entirely on one or two larger, more complicated issues. During these meetings, all discussion of day-to-day affairs will be suspended, and the group will devote its energies to more general problems.

In the case of groups which are meeting for the first time and which have no prearranged procedure for putting together and ordering the agenda, you should cross out the words "Order of" and write "Suggested" on the agenda form. Allocate time at the beginning of the meeting for the agenda items to be modified and given priorities by the participants themselves. This gets people to "own" the meeting and to assume responsibility for what happens.

AGENDA

NAME OF GROUP PRODUCT DIVISION

DATE 3 25 76

STARTING TIME 10:00 AM

TITLE OF MEETING PROBLEM SOLVING SESSION ON COST REDUCTION

ENDING TIME 11:00 AM

MEETING CALLED BY JOE

PLACE ROOM 325

MEETING TYPE PROBLEM SOLVING

BACKGROUND MATERIALS REPORT ON FEBRUARY PRODUCTION LEVELS

DESIRED OUTCOMES 1 IDEAS FOR REDUCING PRODUCTION COSTS

2 A PLAN FOR DETAILED ACTION STEPS

PLEASE BRING ABOVE MATERIALS

MANAGER CHAIRPERSON JOE

MEETING METHOD INTERACTION METHOD

DECISION MAKING METHOD CONSENSUS MANAGER

FACILITATOR TOM

FINAL DECISION MAKER JOE

RECORDER MARY

GROUP MEMBERS RICO, JUAN, MARTA, BILL

SPECIAL NOTES THIS IS AN IMPORTANT MEETING.

PLEASE BE ON TIME

OBSERVERS NONE

RESOURCE PERSONS NONE

ORDER OF AGENDA ITEMS	PERSONS RESPONSIBLE	PROCESS	TIME ALLOCATED
1 REVIEW OF FINANCIAL SITUATION	JOE	REPORT	5 MINUTES
2 DEVELOPMENT OF COST REDUCTION APPROACHES	TOM	BRAINSTORMING	20 MINUTES
3 PRIORITIZING AND ASSIGNING FEASIBILITY STUDIES	TOM	RANK ORDERING	30 MINUTES

AGENDA

NAME OF GROUP: P.T.A.

DATE: 4/15/76

STARTING TIME: 7:30 PM

TITLE OF MEETING: MONTHLY MEMBERSHIP

ENDING TIME: 9:00 PM

MEETING CALLED BY: JUDITH CRENNA, PRESIDENT

PLACE: CORBETT SCHOOL, ROOM 6

MEETING TYPE: PROBLEM SOLVING

BACKGROUND MATERIALS: NONE

DESIRED OUTCOMES:
1. PRIORITIZED LIST OF SCHOOL PROBLEMS
2. PARTICIPANT UNITY ON PRIORITIES
3. A PLAN FOR INCREASED PARENT PARTICIPATION NEXT YEAR

PLEASE BRING:

MANAGER/CHAIRPERSON: JUDITH CRENNA

MEETING METHOD: INTERACTION METHOD

DECISION MAKING METHOD: CONSENSUS/MAJORITY VOTE

FACILITATOR: MS. LESLIE CHIN

FINAL DECISION MAKER: GROUP

RECORDER: MR. PAUL ROSENTHAL

GROUP MEMBERS: ALL P.T.A. MEMBERS IN ATTENDANCE

SPECIAL NOTES:

OBSERVERS: NONE

RESOURCE PERSONS: NONE

ORDER OF AGENDA ITEMS	PERSONS RESPONSIBLE	PROCESS	TIME ALLOCATED
PRESIDENT'S REPORT	JUDITH CRENNA	PRESENTATION	15 MINUTES
FUNDRAISING COMMITTEE REPORT	MR. JONES	PRESENTATION	15 MINUTES
LIST OF SCHOOL PROBLEMS	MS. CRENNA/MS. CHIN	PROBLEM SOLVING	½ HOUR
PLAN TO INCREASE PARENT PARTICIPATION NEXT YEAR	MS. CHIN	BRAINSTORMING	½ HOUR
COFFEE	MS. FRANK		

CHAPTER 16

Solving Problems in Groups: The Tools

Once you have facilitated a few meetings, you'll start wondering why some work better than others. Sometimes your group bogs down trying to define a problem; or it seems uncreative in trying to think up solutions. Other times the group is alive and creative, moving smoothly from one problem to the next and accomplishing a lot of work. Why the difference? How can you help your group when, say, it gets hung up over definitions? What other ways are there to define a problem?

It's at that point, if not before, that you will experience a need to know more. You will realize that a good facilitator knows how to help a group when it gets stuck. This is a second set of facilitation skills: understanding the dynamics of problem-solving and knowing how to use a number of group problem-solving and decision-making tools.

The Interaction Method is not a method of problem-solving and decision-making. It is a method of running meetings.

Group members, assisted by the facilitator, can choose any of several hundred problem-solving techniques. The Interaction Method does not dictate any approach. It is compatible with all group problem-solving methods, including brainstorming, lateral thinking, synectics, Kepner-Tregoe, management by objectives, and many others.

A word of caution: Beware of anybody who tries to convince you that there is one "right" or "best" method of solving a problem. Human problem-solving, we have to say again, is educated trial and error. There is no system that works every time. There is no "right" way of developing a plan, designing a house, or writing a book. These problems, like most of the ones we face every day, are open-ended: Many solutions are possible, some better than others.

BUILD A BETTER TOOL KIT

Your skill as a problem-solver, and particularly as a facilitator of group problem-solving, depends on your repertoire of tools and your knowledge of how to use them. With just hammer and nails, a carpenter can make few things. The more tools he acquires, the better he can deal with various woodworking situations. As his skill develops, he knows better which tool to try at any time. He can cut out a piece of wood with a jigsaw or a crosscut saw; each tool offers certain powers and limitations. When he picks one up, he knows ahead of time what to watch out for. When the jigsaw begins to bind or the crosscut saw is too hard to control, he changes tools. A good carpenter, like all skillful problem-solvers, is inventive and flexible. He is a master of his tools, not limited by them.

It is important for you, as a problem-solver, to be aware of the various problem-solving strategies, so you can avoid panicking when you get stuck, analyze what you have been doing, and consciously choose an alternative approach.

Awareness of different methods is even more essential for you when, as a facilitator, you want a group of problem-solvers to use the same tool at the same time. You can't do that without being explicit about which tool to use. The facilitator has to be able to suggest one or more methods from experience. When you see that your group is having trouble generating alternative solutions, you should be able to say, "I don't think we're getting anywhere by considering old solutions. Let's try to work together to think up some new ones. We could try brainstorming or the checkerboard approach." (The checkerboard approach is explained later in this chapter.)

We have defined "problem" as a "situation you want to change." "Problem-solving" therefore means "situation-changing" and includes all the traditional steps: problem perception, definition, analysis, generation of alternatives, evaluation, decision-making, planning, and implementation. But what are these so-called "steps," anyway? If problem-solving is really educated trial and error, how can there be formal steps?

IT'S NEVER NEAT

Well, you know from experience that you don't solve problems neatly step by step. Human problem-solving is a messy business. Sometimes you may have a solution before you know what problem it solves: You decide to move your bed against a different wall and discover the next morning that the sun doesn't wake you up so early. Or you think of a new way of defining a problem while you are evaluating some alternatives: Where should you park today, at a meter or on the street or in a public garage? Hey, maybe you could get a ride into town!

These steps are sub-problems that you face as you wind your way from problem to solution. Each requires a different focus. When you define a problem, you ask yourself, *"What is my problem?"* When you analyze, you are concerned with the question *"Why is it a problem?"* When you generate alternatives, you ask, *"What are some ways I might solve my problem?"*

At any point, if you stop to think about what you're doing, you could figure out what step (or more accurately, phase) of problem-solving you are in. Once you have solved the problem, you can work out in retrospect how you handled each phase. Every solution implies a definition of the problem and some implicit criteria by which you chose this alternative over the rest. In other words, all phases of problem-solving get dealt with implicitly or explicitly.

Example: When you buy a pair of shoes, you make a number of implicit decisions. Your problem is you need a new pair of shoes; your problem is *not* that you need to repair some old shoes; according to some criteria and personal preferences, a certain pair of shoes is better for you than the rest in the store.

As we have seen, individuals can jump from one problem to another without becoming confused because the mind can focus on only one thing at a time. Not so for a group. To work collaboratively, all minds must focus on the same problem in the same way at the same time; and everyone must focus at the same time on the same sub-problem. That's why, as facilitator, you must understand each phase of problem-solving and know how to move a group from phase to phase.

Therefore, we have devoted a section of this chapter to each phase of problem-solving and to a few of the methods we have found most useful.

PROBLEM PERCEPTION: WHAT IS IT?

When you're in the phase of problem perception, you ask yourself: Is there a problem? Where is the problem? Is it really a problem? Whose problem is it? What does it look like, feel like, etc.? It's the sniffing, groping, grasping phase. It includes whatever you do to get a handle on a problem, to stake out the general problem area. Something is going wrong. Sometimes the only indication is a strange feeling or, as in the case of an engine problem, a strange noise. The first thing you usually perceive is a symptom: People are looking unhappy, no one is buying, there is a change in the rate of growth, etc. You've got to find out what the problem is.

Problem perception is closely related to problem definition and problem analysis. In all three phases your focus is on the problem itself; afterward you start thinking about solutions. In practice, you'll find yourself cycling back and forth between understanding more about the problem through analysis, getting a sharper definition of the problem, and seeing and accepting it more fully. Until these three phases have been covered thoroughly, don't let your group proceed to solutions. (If people don't agree on the problem, they will never agree on a solution.)

One of the main objectives of the facilitator during this phase is to help the group recognize whether it has a problem and, if so, to accept it and agree to try to solve it. Is there a situation that the members of the group want to change? Group members have to buy into the problem, to own it. Otherwise they'll have little energy to proceed. In fact, a lack of energy in a meeting is often a symptom that you haven't dealt adequately with this phase of problem-solving.

PROBLEMS AREN'T "BAD"

As a facilitator, you have a continuing responsibility to educate your group. The more your group understands problem-solving and the Interaction Method, the easier your job will be. One of the first messages you must get across is that problems are okay. Everybody has problems; they are a fact of life. Human beings couldn't live without change in their environment, without stimulation, and all changes require responses, which involves problem-solving. So it's all right to have a problem, as long as you're willing and able to do something about it.

Many individuals and groups are afraid of problems. To admit to having a problem is often regarded as an admission of failure. People like to say, "Everything's all right—no problem!" So some refuse to recognize they have a problem or keep ignoring it or hiding it. If you point it out to them, they'll say it's unsolvable, that that's just the way things have to be. Often there is an underlying fear that any change will be for the worse, and it's better to hold on to an old familiar problem than to have to cope with a new one. Besides, if this problem were solved, maybe there wouldn't be anything left to do!

So you must convince your group that it can solve its problems collectively in a meeting and that there are real benefits in doing so. It's your responsibility to create a positive, supporting, and secure climate in the meeting so that problems can surface, be accepted, and be solved. Here are five problem-solving methods for the perception phase.

HOW TO LEGITIMIZE

Everybody sees things differently, especially problems. Did you ever stop a children's fight and ask them what the problem was? The response is usually a discordant chorus: "He started hitting me and I'm fighting back." "No, she started it by calling me names," etc. In a way there is no such thing as the "real" problem. Everyone's view of the problem is "real" to him or her, and everybody's view is somewhat different. The objective in collaborative problem-solving is to get agreement on a common statement of the problem (see "How to get the problem defined," later in this chapter). But, before you can do that, you have to understand how each person perceives the problem. The expression of personal views, no matter how divergent, has to be legitimized.

One technique for legitimizing individual perceptions is to ask all group members to state their personal view of a problem. Accept and support each statement as a legitimate view (which it is) and protect it from attack until it has been recorded in the group memory and has been somewhat depersonalized.

Facilitator: What do you think the problem is, Maria?

Maria: Nobody follows procedures around here.

Facilitator: Okay, that's how you see the problem. What's your view, Harry?

Harry: No, Maria's wrong. That's not the problem. The procedures don't make any sense.

Facilitator: Hold on, Harry. We're just trying to see how everyone sees the problem. Maria sees the problem as nobody following procedures and you see the problem as the procedures not making sense. You're both entitled to your opinions. Both views are legitimate, and maybe we will discover that both the procedures and the way they are followed are at fault, or maybe there is a more basic problem here. Right now, we're just gathering information. What do you think, José?

Once you have heard and recorded everybody's point of view, the tension should relax and you may be able to find areas of overlap or, with further analysis, some underlying cause.

HOW DOES IT FEEL?

It's very important that group members not only hear but also understand how other people feel about a problem, particularly if the problem is interpersonal. There are many ways to experience a problem from different points of view. If the various sides are present in a meeting, people can exchange roles and try to express the other person's concerns. "If I were Alfred, I think I'd be worried about being left out of this new agreement." Then you can get Alfred to confirm if his concerns were represented accurately and repeat the process until there seems to be an understanding.

If critical views aren't present in the meeting (as in a homogeneous group), you could role-play to simulate how others might see your problem. There is always a danger when you try to speak for someone else, but as long as you realize that a role-playing situation is not necessarily an accurate representation of reality, a lot can be learned.

Other ways to express a problem from other points of view include going on field trips to see the problem firsthand, interviewing people who are closely involved, and watching slides or movies that convey some other aspect of the problem. The more you can understand the general situation, the more chance you have to perceive and solve the "right" problem.

WHAT'S THE "REAL" PROBLEM?

Sometimes group members will skirt around a central problem, hinting at it but afraid to discuss it openly. If you're a member of a group yourself, it should be obvious what is happening. If you are new to the group, an outside facilitator, you can diagnose the situation because you'll sense a general feeling of nervousness and caution. The more the group avoids the issue, the scarier the problem seems. Meeting after meeting can go by without ever getting to the core of the problem.

When you see this happening, a more direct strategy may be called for. You can begin by pointing out the group's behavior: "It seems to me you're avoiding something. Is there something else you haven't brought up?" Or, "Sometimes when people are silent, it means there is something they don't want to talk about." Or, "Why is everyone suddenly yawning and getting fidgety? What's going on? What are you afraid to talk about?"

Then, legitimize: "It's all right. It can't be that bad. In the long run, it would be much better to deal with the 'real' problem than to continue ignoring it." Often just commenting on what is happening is enough to get people to leap in and address the issue. If this doesn't work, you may have to take off the facilitator's hat and do it for them. "Is it that you're afraid someone has been *stealing?*" Speak the unspeakable, and then put your hat back on quickly. Don't acquire a stake in your statement of the problem. A little nudge in the right direction may be enough to get the ball rolling.

THE BEST, THE WORST, AND THE MOST PROBABLE

People have the strangest reasons for not wanting to face problems: fears, fantasies, and unrealistic worries. If you can bring these concerns to the surface, they may melt in the light of day. When a group is balking at tackling a problem, you can suggest a look at the best, worst, and most probable consequences of solving and not solving the issue. Ask: "What's the best thing that might happen if we could get a solution? What's the worst thing that might happen? What's the most probable thing that might happen?" Then do the same for not solving the problem. Sometimes, when questioned directly, people can't think of any terrible consequences and become more willing to grapple with an issue. The payoffs for solving a problem become convincing when compared to the probable consequences of not solving the problem.

WHOSE PROBLEM IS IT, ANYWAY?

One question you should ask a group in this phase of problem solving is: "Whose problem is it?" Countless meetings have been devoted to arguing over issues that group members were powerless to affect or incapable of resolving. As a rule, you can't solve someone else's problems. If you uncover a problem that involves other persons or groups, wait to include these parties before continuing with your problem solving. Ask: "Can this group deal with this problem in this meeting? Who else should be involved?"

HOW TO GET THE PROBLEM DEFINED

In group problem-solving, once you've perceived a problem, the next logical step is to get a working definition of it. When you define something, you set boundaries around it; you say what it is and what it isn't. You describe without necessarily naming: it's smaller than a breadbox but larger than a matchbox; it's red and round and edible. Each definition limits the possibilities. In problem definition the set of possibilities is called the problem area.

There is a great danger that if you narrow the problem area too quickly, you will exclude the real problem. If you can't start the engine of your car, and leap to the definition that you have engine trouble, you will be excluding the possibility that the problem is an empty gas tank. If you define a problem as "how to increase the supply of energy by 1990," you may overlook the problem of how to decrease energy consumption. "Where to build a new school" is a narrower definition than "where to find more classroom space"; it excludes the possibility of converting existing warehouse space to classrooms or using portable classrooms.

Definitions are doubly important because they also determine the range of acceptable alternatives. Problem area is linked to solution space. In the example above, the definition of "engine problem" excludes the solution "more gas"; "more energy" excludes "reduced consumption," and "building a new school" overlooks "conversion of existing space." That's why you have to be very careful when you define a problem. Try to avoid all unnecessary assumptions which can blind you to other causes and innovative solutions. But do make sure that you are defining a problem, not a solution. "Hiring two more secretaries" is not a problem but a solution to some other problem still undefined.

Experiment with a number of definitions, continually testing your definition with the known facts that have been discovered through analysis. You want to build your definition on the foundation of hard evidence, not speculation or blind assumptions.

STATE THE PROBLEM AS A QUESTION

When you first ask group members to suggest definitions of a problem, you may get responses like "I think the problem is that we need a new filing system," or "No one likes the filing system." These contributions are either disguised solutions or statements about the problem; they aren't useful definitions. One effective technique for sharpening definitions is to ask people to state their definitions as open-ended questions, preferably beginning with "how to": "How to change or modify the filing system so that we can find everything we need efficiently." Or, "What is the best way of storing and retrieving this kind of information?"

Each definition has a different slant, a different implied solution. But if they are stated as open-ended questions, then they can be used in an alternative-generating session. A question like "Should we change our filing system?" is not so useful because it is a yes/no question. It doesn't leave room for alternatives. Remember, most problems don't have one "right" solution, just a range of possible solutions, some more suitable than others. Don't let your definitions become too limited.

When you use this technique, get people to generate a list of possible definitions and then choose one as a place to begin. Don't let people argue over which definition is best until you have completed some analysis.

PAG/PAU

This technique of defining a problem is part of a more complex problem-solving method called synectics (see Bibliography). The original definition is written up in the group memory as the Problem As Given (PAG): "How to improve the functioning of this office." That particular wording is preserved and defended as the way the originator defined the problem. Then other group members have an opportunity to offer their definitions of the Problem As Understood (PAU): "How can we stop the busy work?" "How can we cut down on the backbiting and gossip?" "How can we make the office a more pleasant place to work?" Notice how this technique can be combined with the previous one by asking people to state their PAU's as questions.

LASSO

If you want to tighten up a definition, the lasso method works well. Write the definition on the wall and then circle or lasso key words, asking the group to be more specific. If the definition is "How to solve drug abuse in the schools," you could lasso "drug," "abuse," and "schools." What drugs, what do you mean by abuse, which schools, what age levels, and even what do you mean by solve: reduce, eliminate entirely, prevent, etc.

Each time you clarify a key word, you sharpen the definition. If there is an "and" in the definition, check to make sure you are not trying to solve two problems at once.

IS/IS NOT

This technique is drawn from a more comprehensive method developed by two former researchers at the Rand Corporation, Kepner and Tregoe (see Bibliography). It's another way of clearly stating what you know about a problem.

In one column, write down facts you know about the problem: where it is, what its effects are, when it occurs, etc. Then do the same for what you know is *not* part of the problem. Example: The telephone problem is "can't hear some of the incoming calls, occasionally can't get a dial tone, happens more often in early morning." The problem is not "callers can always hear clearly, problem does not affect other lines in the building, the intercom works well." Collectively, these statements build up to a definition of the problem without running the risk of assuming something that is not verified.

HOW TO USE DIAGRAMS

Particularly if you are working with a design problem, it is a good idea to get away from words, to draw what you know about the problem. Diagrams can be simpler and more direct than verbal statements without becoming too specific. If you struggle with planning your new office space, develop diagrams that express what you know about the problem as well as what you know about the solutions. You can diagram what you want as well as what you don't want. Example: We want the reception desk near the main entrance, we don't want the storage space to use up a window area, we want the director's office in the corner of the building and the assistant's office nearby, etc.

These simple diagrams can help to bridge the gap between breaking down a problem and building up a solution. In fact, the verbal statements become what are known as performance specifications, definitions of a good solution, which you can use as aids to generate alternatives and as criteria to evaluate them. Try to get the group members to switch between expressing themselves verbally and graphically. Remember, the group memory exists for group members to come up and draw ideas whenever they feel like it.

DON'T GET IMPATIENT WITH PROBLEM ANALYSIS

In the analysis phase your objective is to break down the problem into component parts and to examine how they go together. You are trying to learn about the problem, not describe it, although the more you understand the problem, the more accurately you will be able to define it.

People tend to be impatient with analysis. They feel an urge to rush on and try to solve the problem. We are a solution-oriented society. Ask anyone on any street corner and he or she will seem to have an answer to almost everything: crime, drugs, nuclear power plants, marriage. You name it, and you will be offered a solution. It's our shoot-from-the-hip mentality. It's the age of instant dinners and instant answers. But the problems we face today are growing more complex and interconnected. There are, in fact, no simple solutions. Everything is part of a larger system, and you have to understand the larger context and how one part affects another.

Everybody knows that decisions are no better than the information on which they are based. If you have faulty data, your solutions will be faulty. They won't work, or worse, will compound the problem. As a facilitator, you have to keep asking your group whether it has the necessary data to proceed. If it doesn't, it's better to stop and figure out how to get the facts before the next meeting. Help your group separate hearsay and gossip from the facts, too.

Fact-finding and research are more efficiently accomplished by individuals than by groups. Make a list of required information and encourage the group to assign to specific group members the tasks of researching the questions and presenting their findings at the next meeting. If there is a major gap in the collective knowledge and experience of the group, it may indicate that other people should be in the meetings.

ANALYSIS: FIRST, THE BASIC QUESTIONS

This approach is as old as the hills, but it's always useful. To understand a problem, you have to be able to answer the basic questions of who, what, where, when, and why as well as such related questions as how many, how big, how much, etc. This is particularly effective in groups because you can get agreement on a procedure in advance. Ask group members what questions need to be answered to build a complete picture of the problem. Suggest the who-what-when sequence and ask for additional, more specific questions. A list can be sorted and serve as a mini-agenda: "First we will investigate what happened, then who was affected, followed by why it happened." Let the recorder write the questions as headings on separate sheets of paper and when information relating to several different questions emerges, it can be recorded under the right heading.

NOW BREAK IT DOWN

Any problem can be broken down into smaller and smaller sub-problems until you reach a size you can handle. That's what analysis is all about. The trick is to discover a good way of slicing a problem so that the parts are relatively independent of each other. Otherwise the solution to one part may interfere with the solution to another.

Suppose you're planning meals for the rest of the week. You could partition the problem into planning a vegetable for each meal and then a meat for each meal. The difficulty would be that you might end up with spaghetti and mashed potatoes in one meal and steak and applesauce in another. It makes more sense to break the planning problem into a menu for Saturday night, a menu for Sunday lunch, etc., and then add up the quantities of various foods at the end.

Medical problems can be subdivided into specialties; organizational problems into functional responsibilities (sales, production, design, etc.); and distribution problems into areas, all of which could be broken down into further sub-problems.

For group problem solving, work with your group to come to some conditional agreement on a way to divide the entire problem before focusing on any sub-problem. If group members know they are going to have a chance to address other aspects of the problem later in the meeting, they will have more patience working with one particular sub-problem. Remember, once you have isolated a sub-problem, problem-solving begins all over again. You may have to lead your group through all relevant phases for just one sub-problem (i.e. define it, analyze it, generate alternatives, etc.).

TRY FORCE-FIELD ANALYSIS

This method has been developed by National Training Laboratories (NTL). One way of looking at a problem is to visualize it as a boundary between forces that are *sustaining* it from getting worse and forces *restraining* it from getting better. The argument goes that if you want to induce a permanent change and reach a new dynamic balance, you should increase the sustaining forces while reducing the restraining forces.

Suppose the problem is defined as inadequate fire protection in the city. The restraining forces (contributing to inadequate fire protection) might be that the city is growing very fast, that arson is increasing, that the fire department is understaffed, that the quality of training has been dropping. The sustaining forces (keeping the situation in check) might be the dedication and commitment of existing personnel, cooperation between police and fire department, new firefighting technology, changes in building codes, etc. Figuring out what the various forces contribute to the problem is the analytic part of the method. When you begin to figure out how to change the forces, you move on to the next phase: generating alternatives.

ASK THE EXPERT

At times it will become clear to you, as facilitator, that your group is out of its depth, or, more bluntly, doesn't know what it's talking about. As analysis gets more specific and technical, it's natural that any group will reach a point where most (maybe all) members get lost. Unfortunately, some people aren't bothered by discussing something they know little about and don't like to admit it when confronted. When it becomes obvious that people are getting confused or that the argument is going in circles, interrupt the cycle by asking, "Who *would* know the answer to this question? Who's the expert? Who could we invite to our next meeting?" Point out that it's okay not to know something. It's better to get accurate information now than to waste time continuing without it. Another point of view won't hurt. One group member may feel responsible for having answers on the subject, and you may be able to get him or her off the hook by suggesting that someone else be consulted.

TWO WAYS TO GET MOVING AGAIN

Groups, like individuals, can get stuck or fixated in problem-solving and spend hours arguing over generalities or fighting over specifics. When you are involved, it is hard to see what is happening, to disengage and come back at the problem from a different direction. The function of the facilitator is to recognize this state of fixation and to nudge the group out of its rut.

Keep in mind two opposing strategies, generalizing and exemplifying, which balance each other. When your group gets locked into abstractions or generalities, you can bring the conversation down to earth by asking for specific examples. "What do you mean by unfair restrictions? Why don't you give some concrete examples of what you are talking about?" Or when group members are in disagreement about whether a particular dress requirement is fair or not, you can gain some headway by asking, "What's the overall problem? Is there a more general situation that needs to be changed?"

Keep the focus moving from the concrete to the abstract until the whole problem has been given a complete examination. (And before you devote a lot of meeting time to an issue, be sure it's essential.)

WATCH FOR THE GO/NO GO POINT

If your group has perceived and agreed upon a problem as well as defined and analyzed it, you are ready to go on to the next phase. If not, you may be doing more harm than good by letting your group charge on to generating alternatives. Generally, the majority of time in group problem-solving should be spent coming to an agreement on a definition and analysis of a problem. A good foundation here should make the rest of the phases of problem-solving go smoothly. Otherwise, you may be headed for trouble.

THE FUN PART: GENERATING ALTERNATIVES

This is the "thinking up" phase. It's the bridge between perceiving, defining, and analyzing a problem, and evaluating and deciding on a final solution. It's a time for creativity and originality, and as in other phases of problem-solving you can learn methods to help you and your group become more creative.

Thinking up alternatives can be lots of fun, particularly in group situations. If the meeting is being run by the Interaction Method, the disadvantages of groups will be minimized and you will find yourself being more creative than if you were working by yourself. There is less chance of getting fixated and bogged down. Another person's idea will trigger a new thought and your mind will take off again. This connective creativity was first described and popularized by the advertising profession, where new ideas are always in demand. The ad people found that under the right conditions groups can achieve "synergy" and produce more creative ideas than group members could generate individually.

Two big barriers to creativity exist in group problem-solving. One is premature evaluation.

Everybody knows ideas are delicate. They have to be protected and nurtured. If one person suggests an idea and another person jumps on it and says, "No, that's stupid. It'll never work," several destructive things happen: A potentially important idea may be dismissed; the originator may be turned off; and the momentum of the group may be interrupted. Remember again: It's the function of the facilitator to keep this from happening; to protect ideas and individuals. As a rule, all forms of evaluation should be banned from this phase of problem-solving. Encourage people to turn off their "criticizers" and to let go and use their imaginations. There will be plenty of time in the next phase for bringing judgment to bear.

We've also met the second barrier to creativity: fixation—getting stuck in a rut and seeing the problem from only one point of view. This happens to groups as well as individuals. As a facilitator you must keep your group moving like a boxer, dodging and moving at the problem from different directions. Remember, one of the causes of fixation may be your definition of the problem. Experiment with different definitions. If you aren't getting anywhere, maybe you should return to the analysis phase or tentatively move on to evaluating your existing alternatives.

By now, you may have experienced personally that each phase of solving a problem is a problem in itself. Once you have *perceived* the need to define your problem, you have to generate *alternative* definitions, *evaluate* them, and *decide* which ones to use. That's why many of the methods we have described under one phase can be used in all the rest as well. For example, brainstorming can be used to generate problems, definitions, criteria, and even alternative methods. In other words, brainstorming can be used in the mini-phase of generating alternatives which exists in all other major phases of problem-solving. Since brainstorming is such an effective method for group problem-solving, we will describe it in more detail.

REMEMBER BRAINSTORMING

Brainstorming is perhaps most useful to learn as a beginning facilitator because it is simple and effective and has so many uses. Its power stems from a combination of the strategy of deferred judgment and the natural connective creativity of groups. The rules are simple: Everyone tosses out as many ideas as possible. The ideas are written down by the recorder. Nobody is allowed to criticize or evaluate any ideas until after the brainstorming session is over.

That's all there is to it. However, you can also use the following techniques in a meeting, as a facilitator, to improve the effectiveness of a brainstorming session. (Most of these are also applicable to the other methods we have described.)

CLEARLY STATE THE CONTENT FOCUS

Make sure everybody knows what the subject is, i.e. what the focus of the brainstorming session will be: "Okay, the problem is what skills and knowledge leaders will need in the year 2000."

EXEMPLIFY THE METHOD IN ACTION

Try: "What would be a typical answer to this question? Yes, Maria." "Okay, leaders will still have to know how to communicate with their people. Does everyone understand what we're going to be doing?"

GET EVERYTHING READY

Before you begin a new procedure, think ahead to see if you are going to need any assistance or special equipment. You know brainstorming can be a strain on a recorder, since ideas come out fast, so arrange for an assistant recorder: "Okay, we're going to need another recorder to help out during the brainstorming session, since we are going to produce a lot of ideas and we don't want to be held back by the recording. Any volunteers? Thanks, Nette. A good coordinating technique for you and Robert is to take separate sheets of the group memory and alternate with the recording, writing down every other idea. Talk to each other, so you know who's recording which idea."

SET A TIME LIMIT

"Okay, in the next seven minutes . . ."

AND AN OBJECTIVE

". . . I'd like to see if we can produce seventy-five ideas."

ENERGIZE THE GROUP

"I'm sure we can do it. Think of yourself as popcorn kernels and the room as a giant popcorn popper. I'm going to turn on the heat and I want you all to begin popping with ideas."

MAKE A CLEAR START

Make sure everybody knows when you are beginning with the method. Don't let some people start before others. "Okay, the question is, 'What skills and knowledge will leaders need in the year 2000?' Remember, no evaluation. Let's begin. Who's got an idea?"

REMAIN NEUTRAL—DON'T EVALUATE IDEAS OR OFFER YOUR OWN

In other words, perform the normal functions of the facilitator.

REINFORCE THE GROUND RULES OF THE METHOD

"Hold it, George! Don't evaluate Maria's idea. Do you have another idea? . . . Good. Who's got another?"

HELP THE RECORDER

If you repeat an idea when it comes out, it gives the recorder a chance to hear it twice. When there are two recorders, you can keep track of who is recording what, and direct your voice to the next person to record. Slow people down when the recorder gets behind. "Who's next? Yes, Barbara? 'Leaders will need to know how to work in groups.' Got that, Nette?"

ENCOURAGE AND COMPLIMENT YOUR GROUP

"Hey, you're doing fine! You've got sixty ideas already. Only fifteen more to go. Last ones are sometimes the best. Keep pushing!"

KEEP STIMULATING CREATIVITY

When the production of ideas begins to slow down, you can stir up the action: "Try to think of the questions in a different way. For example, imagine what the world will be like in the year 2000. Will there be as many countries as there are today? Or one worldwide country? What kind of communication systems? What implications will these things have for leaders?"

DRAW PEOPLE OUT

Watch people's body language. Help people along, call them by name. "Francis, you look like you have an idea. How about it?"

MAKE A CLEAN ENDING

"Okay, one more . . . Wonderful. We have seventy-five ideas. Well done. Let's close the brainstorming session. If you think of any other ideas, we can always add them to the list later."

You see, there are many techniques to help your group. That's why we keep reinforcing the fact that facilitation is an open-ended skill. There is always more to learn.

READY FOR THE CHECKERBOARD APPROACH?

This method, sometimes called morphological analysis, is a systematic way to analyze a problem and generate alternatives. It forces you to look at different interactions and combinations of two sets of variables.

Suppose you're trying to design a new kind of hammer. You might draw a checkerboard (or matrix) listing the desired functions of a new hammer across the top (hammering nails, pulling up nails, turning screws, prying, etc.) and the basic parts of the tool down one side (head, shaft, end of shaft, etc.).

The squares formed by the intersection of two variables become design possibilities. They force you to think about seeing how you might solve the problem in different ways. The intersection of turning screws and end of shaft might give you the idea that the end of the handle could taper into a screwdriver. In fact, each square can be the subject of a little brainstorming session: "How could we turn screws with the end of the handle?" The checkerboard approach can be used with any two sets of variables: different products versus different sales approaches, alternative services versus different forms of pricing, etc.

ASK: WHAT HAVE OTHERS DONE?

What people don't often realize is that creativity is as much the appropriate selection of whatever "exists" as the development of the totally "new." Many of our most popular designs are the product of modifying or adapting something that existed before. Hula hoops are nothing more than hoops of plastic. Frisbees are a modification of a disk. Roller skates and surfboards were around for a long time before people thought of combining the two and surfing down hills on skateboards. Can you think of anything worse than spending hours designing something that you can buy at the local hardware store?

It's a good idea to look at what others have done before. By studying other solutions, you may either find one that meets your needs or get an idea of how to adapt it. Develop a list of previous solutions to your problem; then study the advantages and disadvantages of each. You may find that a new, more appropriate alternative evolves naturally out of this process.

TRY CUTTING UP AND MOVING AROUND

Many problems involve sorting out a number of known entities: figuring out the seating arrangement at a party, designing a new letterhead, rearranging furniture, planning a complex series of events, etc. It's easy to get locked in to a mental image of how things should go. This is called "figural fixation." One of the best ways to break fixation is simply to write down the names or draw the shapes of the entities on cardboard, cut them out, and physically move them around on a desk or pin them to a wall. If you're working at seating arrangements, cut out name tags and shapes to represent the tables and move the tags around until you've come up with an appropriate arrangement. It's much easier than trying to work with paper and pencil; you lose track of which names you have already used and the paper begins to get very messy. This method works very well in designing a network of activities.

EVALUATION: THE ART OF JUDGMENT

What's actually going on in your mind when you say, "I like that" or "That one is the best"? Why do you select one alternative over another? How can someone else say with some certainty, "I know which one you'll like"?

When you make a judgment, you are consciously or subconsciously consulting a set of personal criteria or standards about what is good or bad. When you say, "I like that," you're saying, "That one is consistent with my set of personal preferences."

Most people aren't aware of their criteria, but they have them nevertheless: Jazz is better than classical music, red is nicer than blue, don't trust anything plastic, spinach is yucky, don't pick up hitchhikers. Otherwise, people wouldn't be able to make the countless decisions they do every day. Each value judgment would have to be made from scratch. Each time you'd have to stop and ask, "What do I believe in, what do I care about?"

Except for periods of serious reassessment, most evaluations and decisions are made by testing the alternatives against personal criteria and selecting the one which most conforms: without stopping to deliberate, you turn the radio to the classical station, choose the blue bathrobe, buy the wooden toy, order peas instead of spinach, and drive on past the hitchhiker.

Intuitive evaluations are fine for individuals, but they raise havoc in groups. If one person says, "I like alternative A," and another says, "I like alternative B," where do you go from there? Usually what follows are a lot of "whys" and "becauses," which often only lead to more entrenched positions.

What's happening? Personal criteria are beginning to surface *after* preferences have been expressed. That's too late. The lines have already been drawn, the win/lose attitude established. The key to evaluating in groups is to work for agreement on common criteria *before* judging alternatives. This important step is often left out of group problem-solving and decision-making sessions.

HOW CRITERIA PAY OFF

The development of explicit criteria has important benefits:

1. It forces all group members to externalize their values and to reexamine them. Sometimes, when you stop to think about the basis of your judgments, you find assumptions which may have been true once, but are no longer valid: He's too young for responsibility, electronic calculators always break down, there's no problem with theft around here.

2. Being clear about your personal criteria helps others to understand how you make your decisions. If you're a manager, this is a subtle way to educate your people.

3. The procedure of developing criteria for evaluation creates a useful interlude between generating alternatives and the evaluation of alternatives. Time away from alternatives helps to create some distance and a better perspective.

4. It's much easier to reach consensus about criteria before alternatives are discussed than to try this afterward.

5. If you can't reach consensus on criteria, it's not likely that you'll reach agreement on an acceptable alternative.

6. If you can reach consensus on criteria, future decisions concerning this problem should be greatly simplified. New alternatives can be tested against agreed-upon criteria, and decisions should be more consistent. In fact, if a manager or any group member is absent from a future meeting, that individual should have some confidence that if the same criteria are used, the resulting decision will be acceptable.

In theory, once you have your criteria, evaluation should be simple. All you have to do is to rate each alternative according to how many criteria it meets. Whichever scores best should be your selection.

In practice, evaluating is more complicated. Some criteria are more important than others. So, you need to rate or rank-order them. And often the solution you intuitively feel is best doesn't score well, so you have to go back and reexamine your criteria. In other words, evaluating means modifying, adding or substracting criteria, and then reapplying them to alternatives. Even if you end up choosing the alternative you liked from the beginning, the procedure of criteria development forces you to examine your values and rationale. Sometimes, no alternatives will score very well and you will have to generate other alternatives.

There is another way to evaluate. Test the alternatives first, and then evaluate them. Rather than working hard to figure out which alternatives will be best, eliminate the obviously inadequate, and try the rest and see which one does work best. Of course, you still need criteria, but they are now criteria of "working" or performance specifications. This replaces many of your assumptions about alternatives with verifiable data. For group problem-solving, that means some of the arguments about how well things will work can be avoided. Caution: The testing procedure can be prohibitively time-consuming and expensive. Sooner or later you will have to implement one or more alternatives. At that point you should evaluate performance against expectations to see if things are working as planned.

IDEAS, IDEAS, IDEAS: THE CRITERIA CHECKERBOARD

Generating criteria is really a miniature version of the alternative-generating phase. You can use any of the methods we have described. Probably the simplest is brainstorming. As a facilitator, your biggest problem is to explain what criteria are. To give the brainstorming session focus, try asking: "What qualities would a good solution have?" Or "What would help us to distinguish between a good and bad alternative?" Or "What standards does an alternative have to meet in order to be acceptable?"

After brainstorming, get your group to examine the list of criteria, eliminate items that are redundant, and prioritize the rest. If there are arguments over particular criteria, work on resolving them now—before you try to apply them to the alternatives.

Suppose your group or organization is considering changing its office space. The alternatives you have generated are:

1. Leave the office as it is.
2. Construct partitions in two specific locations.
3. Rearrangement Plan A.
4. Rearrangement Plan B.
5. Buy new furniture.
6. Repaint the office.

Then, putting the alternatives aside, your group works out the following criteria:

1. Must cost less than $2,000.
2. Reduces background noise level.
3. Reduces movement between work areas.
4. Reduces typewriter noise.
5. Livens up the office.
6. Increases communication.

To apply the criteria, draw a checkerboard (matrix) listing the alternatives down one side and the criteria across the top. As a group, work your way through the squares, seeing if you can agree on whether the alternative does or does not meet the criterion. If a yes/no rating is not accurate enough, assign a numerical value to how well an alternative satisfies each criterion. The sum of the values will give you an overall rating for each alternative which may be helpful when it comes to a final selection. Since this procedure can be time-consuming, only use it when a systematic evaluation of each alternative seems advisable.

HOW TO RANK FOR PREFERENCE

In group problem-solving you often face a list of alternatives and need a way of ordering them. Maybe it is a list of alternative methods (Which one do we want to try first?), a list of agenda items (In what order do we want to deal with them?), or a list of alternatives (At the moment, which one do you prefer?). As your problem-solving moves along, it's useful to take a look to see which items seem more important than others at the moment.

Since this is *not* a way to make a final decision, but only a way to take the temperature of a group, you can vote. The simplest way is to ask group members to vote for one alternative by raising their hands. Read the list and have the recorder write down the number of votes next to each alternative. The sequence (or rank order) is determined by the resulting numbers from high to low.

SORT BY CATEGORY

Sometimes, particularly after a brainstorming session, you end up with so many alternatives that it's hard to know where to begin evaluating. If so, your group might work out some general categories of alternatives, some natural groupings. If you are trying to decide how to finish the walls of an office, you could categorize the alternatives according to color (browns, whites, blues, etc.) or materials (paint, paneling, wallpaper, etc.) or cost for the job ($50–$100, $100–$300, $300–$1,000). Then, rather than starting to evaluate individual alternatives, see if you can reach general agreement on which category of alternatives seems most appropriate.

LIST ADVANTAGES VS. DISADVANTAGES

Often, you and your group will want to get right into evaluating alternatives and bypass the development of criteria. That's okay for relatively unimportant decisions. If it's a major decision, ask the group to list the advantages and disadvantages of each alternative. It's a way of organizing the evaluation and making sure that you examine all aspects of each alternative. Don't worry about contradictory evaluations at first. Record them anyway and complete the first cycle of evaluation. Sometimes when all the alternatives have been examined this way, one or two will emerge as most acceptable.

"WHAT I LIKE ABOUT . . ."

This is a useful technique we have discussed before. It is drawn from the larger method of synectics *(see Bibliography)*. Particularly when a meeting is being run informally and people are generating alternatives and evaluating them at the same time, you can use this technique to avoid some of the problems of premature evaluation. Establish a rule that before group members voice criticisms they must first say what they like about an idea. As a facilitator, keep reminding and pushing individuals to come up with more likes ("What else do you like about the idea?"). When you have to look for the good in an alternative you are forced to break fixed positions and consider a different point of view. It also keeps you from putting down the originator of the idea. After you have come up with a number of likes, then phrase your dislikes as concerns. "What I like about that idea is that . . ." or "My concern is that . . ."

FINALLY: DECISION-MAKING

In the decision-making phase of problem-solving a group should review the results of evaluation and commit itself to one or more courses of action. Decision-making is often regarded as a separate activity (distinct from problem-solving), which is why decision-making meetings assume a crucial importance. If you see decision-making as one more phase of a problem-solving process, these meetings become more comprehensible and less scary. In fact, if you have followed some of the procedures presented so far, the foundations of a decision should have been set by the time you reach this phase. If your group has been able to agree on a common problem, a common definition, and a common set of criteria, the decision-making phase may even be anticlimactic.

In Chapter 4 we defined two ways to make decisions: win/lose and win/win. Remember the benefits of the win/win approach: the quality of decisions as well as the extent of the commitment to decisions. The Interaction Method of running meetings is designed to produce win/win decisions, which makes it fundamentally different from traditional methods.

You'll realize by now that consensus can be reached so consistently by the Interaction Method mainly because the group moves together through a complete problem-solving sequence rather than being presented with limited alternatives developed by individuals or subgroups. The key to attaining win/win decisions lies in authentic collaboration, not in some special method of decision-making.

If your group is falling apart trying to make a decision, it may be that you have tried to move too fast or skipped some previous phase. Perhaps it's time to back off and analyze where things went wrong. Maybe you have to redefine the problem, generate more alternatives, or try to reach agreement on some more criteria.

IT NEEDN'T BE ALL OR NOTHING

Assuming now that your group is ready to make a decision, here are some ideas to facilitate the job. First, don't assume that you have to choose a single alternative. Sometimes several alternatives can work together. It does not always have to be either Plan A or Plan B, but both A and B: price cuts *and* salary reductions, high-rise *and* low-rise buildings, cleaning the house *and* going to the movies. Don't force your group to choose between two or more compatible and feasible alternatives.

Secondly, always strive for a consensus before resorting to such win/lose tactics as voting or executive decision. Remember: Group consensus means that every participant can buy into (live with) the decision; it does not mean that everyone believes the solution is the best, but that everyone is satisfied.

Encourage people to surface and keep voicing their concerns until their fears have been dealt with. They are doing the group a valuable service by pointing out shortcomings of the solution; in the end the quality of the final solution will be higher. Spending some time now to develop a win/win solution will save a great deal of time and expense that would be wasted later in efforts to put a mediocre and only partially supported decision to use. Guard against the dangers of groupthink. Groups tend to focus on areas of disagreement. Counter that: Get people to start by looking at where they already agree. Build on success: "Look how many points we agree on." Try to keep people from dwelling on the negative. Encourage flexibility. Keep dancing around the problem. Try different approaches.

FOR DECISION-MAKING: BUILD UP AND ELIMINATE

Consensus-seeking is a delicate process. You don't want to begin it unless you are fairly sure that the foundations for consensus are set and that at least a framework for a win/win solution exists. As a facilitator, you must keep your group moving toward a point of agreement without getting hung up in destructive arguments.

Let's assume your group has generated and evaluated a list of alternatives. If you think that one alternative, solution A, is clearly favored, you could shoot directly for consensus by asking, "Who would like to propose a solution?" Someone volunteers solution A. Then ask, "Is there any one who could *not* live with solution A?" Notice that you don't ask, "Does everyone think A is best?" Often there may be a number of preferred alternatives, but only one that is acceptable to everyone. Someone might think that solution B is a little better but that A is a good solution too. This doesn't mean A is a compromise; it's one of several good alternatives. A compromise implies that you are giving up something you believe is important. Urge group members to voice any reservations they have. You are not looking for a compromise; rather, a solution everyone feels good about.

If no one raises any objections to solution A, you're home free—consensus has been reached. If one or more persons has strong reservations, you can build up or eliminate. By building up, you focus on what you know should be in the solution and slowly add to it; you work with your group to uncover what parts of solution A are acceptable to everyone, and then begin to deal with the reservations.

Ask questions like "Can you think of any changes in A that would satisfy your concern?" Or, "Can anyone see a way that this could be dealt with?" After each proposal or addition, you return to your basic question: "Can everyone live with that?" "Is there anyone who could not buy into solution A as it now stands?" In other words, you can try to keep modifying solution A to see if it can be worked into a form acceptable to everyone. If A doesn't seem to be workable, ask for another proposal and try to build onto that one.

If many alternatives are listed or the building-up method doesn't work very well, try the opposite strategy, elimination. Focus on what people know they *don't* want. Ask, "Is there any alternative that you know now you couldn't accept?" If someone suggests solution C, check out with the group whether C can be eliminated from the list: "Does everyone agree we can cross off C from the list? Does anyone feel strongly about solution C?"

If everyone agrees, C gets axed, and you have one less alternative to deal with. If someone objects, forget C for now, and see if other alternatives can be eliminated. Sometimes this can help you reduce alternatives to one or two. Then you can switch to the build-up strategy, knowing that there is basis for consensus. Remember, before you force a selection between the remaining alternatives, check out whether it has to be either/or. Maybe a final solution can be built from a combination of several alternatives.

WHEN TO TRY STRAW VOTING

At the beginning of the decision-making phase it's sometimes useful to know how everybody feels about the existing alternatives. In this case, straw voting can be used, but with caution. As a facilitator, explain that a show of hands is only a way of taking the pulse of the group, of seeing how much agreement already exists. If your group is considering five alternatives, a straw vote might show you that everyone favors either alternative 1 or alternative 2. The other three alternatives can be eliminated. Then you can use another method (build up) to try to develop a win/win solution from the two remaining alternatives.

We have covered one specialized use of straw voting in the method of rank ordering: voting to see which alternatives are preferred more than others. Sometimes you are faced by a simple yes/no question but don't want to make the choice for the group. "Do you want to take a break now? Which problem do you want to deal with first, A or B? Are you willing to try a morphological approach and see where it gets us?" None of these decisions is very important, but they need to be decided quickly to keep up the momentum of the meeting.

Don't waste the valuable time of your group by struggling for consensus over minor issues. If it's a question of process, make the decision yourself and check it out with the group. "I think we should try brainstorming. Any objections? . . . Okay, let's go." If it is a content question, ask for a suggestion, check it out, and move on. "Which day seems best for the next meeting? . . . John says Wednesday. Any objections? Okay, the next meeting will be Wednesday. What time? . . ." And so on.

WHEN TO BACK OFF

If your group is having trouble reaching consensus, don't push too hard. Maybe it hasn't come up with a workable alternative or found a good way of distinguishing between alternatives. It's much better to return to an earlier phase of problem-solving than to let positions harden, arguing over existing alternatives. When you sense that your group is laboring too hard trying to make a decision, it's a good idea to back off and do some more problem-solving.

During the decision-making phase, a facilitator must try to maintain a delicate balance between pushing for consensus and protecting individuals who still have strong reservations. Since your role is to help your group solve the problem and make a decision as efficiently and as creatively as possible, you sometimes have to hold hands and encourage people to make commitments. Yet you don't want the group to steamroll over valid concerns. Your function is to protect individuals from personal attack. Stress the importance of raising questions and looking at all sides of an issue.

Ask for help from your group. Let people know how hard it is to maintain this balance. You can say, "I'm going to be pushing you to reach closure on this issue, but please let me know if you feel I'm pushing too hard. It's important not to let go of valid concerns until you are satisfied they've been heard and taken into account."

If you see that one or more people are totally opposed to the will of the rest of the group, don't prolong the agony. Sometimes consensus isn't going to be possible, and the sooner you recognize the fact, the sooner you can move on to another method of decision-making.

WHEN TO GO FOR AN EXECUTIVE DECISION

In hierarchical organizations, group consensus is sometimes neither possible nor necessary. Many people are satisfied if they have a chance to contribute their views on an issue and are relieved if the final decision is left in the hands of the senior manager ("Boy, am I happy I don't have to make that decision!").

Throughout this book we argue for the many benefits of participation and consensus, but we know that win/win solutions are not always possible. If you see that your group is strongly split over a decision, you can remind members that if a win/win solution is not found, the senior manager will have to decide.

Sometimes the implications of having to resort to a win/lose method are enough to break a deadlock. Otherwise, as facilitator, you turn to the person who is in the role of decision-maker and say something like, "Well, Frank, it doesn't look like consensus is possible at this time. You're going to have to make the decision yourself. Is there any other information you need from this group?"

Encourage the decision-maker to be as explicit as possible

about how and when he or she is going to make the decision: "Do you know now when you are going to make a decision? How and when will this group be informed?" Make sure everybody knows what the next steps are. Then go to the next agenda item or bring the meeting to a close.

WHEN TO GO FOR MAJORITY VOTE

In a horizontal group, everybody knows that if consensus cannot be reached, the decision will be made by the vote of the majority. You don't want to use this fact as a club to knock the minority into submission. In fact, as facilitator, you want to remind the group that by resorting to a vote, it may become less cohesive and certainly less supportive of the decision. On the other hand, it may be necessary to point out to certain individuals that if they continue to maintain extreme positions, they may end up losing more than if they try to modify or adapt the existing alternatives.

In any case, when you have exhausted the courses of action previously described and the deadlock still persists, turn the meeting back to the chairperson and step down as facilitator. The chairperson then runs the meeting according to parliamentary procedure until the vote has been taken and the issue resolved. If there is another item on the agenda, the chairperson can continue to deal with it by parliamentary procedure or hand the meeting back to you so you can facilitate the problem by the Interaction Method.

PLANNING: NO MORE CRYSTAL BALL

Planning is really problem-solving. When you plan, you generate and sort out actions for the future. Rather than solving a problem in the present, you are figuring out how you are going to solve a problem in the future. When you plan your work for the day, you're not actually doing the work, but figuring out how and when you are going to tackle your duties. When you design your planning, you are solving the problem of how to organize people and activities to accomplish the job.

Since meetings often involve planning future activities, we discuss planning as a separate phase. Actually, some planning usually occurs during each phase. Any time you stop to figure out how you are going to proceed, you are planning. Here we place planning after decision-making because many planning meetings are devoted to figuring out how to implement a decision once it has been made.

LOOK AHEAD VIA THE PRECEDENCE NETWORK

The key to planning complex procedures is to develop some way of visualizing the relationship between activities in the future. Much like physical design, it's easy to get lost trying to keep in your head which comes before what. A graphic representation is necessary.

Several highly developed planning methods exist, including the critical-path method (see Bibliography). If you do a lot of complex planning, engineering, or construction management, you are probably familiar with these methods. At the core of most planning techniques is the development of a flow chart (or precedence network)—a diagram representing activities as boxes and sequences as connecting lines. The passage of time is usually represented by movement from left to right along a horizontal axis. If activity B must come after A but before C, then the network would be presented as $\boxed{A}$—$\boxed{B}$—$\boxed{C}$. If activity D can only start after A has been completed but does not need to be finished until the end of C, then the network would look like this: $\boxed{A}$—$\boxed{B}$—$\boxed{C}$
  $\boxed{D}$

Get your group to generate a list of all activities that need to be performed from beginning to end of a program. Then, using the method of "cutting up and moving around" (described earlier in this chapter), write up each activity on a file card and pin the cards to a large sheet of paper mounted on the wall. For each activity ask the questions "What has to be accomplished before this activity can begin? What activities can't begin before this activity has been finished?"

By trial and error, manipulate the cards until they form a rough precedence network with the connecting lines drawn on the background paper. A final diagram can later be redrawn smaller for reproduction.

Once you have developed a precedence network, you can work out the time necessary for the project by assigning time estimates to each activity: A will take three days, B ten working days, etc. If you want, each activity can be redrawn to scale.

HOW TO WORK BACKWARD

Working backward is simple but useful strategy in a planning session. The natural instinct is to figure out the first thing to do, then the second, and so on, working forward. Sometimes you can get bogged down this way and waste a lot of energy planning a project which will turn out to be physically impossible to implement. Try working backward. Suppose the project has just been completed. What would have been the last activity? What would have been the next-to-last activity? Sometimes you will discover that the final event is so improbable or difficult or expensive that the whole project is unrealistic.

You can also alternate between working backward and working forward until you connect up in the middle. This is a good strategy for designing precedence networks.

AGAIN: ASK THE BASIC QUESTIONS

We have already discussed this method under problem analysis, but it has particular relevance to short-term planning. When your group decides on something that's to be done before the next meeting, make sure that the basic questions of who, what, when, and where are answered before going on to the next agenda item. It's the joint responsibility of the facilitator and the manager/chairperson to see that this has been accomplished: "We've all agreed we need more information on policy X by the next meeting. Who's going to be responsible for getting this information? . . . Okay, George says he'll do it. When will you have this done, George? . . . By next Monday? When can the rest of us get this information? . . . You say it will be posted on the door of your office by next Monday afternoon. Fine. Any more questions? . . ." Be sure all of this critical task information is recorded in the group memory for future reference and accountability.

APPLY THE GOALS-AND-OBJECTIVES METHOD

Long-range planning sessions are usually focused on the development of general directions and strategies rather than specific actions. The question is: What events should happen during the next time period? The actual sequencing of these events is left to other planning meetings. Several policy-making and goal-setting methods have been developed by schools of management; perhaps the simplest is what we call the goals-and-objectives method.

If you're trying to plan the direction of your group or organization for the next year, the first thing is to generate or restate your basic goals. The words "goals" and "objectives" have different meanings in different contexts. Here the word "goals" means "long-range directions," points that you aim for but might never completely reach. Examples: providing total service for customers, developing new software applications for the retail business, becoming experts in low-cost housing, being a watchdog for all forms of discrimination, etc.

Once you have generated an agreed-upon list of a few basic goals for your organization, you brainstorm specific objectives for the next time period. An "objective" is an event or point that is demonstratably attainable within a specific time. Example: writing a new program, designing an advertisement, hiring a new employee, getting a new contract, preparing a proposal, etc.

Then, just as we described under "evaluation," leave the objectives and generate a list of criteria for selecting (or distinguishing between) objectives. Since objectives should be consistent with goals, add your goals to the list of criteria you will use to evaluate your objectives. After the criteria have been developed and accepted, test the objectives against them. And using the various evaluation and decision-making methods we have covered, you choose objectives that your group is going to try to accomplish for the next year.

If you work your way through these steps you should end up with a consistent set of long-range goals and short-term objectives as well as a set of criteria to evaluate any new alternatives that emerge during the next time period. This procedure makes the rationale for your choice of directions explicit so that your group and others can consciously examine, understand, criticize, and revise them.

MAKING YOUR SOLUTION WORK

Problem-solving is a cycle of three activities: (1) figuring out what you are going to do (concept formation); (2) doing it (implementation); and (3) reacting to what happens (feedback). We have covered the first part, which is usually hardest. But sooner or later you have to try out your idea.

Many people think their job is done when they have finally decided on a course of action. But the problem isn't really solved until you (1) implement the solution and (2) monitor the implementation to see if any changes need to be made in the original solution.

Once you realize that your present problem-solving is only a step (or phase) in a larger cycle, you also realize that whatever decision you make may have to be changed shortly. The decision loses its preciousness, and you can accept the attitude of "Let's see if this solution works; we can always try something else."

This doesn't mean that you should take your problem-solving and decision-making lightly. It does mean that you'll never know if an idea works until you've tried it. Thousands of person/hours are wasted arguing over whether something will work or not; the time could have been used to go out and test the idea.

You will reach a point in problem-solving when you can't go any further until you take some action and see what happens. However, there are ways of limiting dangers and costs of the implementation phase by designing control tests, prototypes, pilot programs, etc. You don't have to implement your solution across the board before you test it in a limited area.

FEEDBACK: DID IT WORK?

Even after trials, some of your actions will turn out to be partial or even total failures. That's all right as long as you are prepared to react quickly and make the necessary changes. Many groups and organizations wash their hands of all responsibility once a decision has been made, the rules are laid down, or the design is under construction. They close their eyes to what's really happening and insist that the decision was right

—a symptom of groupthink. One way to avoid this situation is to appoint immediately a group to monitor the results of the implementation and to pick up and solve new problems as they show up.

Feedback is the return link back into the problem-solving process. It closes the loop. You solve a problem, make a decision, implement it, and then, depending on the feedback, you may have more work to do. If you do, you have to define your problem, analyze it, generate alternatives, etc.

Feedback is information you receive back from your trial or implementation. You have to analyze and evaluate it to see whether your trial is successful or not, using the methods described under the phases of analysis and evaluation. The criteria you used to select alternatives can now be used as performance specifications. If one of your criteria was "keep absenteeism below 5 percent," you can now judge the performance of your solution to see if it does, indeed, keep absenteeism below 5 percent. If it doesn't, perhaps you should analyze why not and begin new problem-solving.

You should also analyze the successes and failures of your solution to feed this information into your next design cycle. A failure in this round can lead to a success in the next. The group should take the trouble to study the performance of their products and services and learn what to do and not to do the next time.

So problem-solving is an endless process. The solution of one problem leads to the birth of new ones. You can always do more to improve the performance of your solution. Groups and organizations do best when they learn to see themselves as problem-solving organisms. A healthy organism is able to live in a world of change, dynamically acting and reacting to internal and external forces.

CHAPTER 17

How to Make a Presentation

In many meetings, much time is spent on presentations—too much. Many reports could have been submitted to group members in writing or on a one-to-one basis. And of the essential presentations, a large number are poorly prepared and delivered.

Most oral presentations are given to inject new ideas and information into a group's problem-solving and decision-making. Poor presentations waste participants' time even after they are delivered because the relevant information is not in a form that can help the group in its deliberation and so people spend a lot more time wheel-spinning, trying to reorganize and digest it before they can make a decision. Therefore, a book about meetings would not be complete without guidelines on how to make short and effective presentations so organizations can function more effectively.

What's so difficult about making a presentation, anyway? All you have to do is to get up in front of a group and say what you want people to know and they will get the message. Wrong! You may say X, but they may hear Y. And what's worse, they may think that Y really means Z. Communicating is a two-way street. You haven't communicated until you know that the other person has heard you correctly and comprehended what you really mean.

Communicating is also problem-solving. The situation you want to change is the difference between what you know and what you think someone else knows. Until you have changed the situation to a point where you believe the other person knows what you wanted him or her to know, you haven't solved your communication problem. And you can't do that without some feedback, some response from the other person. It's like trying to find out what's wrong with a child. Until the child responds in some way, by talking, nodding, pointing, or stopping to cry, you won't know what's wrong. Problem-solving is trial and error. But until you know the results of one trial, how can you decide what to do next?

The point is that to solve a presentation problem, you must consider the total interchange between you and your audience, not just what you do and say during your report. You must analyze the situation and design your presentation the same way you plan a meeting. You must ask yourself the same design questions: what, why, who, when, where, how, and how many.

WHO IS YOUR AUDIENCE?

There is no one right place to begin designing a presentation, but certainly one of the questions you should ask early is "Who is my audience?" Who are these people? What are their expectations? More specifically, why do they want this presentation? What do they need to know? How much do they already know about this subject? What language do they speak, what terms and jargon do they understand? What level of detail do they want—very specific or very general? What will they do with this information after this presentation? What do they know about me and who do they think I am?

There are two sets of expectations—yours and theirs. And they almost always differ. Active learning and communication take place when there is an overlap between what the sender wants to send and what the receiver wants to receive. There is no point wasting your time and the time of your audience by presenting information that it is not interested in hearing or knows already. So find out ahead of time what is really needed. Maybe a presentation or report isn't necessary at all. Or maybe there is a better way of communicating the information: a written report, for example.

If you can, talk to some of the members of your group or your audience ahead of time and find out the answers to these questions. It may save you a lot of trouble and embarrassment later. By involving group members in the process of helping you define and prepare your presentation, you are also gaining their support and commitment to the final form of your presentation.

IS THIS PRESENTATION REALLY NECESSARY?

Once you know something about the expectations of your audience, you should examine your own expectations! Why are you doing this presentation anyway? What do you want to happen? There is a wide range of possible answers, and the clearer you are about your reasons for giving a report or presentation, the easier it will be to decide what to include and how to present it.

Are you only presenting because you've been asked to? If so, why? If you don't know, you'd better find out.

Do you want to show your group or your boss that you have completed a task? Are you out to impress somebody?

Do you want to communicate some information or ideas? If so, why? Ideally, what do you want your audience to be able to do with your information? Use it to solve separate individual problems? Use it as a basis for collectively solving a common problem? Use it to make a decision to select an alternative? React to it, offer comments? Simply to be exposed to and aware of it? Communicate it to others?

Are you asking for help? Are you presenting a problem that you want your group to work on with you?

WHAT TO PRESENT

Given what you know about the expectations and needs of your audience, and given your own motivations, is there some information that you want to communicate and that this group wants to know? If there is no overlap, you may be setting yourself up for failure.

If there is a body of relevant information to communicate, your next task is to give the various items priorities. What are the main points you want to be sure to get across? Many presentations flop because too much information is spilled out. People get overloaded with data and end up retaining and understanding very little. What is really essential for your audience to get? If possible, pick out a few key ideas and save the rest of the information for background materials.

Handouts can be helpful if you keep them short. Either send them out with the agenda well in advance or hand them out at the end of the meeting—not at the beginning. People will just bury their heads in the handouts, and you will have lost your audience, unless you want to "walk" people through technical materials (a budget statement) or to receive detailed criticism (the editing of a proposal).

Think about how much time you're going to have. What's the total amount? How much of that time are you going to reserve for questions and discussion? How much time does that leave? Try to keep your presentation as short as possible. If you talk for over half an hour without interruption, you are going to start losing people's interest. (Five to fifteen minutes is preferable.) If you have a lot of information to get across, it may be better to break it into several presentations over several meetings, or at least schedule discussion periods in between segments.

HOW TO ORGANIZE YOUR INFORMATION

Once you know what you want to present, you've got to figure out how to organize it. There will probably be several feasible alternatives. The main thing is to be sure to state at the beginning of your presentation why you are giving it, how it's organized, and what you want people to do with it. Sometimes, everything seems to relate to everything else. (This book, for example.) There is no "right" place to begin. If you open your presentation with a brief outline, people will know what's coming and be able to relax.

One of the worst traps that people fall into when they present their work is to offer only their solutions, thereby excluding the audience from how they arrived at their conclusions. The audience can either take it or leave it. And the tendency is to leave it. It's hard to accept a solution when you are not even sure what the problem was.

If you want the support and commitment of a group, it is almost always best to involve its members in the process of solving a problem. If you've gone ahead and solved the problem by yourself and aren't willing (or don't have time) to repeat the process with your group, at least you can reveal your own thoughts step by step in your presentation. One good way of organizing your report is to organize it according to the standard phases of problem-solving: "This is how I perceived the problem. This is how I defined and analyzed it. These are some of the alternatives I came up with. Here are my criteria for evaluating them. Here are some of the advantages and disadvantages of each alternative. Based on all this, here are my conclusions." Now others understand your reasoning and they can indicate where they agree or disagree with your logic. It's much easier to isolate the points of disagreement and build on what you've done, rather than throwing out all your hard work because there isn't agreement on your conclusions.

Whenever possible, present all sides of an issue, not just your own point of view. Offer the main alternatives with possible advantages and disadvantages. Don't stack the deck. Let your ideas stand on their own merits. People will respect you for your honesty and fairness and will be less likely to make snap decisions themselves.

HOW TO INVOLVE YOUR AUDIENCE

To increase the effectiveness of your presentation, allow your audience to get involved: to question, clarify, or to redirect what you are saying. You can allow questions before, during, or after your presentation; each time has certain advantages.

TAKING QUESTIONS AT THE BEGINNING

This assumes your audience knows a good deal about your subject and has questions before you begin. By getting these questions out ahead of time, you get an idea of what people want to know and can reassure them that their questions will be answered during your presentation. It allows you to tailor your material to the needs of a particular group.

Like any strategy, taking questions before you talk has its limitations. You really have to know your subject matter well and be able to think on your feet so your presentation will be responsive to the concerns of your audience. Your prepared material should be broken down into chunks which can be rearranged as you go along.

It's good to record the questions as they come out. Use sheets of butcher paper or an overhead projector for a large audience. Then you can say, "Okay, we captured your ideas over there. I'll try to cover them in the course of my presentation except for numbers five and eight, which I am not prepared to deal with at this time."

Taking questions before a presentation is not recommended unless you have lots of experience making presentations.

TAKING QUESTIONS DURING

If you're talking to a small group of people (less than seven) and want to keep it informal, you can say something like "Please feel free to raise questions as we go along. I don't want to lecture to you." This keeps people involved and lets you know if you are getting your message across. The questions can get out of hand, though. If there are too many interruptions, your presentation can become fragmented and lose its continuity. You can get thrown off your train of thought and brought to a standstill by an embarrassing question. There are ways of buying some time to think, like repeating the question: "Do I understand you correctly? You want to know if . . ." This gets you a couple of precious seconds to think, but in general, you or the facilitator have to keep some control.

If your presentation is getting bogged down by questions and you see your audience getting restless, you may have to say, "Okay, I want to be able to deal with all your questions, but I think it may be best now to complete my presentation and then use the rest of the time for questions and discussion. So please hold your questions until the end of my report."

You can also stop periodically and ask your group how you're doing: "Have I been clear so far? Am I getting across? Are there any questions?" If heads nod, you can proceed with more confidence. If there are questions, you can field them until you have made up your mind how to proceed and then turn them off: "Okay, now that I have a better idea of your concerns, let me continue with the presentation."

TAKING QUESTIONS AT THE END

A question-and-answer period at the end of a presentation is the traditional way. Its advantages are that there is a clear transition between presentation and discussion; you can give a prepared presentation without interruptions; people can leave if they don't have any questions; and it's a good way of dealing with very large audiences. Of course, the big disadvantage is that your presentation may have been misdirected in some way, and you won't know it until you're finished. Your audience may be totally turned off and have forgotten any questions it ever had.

When it comes time for questions and discussion, the format of the meeting should change. Give a brief summary and let people know that you are finished. Once the floor is open for anyone to ask a question or give comment, all the basic meeting problems arise. Turn the meeting over to the facilitator or chairperson and step out of the limelight. Let the facilitator field questions, recognize people, and clarify communication. It's easy to get defensive when tough questions come your way, and the facilitator can help protect you and keep the meeting on a positive note.

HOW TO MAKE IT VISUAL

People retain only about 10 percent of what they hear in a presentation and 20 percent of what they see, but about 50 percent of what they both see and hear. That's what the 3M Corporation reports from its research. That's such an astounding increase in audience comprehension, you can't afford not to make your presentation visual as well as verbal. Graphics have other advantages:

1. They provide a focus of attention for your audience, just like the group memory. By controlling what you reveal, you can keep people focused on the point you are covering and no other.

2. By getting people to look at your visual presentation, you can step out of the focus of attention for a while. In a small group this can help alleviate the uncomfortable business of being stared at while you talk. In a large group it can give you an occasional chance to think while people take in the graphics.

3. The process of preparing graphic material forces you to organize your information and to simplify and shorten it.

4. A graphic presentation demonstrates to your audience that you are prepared and well organized.

5. The graphics serve as notes. When you turn to the next transparency or page, the display will remind you of what you were going to talk about next. This can help to lessen the "presentation jitters."

Putting together visuals to support your presentation doesn't have to be a big production. Many people shy away from doing anything graphic because they think that "to do it right" would take a lot of time, expense, and skill. Just a few sheets of clear hand printing in multicolored marking pens can be enough. Anyone who knows how to record can prepare a few sheets on a flipchart for a presentation.

TIPS FOR MAKING VISUALS SIMPLE

Here's what to keep in mind when preparing the visual part of your presentation:

1. Everyone in the group should be able to see and read the visuals easily. Think about the size of the group. The number of people will determine the technology you should use.

2. You want to be able to keep a tight focus on what is presented when. You don't want to display too much information at any one time. Keep to three or four main ideas on each sheet. You don't want your audience to get confused or overloaded.

3. Remember the "wallpaper effect" we discussed in relationship to recording. Vary the size and color of the printing so that everything doesn't look the same. Make sure you have some way of pointing to what you are talking about. It's a way of narrowing the focus.

4. Sometimes it helps to add activity and motion to your presentation, adding to it as you go along. (The weatherpeople on TV use this technique effectively when they draw a weather front on top of a map of the United States.) It creates interest that can liven up what otherwise might be rather boring data.

WHAT MATERIALS TO PICK

Here are some aids to help present your visuals, each with certain powers and limitations:

1. Presentation boards are stiff and can be stood up anywhere, and the order can be shuffled from one presentation to the next. But they are a little harder to prepare than sheets (you can't trace on top of a rough copy), they can be bulky to carry, and, depending on the size of the print, you can use them only for fairly small groups (under thirty).

2. Flip charts are like presentation boards except that you

need an easel to hold the chart, and the sequence of sheets is usually fixed. However, some pads have ring holders that can be opened and closed so that the sheets can be shuffled and new ones added.

3. Large sheets of butcher paper serve as a good informal alternative. If you are going to make a brief report as part of a meeting run by the Interaction Method, you can go to the meeting room early, rip off a few sheets of paper, and write up your display with markers, just as if you were a recorder. The sheets can be rolled up and brought out when you get up to give your report. This is quick and effective. Further more, your sheets can become part of the collective group memory.

4. An overhead projector and transparencies can work very well with larger groups. Overhead projectors permit you to work in a fully lit room, face your audience, point to parts of your presentation, cover up and reveal portions of a transparency, and write on top of transparencies or blank film. The disadvantages are that you can't display much information at one time, it's difficult to carry around the projector, you need a room with a screen, and you need special equipment to prepare high-quality transparencies.

5. Color slides can be used simply and quickly if you have some experience with photography. Once you have the right equipment, and have tried it a few times, you can make small sketches or typewritten sheets, photograph them with a close-up lens (or any lens with a short focal distance), and take the films to a photo lab that offers same-day or overnight service. Be sure to buy film that is corrected for the type of lighting you are going to use and that can be processed by your local lab. The advantages of this technique are that you can mix true-life slides with your presentation, and many places have 35mm slide projectors. But this does require advance preparation, and unless you have a rear-screen projector, you have to darken the meeting room. Anytime you rely on technology, there is a good chance that it can fail at the last moment. Be prepared.

FACING THE MUSIC

While the skills of public speaking are beyond the scope of this book, here are a few hints to make your presentation more effective.

1. If at all possible, don't read or memorize your material. (We are talking about brief presentations or reports, not formal lectures and the delivery of papers.) If it makes you feel more comfortable, you might write out your presentation and read it aloud a few times, but when you give it, talk from notes or the visual presentation. There is a tremendous difference between reading and normal speech in someone's tone of voice, eye contact, and animation.

2. Face your audience. Don't turn your back to people or bury your head in your notes.

3. Unless you need it, don't put a table or podium between yourself and your group. It adds to the sense of distance.

4. Be aware of your body language: how you stand and move in front of the room. Don't pace or slouch. Try to be lively and animated. Move around from time to time, closer to the group when you're asking for questions, back toward your visuals when you want to focus the group's attention on them. Many of the techniques for being a good facilitator apply to you as a presenter.

5. Also be aware of the body language of your audience. Are people yawning, slouching, whispering, or looking bored? These are clues you can use to modify your presentation as you go along. Maybe it's time to ask some questions to see how you're doing.

6. Let people know what's happening. If you're new to the group explain who you are and why you are making a presentation. Let them know what you expect of them. Do you want questions? What do you want them to do with your information? Give people an overview of what's coming, an outline of how your report is organized, and a brief summary at the end.

7. If you have a lot of trouble giving presentations, if you get very nervous, be open and honest about it. Let the audience know that you feel uncomfortable and ask them for their patience and assistance. You will help break the ice and keep everyone from being uncomfortable, including you. If you're worried, practice your presentation ahead of time by yourself and then before a friendly audience (your husband, wife, friend, or associate). Ask people for their advice. Tape your presentation and listen to it yourself.

If you follow these guidelines and take your presentation seriously, we're sure you'll increase your effectiveness and earn the appreciation of your associates.

CHAPTER 18

How to Introduce the Interaction Method into Your Organization

How are you going to introduce the Interaction Method into your organization? You can't go charging into a meeting tomorrow and say, "Hold it, everybody, we're going to change the way we run our meetings!" People and organizations don't like sudden changes. Don't set yourself up for certain failure by rushing off and trying to change your meetings without a plan.

Groups and organizations are changing, living systems. A great deal has been written about systemic change, and we make no pretense of trying to cover the field in this one chapter. Instead, here are some guidelines we have assembled after working with a wide variety of organizations.

1. People don't change unless they want to or have to—and why should they want to these days? There's already too much change going on! Until members of a group or organization recognize and agree that they have a serious problem and understand the consequences, they won't even consider changing.

To want to change, people either have to have some kind of negative experience, a crisis where things don't work the way they used to, or a very positive experience where things work much better than they usually do.

2. People have to see payoffs for changing, both for their organization and for themselves. If there isn't something in it for them, if their lives aren't going to be easier or more interesting in some way, then whatever change occurs is not likely to be lasting.

3. Nothing is more convincing than success. If you can find a way to begin with a little success and keep building, you'll have a much easier time of winning people over.

4. The old argument about which must come first, attitudinal change or behavioral change, is a waste of time. We have seen it work both ways. We have seen some people start behaving differently without being convinced that the new behavior is going to make any difference, only to discover that the new way does work (like the manager who says, "I don't believe consensus is possible, but I'm willing to try"). And we have seen others who wouldn't change their actions until they were totally convinced by some intellectual argument.

5. If you introduce an innovation into only one part of an organization, the system as a whole will tend to protect itself from the threat of change by isolating and detaching itself from the element of "newness." The body will reject a new transplanted organ unless you specifically deal with the antibody reaction; similiarly, if you introduce a new teaching technique to only one teacher in a school, the other teachers will become suspicious and tend to reject the changing one. Unless the system as a whole understands what is happening, unless fear of the unknown is dealt with head on, rejection is inevitable.

To counter this effect, your objective should be to work with several parts of the system simultaneously, and provide ways for the rest to "buy in." People must be constantly invited in to see what is happening and to participate in the changed ways so that a we/them gulf doesn't open up.

6. Like certain chemical reactions, the process of organizational change may have to reach a critical mass in order to maintain itself. This is really another way of looking at the rejection problem. One or two isolated people who change the way they do things in a large organization may meet such resistance that they will succumb to the pressure and drop out or return to their old ways. Once there are enough people with the same ideas to support and reinforce each other, to provide each other with the positive strokes one needs for survival, there may be enough collective energy to sustain the innovation and recruit other supporters.

7. Above all, lasting positive change takes time. Things don't happen overnight. If you push too hard and too fast, you may create waves of resistance. Take your time. Don't burn yourself out. Be patient.

How do these generalizations translate into specific strategies that you can use in your organization to change the way meetings are run? Again there is no one "right" or "best" way. Changing your group or organization is a problem, and you may have to try several ways. We believe in being pragmatic: If it works, fine; if not, try something else. A lot depends on your organizational situation and your present role in the meetings you attend. Here are some of the strategies we have seen work.

START FROM WHERE YOU ARE

Sooner or later you've got to begin someplace. Why not with your own group? Sometimes, because of organizational constraints, the only meetings you can affect are the ones in which you participate. It makes sense to test these ideas in your own back yard. There is no better place to develop your skills and gain experience. If you're going to spend valuable time and energy participating in meetings, why not make them more productive and enjoyable? Here are eight steps you can take as manager/chairperson to introduce the Interaction Method into your meetings.

WHAT YOU CAN DO AS MANAGER/CHAIRPERSON

1. Almost every technique in this book can be employed by itself and should produce some improvement in your meetings. If you feel cautious and want to get your feet wet before trying to swim, continue your role as meeting leader, but gradually introduce a few ideas that seem relevant. At first, you don't have to tell people what you are doing. Just leap in and do it. For example, you could try introducing the distinction between process and content, and get group members to agree on a subject and process before beginning a discussion. Or start sending out an agenda a day ahead of time. Or work for consensus before resorting to a vote. Or start with any of the hundreds of suggestions in the book. Then, as you can see that they work, try a few more, until you are ready to attempt one of the more major changes, such as having a facilitator run your meeting.

2. Here's one small but important change you could introduce: Ask your group to sit in a semicircle rather than a circle. Start recording on a flip chart some of the ideas as they come up. Then tear off the sheets and tape them on the wall. Presto —you have the beginnings of a group memory. This should produce a dramatic change in the focus of the meeting.

3. If you have modeled the role of recorder for a while, get someone else in the group to relieve you. At that time, you could explain the basic ground rules: the recorder should not contribute or edit ideas and group members should check to be sure their ideas are recorded correctly.

4. If your meetings are not working very well, there is a more

direct strategy that will help to lay the groundwork for all the rest. At the end of a particularly bad meeting, reserve some time for a group discussion about why things aren't working. Ask people to list some problems they see or fill out our meeting diagnostic sheet. Then ask for suggested changes in the ground rules. You may be surprised how similiar some of the ideas will be to the basics of the Interaction way. If there seems to be some agreement that changes should be made, this would be a good time to suggest one of the strategies that follow. If you can get your group to buy into the need for change, group members will be more receptive to the Interaction Method and will not regard it as another set of restrictions.

5. Tape-record (or even better, have someone videotape) one of your meetings. It's an effective way to initiate a discussion about meeting problems. Play back the recording and ask people to listen and think about what's happening. You will be amazed how much you and your group can discover about the unproductive dynamics of your meetings.

6. The Interaction Method does involve some major reshuffling of roles and the development of some new skills. If it is important that everything go smoothly the first time your group tries the new approach, find an experienced facilitator (and recorder) to come in and run the meeting. Just the presence of someone new can help, and it's easier for an outsider to introduce changes into an existing system.

7. Unless you're in a position to have all your meetings run by an external facilitator, sooner or later you and your group are going to have to learn to facilitate yourselves. The most efficient, effective way to learn is to get an experienced trainer to train your group as a whole, beginning by modeling the roles of facilitator and recorder, and then supporting individual group members as they are rotated into these roles. By getting someone else to do the training, you can avoid having to play teacher along with all the managerial roles you perform already.

8. If outside help is unavailable, your group can train itself. It's really not hard. If group members read this book and understand the roles, the self-correcting system will work so that people who make mistakes will be helped by the rest of the group. Once your group has agreed to experiment with a change in the way meetings are run and you are willing to give up the meeting leadership role, get everyone to read this book (or explain the basics yourself) and ask for volunteers who want to become facilitators or recorders. Many groups have made great improvements in their meetings just learning by doing.

WHAT YOU CAN DO AS A GROUP MEMBER

Most of the suggestions offered to the manager/chairperson are aplicable to you as a group member. You just can't be as directive.

1. First, be a good group member. One positive, helpful person in a meeting can do a lot of good. You can offer process suggestions to your group like "Why don't we figure out how we are going to deal with this issue before we rush off in different directions?" and move on to the facilitating interventions we have discussed.

2. Rather than confronting your boss or chairperson in front of the group, you could talk to him or her after a meeting, offer some constructive criticism, and suggest that he or she read this book. Let the printed page do some of the talking for you.

3. You can wait until a meeting blows up and suggest that it might be worthwhile for your group to spend some time figuring out what just happened and how meetings could be improved. The objective is to get your group to realize its meetings aren't as effective as they could be. Then, when everyone is arguing about what should be done, you can suggest one of the courses of action listed below.

4. As a first step, you could offer to act as a recorder. Get the

group to sit in a semicircle facing sheets of butcher paper. And as the meeting continues in its normal way, quietly create a group memory. Just having a record of the meeting will help your group visualize some of its methodological problems, and the group memory itself will have a beneficial effect.

5. You could suggest bringing in an experienced facilitator to run one of your most important meetings. Point out that it's worth a try and that people can always throw the facilitator out if things don't work. Bringing in a neutral third party is always an effective way to introduce positive change into a group. In preparation for that meeting, you can suggest that interested group members read this book.

6. If you're determined to improve the meetings of your group and are willing to take an active role, you could get some training yourself in the Interaction Method. If necessary, you could develop some confidence by facilitating meetings of other groups with whom you feel more comfortable or more in control. Then, after laying the necessary groundwork, you could offer to run the next meeting of your group. Be sure to explain your role as facilitator as well as the role of recorder, group member and manager/chairperson. If you're willing to make some mistakes as part of the learning process, you will develop the necessary skills quickly, your meetings will improve, and your group will be grateful.

SELLING THE METHOD IN HIERARCHICAL ORGANIZATIONS

In a hierarchical system, the standards and behavior of the top executives have a great effect on the rest of the organization. If they don't buy into the Interaction Method, if they aren't willing to have their meetings facilitated, there isn't much payoff for junior executives to improve the quality of meetings. Sooner or later the chief executive officer must believe in the benefits of improving meetings through the Interaction Method and communicate his or her support to subordinates by doing his own managing in a collaborative and participative way. After all, the goal of our method is more effective collaborative problem-solving and decision-making. If the top people believe in managing autocratically and don't feel a need to change, they probably will feel threatened by the Interaction Method and reject it strongly.

An organization-wide assessment of needs is one way to create an awareness of the magnitude of the problem and a need to change. It can be a simple questionnaire (based on our diagnostic sheets) asking employees how much time they spend in meetings, why they hold meetings, how effective their meetings are, whether there is a need to improve their meetings, and if so, in what way. The survey should help to personalize the problem, yield specific costs, and locate particular areas for improvement.

It is much easier for an outsider to suggest a new way of doing things than it is for someone in the organization. The outsider is not locked into the existing system and does not have much to lose if the change doesn't work. Why should you risk your job by telling your boss that he shouldn't be running meetings? That's why you bring in a neutral third party—to tell it like it is. The worst thing that can happen to an outsider is to not be invited back.

So if you're a member of a top management group and you feel your people might be receptive to the Interaction Method, a relatively low-risk strategy is to get an experienced facilitator to demonstrate what it's all about. Find somebody acceptable to your group, either an external consultant or someone within the organization who has experience in the method.

A good way to start is to have the consultant observe one meeting, catch on to the issues and jargon of your group, and diagnose your most critical meeting problems. After the initial meeting the consultant should give a brief report to the senior manager and help plan the next meeting. If at all possible, design that next session to be a problem-solving or decision-making meeting, not an information sharing one. Pick a problem that is manageable and allow enough time to get into it. It is very important that the first meeting yield a significant improvement over the previous ones. If you plan it right, it almost always will.

DEMONSTRATE THAT IT WORKS

Once the Interaction Method has been demonstrated and there is interest in continuing to test it, the consultant might interview members of your group to find out what each person would do to improve meetings and to answer questions about the method. Then it would be a good idea to retain the facilitator to run the next few meetings so your group can experience the benefits of the Interaction Method under a variety of conditions. At that point, you and your group should be able to decide whether to continue and, if so, how to introduce the new method to other parts of the organization.

Rather than beginning by introducing the Interaction Method into regular staff meetings, you might choose a special setting—a staff retreat, a task force, or a long-range planning committee. These temporary groups won't have developed much protocol and structure, and there may be relatively little resistance to trying something new. These situations may also be viewed as less risky by the newcomers. Your organization won't reap the full benefits until the method has become incorporated in the many meetings held every day. And this can only be accomplished by extensive learning and training. There are a number of ways to get training in the Interaction approach: train yourself, attend a workshop, or be trained in your natural work group.

Going to a workshop may seem attractive. Yes, you can pick

up some skills. But it's difficult to transfer these skills to your work environment. The so-called university model of training (sending employees to outside educational institutions) has proven relatively ineffective. On the average, you can expect to see the transfer of no more than 5 to 20 percent of the desired skills two years after the training program.

When you learn skills in your natural work group, your whole group is learning at the same time and everyone can support and reinforce everyone else. There is no problem of transfer. As part of the training, you're applying the Interaction Method to your everyday real-world problems. People are less likely to question whether it will work. And there is the added advantage of less time off the job. We see at least 40 percent of the skills utilized when we return two years later to a group we have trained in this way.

Since every organization has its own peculiar problems and personalities, the introduction of the method must begin in different places in different ways. However, one series of events must happen sooner or later if this method is going to "take."

1. Senior executives must decide to have their meetings facilitated.

2. Middle-management groups must adopt the Interaction Method as their standard way of running their meetings.

3. A few people at least must receive some advanced training so that they can serve as internal consultants and facilitate top and critical middle-management meetings.

4. Ideally, someone should receive sufficient training to become an internal trainer, continuing the task of training other employees in facilitation. This person might come from the personnel, training, or organizational development departments.

Once all this has happened, change should be self-sustaining, and the organization should not require any further assistance from an external consultant.

SELLING THE METHOD IN HORIZONTAL ORGANIZATIONS

Probably the hardest place to introduce the Interaction Method is in a horizontal group of elected representatives: a board of supervisors, school board, or legislative body. The win/lose mentality of voting and the debate orientation of Robert's *Rules of Order* are usually well entrenched. Your first objective must be to convince group members that there is more to be gained by collaboration and cooperation. If your meetings have bogged down in stalemates and endless arguments, it may be possible to get several members to agree to try collaborative problem-solving and use our method on the next issue to come before your group. Introduce the Interaction Method on a new issue. It's very difficult to get people to move off a win/lose stance once positions have been frozen!

Explain that the group can always fall back on a majority vote. If the level of frustration with the old meeting practices is high, and the groundwork is well laid, it should be possible to get an opportunity to try the method, but it may take effort. A committee meeting may be a good place to begin. If the committee members gain a positive experience, they will be less resistant to trying the method in other situations.

An appointed group (such as a board of directors or committee) may be more open to trying something new. Often the appointees have much in common and are willing to work in a collaborative style. (But watch out for groupthink!) Again, it may be easier to hire an experienced facilitator to run the first few meetings. If the group agrees that the Interaction Method is a more effective way of doing business, then someone from within the organization can be trained as a facilitator, or group members can learn to rotate the roles of facilitator and recorder.

PERSUADING THE INFORMAL GROUP

In our experience, informal, horizontal groups that exist only temporarily (task forces, citizen committees, parents' groups, etc.) are very receptive to our method. These groups know that they can become powerful only if they involve their membership and are concerned about running their meetings in the most open, collaborative, and nonmanipulative way possible. The Interaction Method is ideally suited for this kind of group.

If you're a member of a task force or citizens' group, it shouldn't be difficult to point out how the traditional ways of running meetings are not consistent with the goals of your organization. You can use many of the arguments presented in this book, particularly in the first few chapters. Activities that involve the citizenry at large should operate under rules that allow everybody to feel that he/she "won." The Interaction Method can be a symbol of a new way of solving problems and making decisions.

If your organization has financial resources, getting some training in our method may be one of the best ways to get the most leverage out of your money. When you increase your ability to solve your own problems, you won't need as much technical assistance. And what technical consultants you do hire, you can use more effectively.

CHAPTER 19

How to Train Yourself

No matter how many books you read, how many training programs you attend, or how many meetings you run, you can always improve your facilitating and recording skills. Professionals in any field know this. Famous athletes or performers are constantly experimenting, trying new techniques, striving for perfection which they know, no matter how hard they work, no one can attain. Even if you've been fortunate enough to receive professional facilitation training, if you want to become a topnotch facilitator or recorder, you will have to continue learning by yourself.

Once you have finished your formal education, it is easy to forget how to learn. You forget how difficult learning can be, how hard you have to work, the occasional discomfort, the fear of failure. You may also have forgotten the sense of exhilaration that you experience when you master a new skill, when things become easy, and you can do something you couldn't do before.

Learning a skill requires doing and thinking about doing, analyzing components and then synthesizing them into an integrated whole through un-self-conscious action. A professional athlete doesn't go out and compete every day. Billie Jean King, for example, spends hours every day, many days a week, practicing particular tennis strokes. She understands the awkward feeling that comes over her when she becomes totally focused on one aspect of a stroke; she also knows that the self-consciousness will disappear when she concentrates on winning a game. Don't be afraid of analysis. It's an essential part of the learning and growth process.

Learning is a form of problem-solving, and everyone learns in a different way. Some people like to begin by understanding why a new skill works; some people like to jump in and try it; others like to see it demonstrated first. Like problem-solving in general, there is no one right way of learning. You have to try different routes until you find the one that suits you.

Since recording and facilitating involve other people, you can't learn to facilitate by yourself. You need a group of people, and since the purpose of the Interaction Method is to help groups do what they want to do more effectively, you have to judge your effectiveness in the last analysis by what other people say. The key to learning to facilitate and record is feedback. Until you know what other people like and dislike about how you run a meeting, you won't know what behavior you need to change and what skills you need to learn or improve.

HOW TO GET CONSTRUCTIVE FEEDBACK

Feedback can be constructive or destructive, so one of the first things you need to learn is how to ask for (and give) constructive feedback:

1. Everyone needs positive and constructive negative feedback. Everyone needs encouragement, to know when he or she is doing something well. When you request feedback, ask people

to tell you what they liked about what you did, before they criticize: "I really liked the way you handled Jennifer when she interrupted George, and the way you got everyone to define a problem before trying to solve it. But I felt that you didn't keep the meeting focused after that. I got lost several times." In their rush to criticize, people sometimes forget the things they like.

2. Ask people to comment on specific behaviors and specific times. Try to avoid general comments: "I like the meeting," "I didn't like the meeting." It's nice to be complimented, but generalizations aren't very useful when it comes to developing skills. Get people to pinpoint their criticisms: "When I suggested we try something else, I felt you cut me off without listening to my suggestion." "On page five on the group memory, I couldn't read your writing." "When Phil was talking about hiring practices, I thought you might have recorded more of what he was saying. It would have been useful later on."

3. When someone criticizes something you did, ask what you could have done differently. It's a good way of turning a negative criticism into a positive suggestion: "Thank you, I wasn't aware I was doing that. I was worried about how much time we had left, and was trying to get the group to move on to the next agenda item. What could I have done differently?" The objective is to develop a repertoire of strategies for dealing with particular situations. Don't argue with the feedback; learn from it.

4. Make sure you understand the feedback before you respond to it. It's easy to jump to conclusions and get defensive. If you do, feedback will stop coming. A good technique is to repeat or paraphrase the criticism to see if you got it right. "Let me see if I heard you correctly. You think that I shouldn't have cut Joan off when she started evaluating during the brainstorming session because she stopped participating after that." Thank people when they give you feedback, even if you don't agree with the criticism. You need feedback to learn. You can't afford to turn people off.

5. Don't react too soon. Just because one person didn't like

something you did doesn't mean you weren't effective or should change what you do next time. Respect opinions of the individual, but check out what other people feel. It's not that the majority viewpoint is right, but when you hear how other people see a situation, you get a better perspective. It's hard to be sure of someone's motivations for criticizing you. Someone may feel threatened by the attention you were getting or for some other personal reason. There is no "right" way to facilitate or record. Everyone has a different style. If you can become aware of the limitations of your personal style, you can compensate for this or at least acknowledge some its negative effects.

6. You can only work on so many things at one time. Don't get overloaded. You'll just get depressed and feel like giving up. Facilitating and recording can be exhausting, particularly when you are first learning. While it's important to get feedback as soon as possible after the end of the official part of a meeting, that's also the time you are the most tired. When you feel you've had enough, gently turn the feedback off. Thank people for their comments; tell them that you've heard enough to know what to try next time.

If you don't have the opportunity of learning in the safe environment of a training session, how do you go about training yourself? At some point you have to get up in front of a group and begin. How can you keep from fouling up the first meeting and making a fool of yourself?

IT'S ALMOST FAILURE-PROOF

Keep in mind that most meetings aren't very effective as they are now run. When you get a chance to facilitate or record, it will be because your group has agreed that it is worth trying something new. You are probably going to look good no matter what you do. The mere presence of a facilitator, recorder, and group memory will do wonders. Even if you think you have done a lousy job, your group may well be impressed just because it will all be so new. Explain that you are learning and will make mistakes. Ask people to help you stay in your role and remain neutral. You are there to help them. It's their meeting and they share the responsibility for making it a success.

If you happen to know someone who is an experienced facilitator or recorder and can observe one of the meetings, this would be an excellent boost for your first facilitation or recording job. In any event, you'll make some mistakes and feel awkward at first. Every great professional had to begin sometime. That's part of learning. Don't worry; you'll do a good job.

HOW TO JUDGE YOURSELF

If for some reason you can't ask for feedback from your group or would prefer to criticize yourself at first, here are a couple of ways of evaluating your own performance:

1. After the meeting, you can fill out our meeting diagnostic sheet. It's a way of focusing on the various parts of your job, thinking about what you did and what else you might have done.

2. If you can, videotape or audio-tape your meeting. Be certain to ask permission of your group ahead of time. Some people get very uptight about any kind of recording equipment. Tell them it's for your own use, that you'll stop recording any time anyone wants you to, or erase a portion or all the tape at the end of the meeting. Most of the time, that will be adequate assurance. Once you have a tape, you can go back over it at your leisure. You will discover many things about yourself. You may be embarrassed at first, but once you get over the shock of seeing and/or hearing yourself, the recording will be an extremely valuable educational tool.

Once you're ready for feedback from others, you can encourage constructive criticism in many ways. Here are some:

1. In breaks during the meeting, and particularly at the end of the meeting, you can get together with the other half of your team, your recorder or facilitator, and, using the group memory as an aid, review critical periods of the meeting. Isolate particular segments and share with each other your positive and negative reactions about what happened; then develop alternative strategies and techniques that you might have used. This mutual criticism builds a sense of teamwork and an understanding of each other's working style. You get an insight into how another person deals with particular problems, and together you can usually generate a large repertoire of alternatives.

2. Invite someone who has had experience with the Interaction Method to observe one of your meetings. A trained observer may notice more that could be useful to you than a group member who is involved in the content of the meeting. If you can't find someone in your organization who has had more experience in the Interaction Method than you, you may be able to encourage one of your friends in the group to read this book and serve as your coach. After each meeting, you can sit down with your coach and discuss important parts of the meeting. It's a great help to be able to talk with an outsider who attended a meeting.

3. Then there's what we call the "Howard Cosell Interview." This sportscaster is noted for his pointed interviews with athletes right after a contest, "Well, Mohammed Ali, how does it feel to have lost your first major fight? Which blow was it that really got to you? Take a look at this videotape and tell our TV audience what you were thinking about at this particular moment in time." You can do the same, we hope with a little more tact. After a meeting which you have facilitated or recorded, find willing group members and interview them one by one. Ask them pointed questions about what they liked and disliked. Get them to give you specific examples and ask for suggestions to use in future meetings. Most people will be happy to oblige you, and interviews are also good occasions for dealing with any

concerns that your people may have about the Interaction Method.

4. Once in a while you can ask group members to fill out the meeting diagnostic sheets. In its present form, this questionnaire is quite long and involves some time commitment, so you can't give it to people too often. However, it's possible to develop your own evaluation sheet of ten to fifteen questions and zero in on skills you're currently trying to improve. If you are working on your recording, you can make up a questionnaire asking people to rate the legibility of your writing, use of different colors, completeness of recording, etc.

5. The easiest and in some ways the most direct way to get feedback is to reserve a few minutes at the end of the meeting for evaluation. Stress your desire for constructive criticism; tell the other members of your group the more skillful you and they become, the more productive your meetings will become. At the beginning, the comments may be too general to be useful: "It was a good meeting"; "I liked having a facilitator"; "The group memory was useful." This may be a good time to stress how important the roles of group member and manager/chairperson are and to suggest that everyone read at least some portions of this book. The idea is for everyone to learn together even though some may never want to facilitate or record.

HOW TO LEARN WITH A GROUP

Once you get other members of your group interested in learning more about the Interaction way, constructive feedback will increase and your rate of improvement should accelerate. But we reemphasize, it's much more effective to learn these techniques in a group.

Together with your group, set up a system for giving everyone an opportunity to record and to facilitate. One workable plan is to appoint a new facilitator and recorder for each meeting. Reserve fifteen minutes at the end of each meeting to discuss how the meeting went and offer helpful suggestions to the facilitator and recorder. Once a few people have had a chance to experience the joys and difficulties of recording and facilitating, the level of empathy and respect for these important roles will rise quickly.

It's a good idea to agree not to evaluate the performance of the facilitator and recorder while the meeting is in progress. It's all right to offer suggestions about working methods and keep the facilitator and recorder in their neutral roles, but don't say things like "I don't like the way you're facilitating; I think Mary did a better job last time." As a group member, your focus should be on the subject of the meeting. If a facilitator or recorder is having trouble, he or she can call "time out," stop the meeting, and ask for help or to be relieved. Try to keep such interruptions to a minimum. People who start off shakily may soon gain confidence and do a good job by the end of the meeting.

It's probably wise to ask someone else to facilitate the feedback session. It's hard to facilitate a criticism of yourself; you can no longer be neutral. Let someone else handle the evaluation sessions, perhaps the chairperson or manager.

There is always more to learn. We recommend taking courses in problem solving, psychology, communications, and group dynamics as well as reading books listed in the Bibliography.

Appendix

EIGHTEEN STEPS TO A BETTER MEETING

Before the Meeting
1. Plan the meeting carefully: who, what, when, where, why, how many.
2. Prepare and send out an agenda in advance.
3. Come early and set up the meeting room.

At the Beginning of the Meeting
4. Start on time.
5. Get participants to introduce themselves and state their expectations for the meeting.
6. Clearly define roles.
7. Review, revise, and order the agenda.
8. Set clear time limits.
9. Review action items from the previous meeting.

During the Meeting
10. Focus on the same problem in the same way at the same time.

At the End of the Meeting
11. Establish action items: who, what, when.
12. Review the group memory.

13. Set the date and place of the next meeting and develop a preliminary agenda.
14. Evaluate the meeting.
15. Close the meeting crisply and positively.
16. Clean up and rearrange the room.

After the Meeting

17. Prepare the group memo.
18. Follow-up on action items and begin to plan the next meeting.

MEETING DIAGNOSTIC SHEET
AND CHECKLIST
Questions

Chapter 6: Facilitator Did the facilitator clearly explain his or her role and the social contract with the group?	
Did the facilitator allow the participants to revise the agenda?	
Was the facilitator effective in getting the group to focus on a common task?	
Was the facilitator effective in getting the group to use one method or procedure at a time?	
Was the facilitator able to keep the meeting moving along smoothly?	
Did the facilitator talk too much?	
Did everyone have a chance to participate?	
Did the facilitator protect group members and their ideas?	
Did the facilitator keep the manager or chairperson from dominating the meeting?	
How well did the facilitator handle disruptive behavior of participants (if any)?	
Was the facilitator able to remain neutral and not get involved?	
Did the facilitator become defensive when criticized?	
Was the facilitator effective in bringing the group to closure and agreeing on specific action items?	
Chapter 7: Recorder 33. Did the recorder define his or her role and the function of the group memory at the beginning of the meeting?	
Was the group memory legible?	

Did the recorder capture the basic ideas of the meeting?	
Did the recorder make corrections without getting defensive?	
Did the recorder slow down or inhibit the progress of the meeting in any way?	
Did the recorder enliven the group memory by changing colors, underlining, diagramming, etc.?	
Did the recorder support the facilitator?	
Did the recorder assist the group in organizing the data that was generated?	
Did the recorder prepare a group memo and send it out to the members of the group?	
Was the group memo accurate and understandable to people who did not attend the meeting?	
Chapter II: Meeting Type Was the type of meeting appropriate to the task and the occasion?	
If it was a problem-solving meeting, did everyone recognize and accept the problem being addressed?	
If it was a decision-making meeting, was the final decision-maker involved?	
Did everyone accept the method of decision-making and understand who had the authority to make the final decision?	
Chapter 12: Group Composition Were the "right" kinds of people involved (people who had relevant expertise, were affected by the problem, who had to make the final decision, etc.)?	
Was the group heterogeneous enough (fresh ideas, different opinions, constructive conflict, etc.)?	
Were any of the twelve signs of "groupthink" present in the meeting?	

Chapter 13: Numbers of Participants Was the size of the group appropriate for the type of meeting being held?	
Given the type of meeting and numbers of people involved, was there adequate structure and differentiation of roles to insure participation, productivity, and protection of group members.	
Chapter 14: Meeting Space Was the meeting room of appropriate size and shape for the number of participants involved?	
Were the chairs arranged and oriented effectively for this type of meeting?	
Did the participants sit in a pattern that focused the energy of the group on the task (or did disruptive cliques form)?	
Was the atmosphere of the meeting appropriate for the occasion (too formal or too relaxed)?	
Were the levels of light, heat, and noise adequate?	
Were the required materials and equipment available and functioning properly?	
Chapter 15: Agenda Was there a content and process agenda prepared and sent out to all the participants in advance of the meeting?	
Were there too many agenda items for the time available?	
Were the agenda items appropriate for this group at this type of meeting?	
Were the objectives of the meeting clearly stated in the agenda so that participants came with similar expectations?	
Chapter 16: Problem-Solving and Decision-Making Was the problem clearly defined?	

Was it a problem that this group could and/or should try to solve?

Did the group have enough information or expertise to analyze and solve the problem?

Did the group examine enough alternatives?

Did the group rush prematurely to a decision?

Was the decision already made before the meeting (a rubber stamp)?

Did the group try to reach consensus on a win/win solution before resorting to a win/lose method of decision-making?

Chapter 17: Presentations

Were the presenters adequately prepared?

Did the presenters make the purpose of their presentations clear in the beginning?

Were the presentations well organized and delivered?

Were the presentations visual as well as verbal?

LOST ON THE MOON TEST: THE ANSWERS

Following are the answers to the group problem-solving test, "Lost on the Moon," presented on page 62.

Items	NASA's Reasoning	NASA's Ranks	Your Ranks	Error Points	Group Ranks	Error Points
Box of matches	No oxygen on moon to sustain flame; virtually worthless	15				
Food concentrate	Efficient means of supplying energy requirements	4				
Fifty feet of nylon rope	Useful in scaling cliffs, tying injured together	6				
Parachute silk	Protection from sun's rays	8				
Solar-powered portable heating unit	Not needed unless on dark side	13				
Two .45 caliber pistols	Possible means of self-propulsion	11				
One case of Pet milk	Bulkier duplication of food concentrate	12				
Two 100-pound tanks of oxygen	Most pressing survival need	1				
Stellar map (of the moon's constellation)	Primary means of navigation	3				

Self-inflating life raft	CO² bottle in military raft may be used for propulsion	9
Magnetic compass	Magnetic field on moon is not polarized; worthless for navigation	14
Five gallons of water	Replacement for tremendous liquid loss on lighted side	2
Signal flares	Distress signal when mother ship is sighted	10
First-aid kit injection needles	Needles for vitamins, medicines, etc., will fit special aperture in NASA space suits	7
Solar-powered FM receiver-transmitter	For communication with mother ship; but FM requires line-of-sight transmission and short ranges	5
	Total	

Error points are the absolute difference between your ranks and NASA's (disregard plus or minus signs).

Scoring for individuals:
0-25—excellent 56- 70—poor
26-32—good 71-112—very poor, suggests possible faking or use of earth-bound logic.
33-45—average
46-55—fair

Bibliography

Communications

Berlo, David K. *The Process of Communication.* New York: Holt, Rinehart and Winston, 1960.

Bois, J.S. *The Art of Awareness.* Dubuque, Iowa: W.C. Brown, 1966.

Fordyce, Jack K. and Weil, Raymond. *Managing With People.* Menlo Park: Addison-Wesley, 1971

Gordon, Thomas. *Parent Effectiveness Training.* New York: Peter Wyden, 1970.

Miller, George A. *The Psychology of Communication.* New York: Basic Books, 1967

Phillips, Gerald M. *Communication and the Small Group.* Indianapollis: Bobbs Merrill, 1966

Problem-Solving

Adams, James L. *Conceptual Blockbusting.* San Francisco: W.H. Freeman, 1974.

Gordon, W.J.J. *Synectics.* New York: Harper & Row, 1961.

Interaction Associates. *Strategy Notebook.* San Francisco: 1972.

Kaberg, Don and Bagnall, Tom. *The Universal Traveler.* Los Altos: William Kaufmann, 1972.

Kepner, C.H. and Tregoe, B.B. *The Rational Manager.* New York: McGraw-Hill, 1965.

McKim, Robert H. *Experiences in Visual Thinking.* Monterey: Brooks/Cole Publishing Co, 1972.

McPherson, J.H. *The People, the Problems, and the Problem Solving Methods.* Midland: The Pendall Company, 1967.

Parnes, S.J. *Creative Behavior Guidebook.* New York: Charles Scribner's Sons 1967.

Patton, Bobby R. and Griffin, Kim. *Problem Solving Group Interaction.* New York: Harper & Row, 1973.

Prince, George M. *The Practice of Creativity.* New York: Collier Books, 1972.

Small Groups

Eddy, William B., et al. *Behavioral Science & the Manager's Role.* Fairfax: Virginia, NTL Institute, 1969

Gordon, Thomas. *Group-Centered Leadership.* Boston: Houghton Mifflin, 1955.

Janis, Irving. *Victims of Groupthink.* Boston: Houghton Mifflin, 1972.

Kemp, C. Gratton. *Perspectives on the Group Process.* Boston: Houghton Mifflin, 1964.

Luft, Joseph. *Group Processes.* Palo Alto: National Press Books, 1963.

Miles, Matthew. *Learning to Work in Groups.* New York: Teachers College Press, 1969.

Schein, E. and Bennis, W. *Personal & Organizational Change Through Group Methods: The Laboratory Approach.* New York: Wiley, 1965.

Steiner, Ivan D. *Group Process and Productivity.* New York: Academic Press, 1972.

What Is Interaction Associates?

The authors of this book are the principals of Interaction Associates Inc., a consulting and training firm with expertise in problem-solving. We focus on improving the problem-solving and decision-making skills of individuals and organizations, helping them to become the architects of their own futures.

As consultants, we facilitate intensive planning and creative problem-solving sessions, assist communities to design citizen-involvement programs, and help organizations to develop internal problem-solving centers.

As trainers, we run programs in problem solving, decision-making, process-management, and the Interaction Method. We also train people to become local trainers in the Interaction Method.

If your organization is interested in our services or if you would like a list of training programs in your area, please write to us, PO Box 7862, San Francisco, CA 94120.

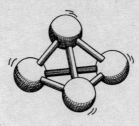

Feedback Form

We want and need your feedback. Your response will help us to make the book more useful to people when it comes time to revise it.

What are the most useful ideas and techniques for you in this book?

What ideas aren't very clear or do you not understand?

What kinds of success have you had using the Interaction Method?

What subjects would you like to see expanded?

What other kinds of materials about meetings would you find useful to increase the effectiveness of your meetings?

Please mail your reply to: Interaction Associates, Inc.
P.O. Box 7862
Rincon Annex
San Francisco, CA 94120

THE BEST BUSINESS GUIDES AVAILABLE TODAY FROM JOVE PAPERBACKS

66A

WOMEN'S
BUSINESS BOOKS

_____ 872-16806-9	THE LANDAU STRATEGY Suzanne Landau & Geoffrey Bailey	$2.50
_____ 872-16816-6	MONEY MANAGEMENT FOR WOMEN Rosalie Minkow	$2.50
_____ 872-16909-X	RE-ENTERING Eleanor Berman	$2.25
_____ 872-16899-9	SUCCESSFUL NEGOTIATING SKILLS FOR WOMEN John Ilich & Barbara S. Jones	$2.25
_____ 872-16835-2	WHAT EVERY WOMAN NEEDS TO KNOW ABOUT THE LAW Martha Pomroy	$3.95
_____ 867-21064-8	WOMAN TIME Personal Time Management for Women Only! Diana Silcox with Mary Ellen Moore	$2.95

Bestselling Books for Today's Reader

____**THE AMERICANS**   07289-3/$3.95
    John Jakes
____**THE BLACK YACHT**   06159-X/$2.95
    John Baxter
____**THE CAPTAINS**   05644-8/$3.50
    Brotherhood of War #2 W.E.B. Griffin
____**A GLORIOUS PASSION**   07071-8/$3.50
    Stephanie Blake
____**THIS GOLDEN VALLEY**   06823-3/$3.50
    Francine Rivers
____**HUMMINGBIRD**   07108-0/$3.50
    LaVaryle Spencer
____**CATCHER IN THE WRY**   07254-0/$2.95
    Bob Uecker
____**SHIKE: TIME OF THE DRAGONS**   07517-5/$3.95
    Robert Shea
____**SHIKE II: LAST OF THE ZINJA**   07518-3/$3.95
    Robert Shea
____**SOMETHING OLD, SOMETHING NEW**   05865-3/$3.50
    Lillian Africano
____**THE ULTIMATE GAME**   06524-2/$3.50
    Ralph Glendinning
____**THE WOMEN'S ROOM** Marilyn French   06896-9/$3.95
____**ACT THIN, STAY THIN**   07118-8/$3.50
    Dr. Richard B. Stuart
____**RIVINGTON STREET**   07149-8/$3.95
    Meredith Tax

Bestsellers you've been hearing about—and want to read